Seeds
Injustice

Violence has a source, and that source is injustice.
Violence is the fruit of the tree of injustice
and hatred is its evil flower.
If we sow seeds of injustice, we reap violence.
If we want to remove violence, we must first remove injustice.

Niall O'Brien

Priests arrested for multiple murder; farm workers tortured; arrest, house arrest, military custody; a unique escape into an Asian prison; a tense court case complete with terrorised witnesses – these are some of the elements which go to make up this eye-witness account of the struggle for liberation in the Philippines.

This struggle of the Filipino people reflects the greater struggle all over the world of crushed people seeking to free themselves from debt, hunger and militarisation.

How does a priest respond to this struggle to be human? A Filipino, an Australian and an Irish priest found themselves in prison because they believe that the work for injustice is an essential part of the Gospel. This is their story, their solution. If it is correct, dangerous times lie ahead for the Church.

A large part of this book is based on the thoughts and facts recorded in Niall O'Brien's Prison Diary.

The Author Niall O'Brien worked for twenty years in the Philippines as a member of the Society of St. Columban. He was born in Dublin.

The Negros Nine in Cell 8 at Bacolod Provincial Jail. Fr Niall O'Brien is on the left, second from the gate. *(Fr Frank Connon)*

Seeds of Injustice

Reflections on
The Murder Frame-up
of the
Negros Nine in the Philippines

from the Prison Diary of

NIALL O'BRIEN

THE O'BRIEN PRESS
DUBLIN

First published 1985 by The O'Brien Press
20 Victoria Road Rathgar Dublin 6 Ireland

British Library Cataloguing in Publication Data
O'Brien, Niall
Seeds of injustice: reflections on the murder
frame-up of the Negros Nine in the Philippines
from the prison diary of Niall O'Brien
1. Philippines—Politics and government—1973-
I. Title
959.9'046   DS686.5

ISBN 0-86278-091-8

Book design by Michael O'Brien
Typesetting by Koinonia Ltd.
Printed by Irish Elsevier, Shannon

para sila nanday

+	+	+	+	+	+	+	+?
Digna	Nato	Arod	Clarita	Lina	Nanette	Boy	Putot

para sa akon Iloy kag Amay

kag para man sa imo Nene

for

+	+	+	+	+	+	+	+?	
Digna	Nato	Arod	Clarita	Lina	Nanette	Boy	Putot	Nene

and for my father and mother

Acknowledgements

To all those from all over the world and from every walk of life who joined us in our struggle, on behalf of Brian, Itik, Boy, Imong, Condring, Erning, Siting and Peter, I wish to say *SALAMAT* (thank you).To list the names would be

impracticable – there were so many,

unfair – some would surely be missed out, and

impossible – so many remained anonymous.

Within the text more could have been mentioned, but ruthless editors stood in the way.

But if you so much as said a little prayer, then you are included here.

For help in producing this book I should like to thank Sister Carmel and Sister Paula of the Presentation Sisters, Father Frank Connon C.SS.R., Séamus Ó Tuathail, Leslie Wearne, Eilis Brennan, Daphne Graham, and Father William Halliden S.S.C.

I should also like to thank *The Irish Times* and *The Far East* for permission to publish material previously published by them.

The names of certain people and places have been altered in this book in order to protect the safety or respect the confidences of some and because of the feelings of the families of others.

The monetary value ascribed to the peso is that value which it had in dollars/punts at the time of a particular event. Since the dates of these events differ, so do the values ascribed to the peso.

From a thousand pages of four diaries I have chosen those parts which will help to tell the story, making minor alterations for the sake of clarity and omitting what I felt was irrelevant, inopportune or too personal for the occasion.

This is, in the last analysis, the story of two harrowing years; it would take more than another book to tell the story of my other twenty years among one of the most generous and hospitable peoples in the world. To them I owe far more than this book has had space to tell, and I regard the Philippines as my second home.

Niall O'Brien

Contents

Preface

The Republic of the Philippines, an archipelago of some seven thousand islands, lies on the western rim of the Pacific basin just below Taiwan and well north of Australia.

Ten thousand years before Christ, people were living in the Philippines; their traces have been carefully documented. How they got there we can only guess – by flimsy boat, or by simply trekking across the landbridges from Asia and Borneo, uncovered by the lowering of the ocean in the last ice age. When the Spaniards reached the Philippines from South America in the early sixteenth century they found a people with a well-developed culture, with religion, laws and the art of writing, and with wide trade contacts with the rest of Asia, and even further afield, for Islam was just arriving too.

The victors write the history, but from what we can glimpse through the 'cracks in the parchment curtain' the first Filipinos whom the Spaniards encountered were non-belligerent, gentle, generous, and brave when aroused. Contact with the aggressive Portuguese and Spaniards soon forced them to be more defensive.

Spain had learned some moral lessons from her early excesses in Latin America, so her policies in the Western Isles (as they were first called) were comparatively enlightened compared with other colonisers. Slavery, which lasted into the nineteenth century in the rest of the world, was by this time outlawed by Spain, and special laws defended the land rights of the native populations. The Indians of North America hardly survive today, whereas the Indios of the Western Isles have grown into a great nation of more than fifty million people. Spain came in search of spices and gold. The voyage was unashamedly commercial and was funded by banking houses of Europe. They found neither spices nor gold in quantity, but they stayed to bring the faith – the personal decision of Philip II, after whom the islands are named. Letters to Philip are still extant in which the first priests who came on the Spanish galleons vehemently attacked the oppression of the native population by the soldiery and by corrupt government officials. However, as time went on the Church was co-opted into the ruling body and became almost identified with it. Things took a decisive turn for the worse in the eighteenth century with the accession of the Bourbon (French) kings to the throne of Spain. Whereas in the time of the Spanish Habsburgs the Philippines had been an unproductive jewel in the Spanish crown, now they became an object of planned exploitation. Tobacco, indigo and other monopolies were introduced and the laws protecting the land rights of the native population began to be abrogated to allow European capital to come in to develop the country.

The process was well under way when the United States, expanding westwards towards China, took the Philippines in 1898. Strangely enough, it was under the US that the plantation system that was to bedevil Negros (one of the Philippine islands) intensified.

Negros had in fact escaped the Spanish colonisation to a great extent – they just did not have enough men, and *Moro* (Muslim Filipino) pirates coming from the south made it a dangerous place to live in. However, around the middle of the nineteenth century three significant things happened: the Suez Canal opened, shortening the distance between Spain and the East and bringing an influx of European entrepreneurs; the steam boat reached the Philippines and could overtake the *More vintas* (fast sailing ships); and Nicholas Loney, agent for the Manchester cotton mills and British Consul in Iloilo, the neighbouring island, 'founded' the sugar industry.

How Loney did this is important, because it gives us a typical example of one colonial method of penetration. At that time (*c.* 1850) Iloilo had a thriving textile industry; its main city, Iloilo City, had sixty thousand hand-looms which produced fine cloth that found markets around the globe. Loney pirated the textile patterns and sent them back to Manchester, where a combination of steam mills and slave labour was able to produce the same textiles at a much lower price. He shipped them back to Iloilo and in a few years had utterly destroyed the economy of the island. Not wanting his ships to go home empty, he planned to fill them with sugar, hence he pioneered the opening up of Negros to sugar plantations. He gave liberal loans to entrepreneurs (frequently those whose textile interests had collapsed) to buy British-made steam mills and move into Negros. In one stroke he strengthened the British economy and wedded Negros to a Third-World economy – a grip it is still in to this day.

With the new steam mills the large sugar farms expanded, and peasants who had cleared the forests of lowland Negros to plant their rice and corn became day labourers on the land they had cleared. There was still a shortage of workers, so peasants from other islands were imported, creating a new class of semi-indentured labourers known as the *sacadas*. The system was consolidated under the Americans, who again re-wrote the laws and introduced the enormous centrifugal sugar factories which, with their tall chimneys, still dominate the landscape of Negros today.

Came the Second World War, and, although US strategy decided that Europe came first and so allowed the Philippines to fall to Japan, the Filipinos stood by the US, putting up a brave guerrilla resistance, and gained their promised independence in 1946. But the independence turned out to be illusory, as colonialism was replaced by neo-colonialism. The US discovered that there was no need to have the Stars and Stripes flying over the Philippines as long as the laws ensured US economic domination and US military bases. These laws were partly achieved in exchange for war damage money (which was owed to the Philippines in any case). In the ensuing years, as Filipinos struggled to make something out of democracy, a genuine nationalism gradually emerged. People began to demand economic independence and reform of the whole social structure. By 1971 the ground was shaking with the call for change; nothing, it seemed, could hold it back. However, it was precisely to hold it back that President Marcos introduced martial law. Martial law opened the gates to international finance, which marched in with vast self-serving projects and full rights to repatriate their earnings. The two-billion-dollar nuclear plant, built in an earthquake-prone area, is a typical example.

Balked in their push for reform, many idealistic students took to the hills and joined the then miniscule New People's Army (NPA). The régime responded by militarising the whole country. The ensuing actions of the military on the innocent population have served to swell the ranks of the NPA further. Effective reform has been rejected and many people have reluctantly taken up the grim alternative of rebellion. Meanwhile, in the Bishop of Bacolod's controversial phrase, Negros became a 'social volcano'.

In 1979 Church researchers found that only 1.5 percent of the Negros population owned any land at all. Among a total of 332,000 families in the province, 330 families owned 45 percent of the sugar land, 20 families controlled 60 percent of the fishing catch, and 14 families held 150,000 hectares [about 350,000 acres] of lumber concessions. And this translated into extreme poverty for at least 82 percent of the province's 1.8 million people.

Alfred W. McCoy, *Priests On Trial*, Penguin Books, 1984.

A hundred years ago the introduction of a European-style land title system served to disinherit the traditional owners of lowland Negros. Many of these people moved to the hills. Now the same and new legal devices are being used to disinherit these people again, and indeed mountain tribes throughout the Philippines. For them there is nowhere left to go. It was with these people that Father Brian Gore, Father Vicente Dangan and I were attempting to build small Christian communities.

Introduction

This is a fascinating book, a great 'love story', without sentimentality. It is life – the truth of life. This report of the distressing, but finally liberating, story of the murder accusation against the Nine of Negros has moved me more than any work of fiction I have ever read throughout my long life. The reader will ask again and again: how can people in power be so wicked, so ruthless, so brutal?

Yet this book also speaks movingly of true humanity. The author, an Irish priest who worked for twenty years with the poor and for the poor in the Philippines, has really fallen in love with this people. In the worst hours of the murder case construed against him and his fellow-priests and lay leaders he experienced the solidarity, courage, generosity and creativity of the Filipino people.

This book unmasks a system of lies, greed, lust for power, cruelty, violence. But against this sad background the power of truth and the hunger and thirst for justice, healing and forgiving love shine through.

This story, told with utmost simplicity, is a great document of the times we live in and a great challenge to us all. It should be read by all those around the globe who work in the service of authoritarian systems – and of course it should be read by those who serve honestly and want to serve more honestly in truly democratic societies. What would happen if Marcos and his partners in the Philippines took the time to read this book attentively? They might never be the same again – they would either change their minds or they would degrade themselves even more. I dare to hope that quite a few, who in one way or another have co-operated with that system of oppression and exploitation, would no longer continue to do so with a good conscience.

The humanised world asks the question: how could tyrants like Hitler and Stalin find so many people willing to associate themselves with their horrifying abuse of power? This story does not raise that question directly, but it gives deep insights. By reporting the facts and circumstances it reveals the main motives: greed, lust for power, sadism. In many situations people are simply crushed by fear or even torture, as in the case of this elaborate murder trial where witnesses were manipulated in order to destroy the credibility of the Church's opposition to injustice and oppression. Like the author, you too may feel compassion for those victimised, crushed people; there are also thousands ready to take any kind of risk and willing to undergo suffering for the cause of non-violence.

11

This book should, for quite some time, be a classic work on non-violence – its spirituality, strategies and tactics – not taught theoretically but told as a lived story of what it is and how it works. Nobody should ever again opt for violence without carefully reading this story of non-violence, of people's capacity for endurance, bravery, serenity, hope. The murder case turned out to be a victory not just for the Nine of Negros but for those thousands who, with unbreakable solidarity, stood behind them.

What has moved me above all is the day-to-day account of life in the prison camp where political prisoners and 'ordinary criminals' lived, loved, suffered and celebrated together. The true humanity of these people (with all their faults) shines through against the inhumanity of their oppressors, against the professional liars and torturers, and, even more, against the inhumanity of those clinging to their power and wealth and forcing weak humans to serve their purposes.

This story also tells us much about the opportunities for non-violent defence and non-violent liberation – what finally forced the corrupt system to give in was not so much the evidence brought out by facts and courageous testimony but the outburst of worldwide opinion and the pressure this brought to bear on the conspirators. The many actors in this drama showed an enormous capacity to mobilise public opinion in the Philippines, Australia, Ireland and far beyond. This story, therefore, is an important moment in non-violent liberation and it tells us what it would mean in today's world were all the modern means of communication used in the service of non-violent defence against usurpation and oppression.

This book should shock the western world. It should make us think about our false tolerance and insane fatalism when faced with inhuman, authoritarian systems. And what impresses me most is that it is hope-inspiring throughout. Injustice, organised falsity, oppression, institutionalised violence can be overcome by the combined force of truth and creative non-violence in a worldwide solidarity between people of good will.

Bernhard Häring
Rome, March 1985

12

ONE

Arrested for Murder

My first and my last visits to the mountain barrio of Inapoy on the island of Negros were very different.

My first was in May 1965, when as a curate I sailed up the river Ilog from the town of Kabankalan in a long river canoe with an outboard motor, landing at Piliopiliohan; from there we trekked overland for a few miles until we came to the makeshift chapel set up for the once-yearly fiesta Mass. Healthy rice land lay all around. That night, kneeling with a group of women on the dirt floor of the chapel, I joined in the last day of the novena of prayers in preparation for the next day's fiesta Mass in honour of San Isidro.

In the morning, the people had arranged a procession, after which I celebrated Mass in Latin, stumbled through a sermon in Ilongo and baptised many children. For some reason or other, that stumbling sermon was about the spear being thrust into Christ's side – I remember that because I used the wrong word for spear.

Food seemed abundant, although life was frugal; the people were numerous, joyous and affectionate. They recalled the previous years when the priest came to visit them, and how one priest would drink only boiled water while another had what was – to them – some other idiosyncrasy.

When my work was done, I set off on my trek again. However, as I said goodbye to the happy scene, I had a deep sense of unease about the pastoral conditions of the whole village – the result of seeing the priest but once a year and having contact with him on a sacramental level only. After all, sacraments celebrate life and I knew so little of their life.

Little did I know, either, that their frugal rural scene was to change radically in the coming years as sugar cane pushed its bitter-sweet stems up into the mountains, displacing the rice and frequently changing the old rural relationships into the realities of plantation life. The gross barrio product was to increase, but the pattern of distribution was to be altered. The increase would go to absentee landlords.

My last visit to the barrio of Inapoy was to be twenty years later. It was 6 May 1983 and this time I was the parish priest, having been so for seven years. The barrio was now divided into thirteen Christian communities.

The Mass had been a grand affair in the morning in the local language, throbbing with song and warmth. Now, in the afternoon, a thousand people thronged into the largish *plaza* cleared by the people.

Eleven of the Christian communities had put on a contest. Each community had dressed up a little girl as a princess and she was drawn on a decorated oxen-cart. Two other priests – Father Terry Bennett and Father Brian Gore – and I were to judge the oxen-cart floats. It was a very beautiful sight for the three of us, who were standing on a platform erected for the visitors.

It was when we were addressing the crowd that the helicopter appeared. It was a large green gun-ship of Vietnam vintage with a fifty-calibre machine gun sticking out of each of the open sides. It was passing over us – not an unusual sight in Negros, where a virtual war is on between the New People's Army (a growing band of rebels in the inner mountains) and the military government of President Marcos.

However, the helicopter did not pass over. It turned and began to descend.

Panic set in among the illegal cockfighters, who fled in all directions, still holding on by strings to their terrified birds who were hurtled through the air squawking wildly. The helicopter made straight for the *plaza* as if to dash us, but stopped abruptly about fifty yards from the platform, the screaming propellers flinging dirt and dust at us like a sandstorm. Out jumped some soldiers in full fatigues, bearing machine guns and led by a colonel holding a small, chrome, hand-machine gun. The people panicked. One woman clung to me, shouting, 'Save us! Save us!'

We decided to move quickly and, while Terry Bennett stayed with the people to calm them, Brian and I walked straight towards the colonel to make sure that our altercation, whatever it was to be, would take place before the soldiers reached the people.

I said: 'Welcome to our fiesta, Colonel.'

'I want you and Father Gore and his lay leaders to come to a conference in Kabankalan,' he answered. (Brian had brought six of his lay leaders with him to the fiesta.)

We knew this to be a euphemism for arrest, but Brian stepped in, saying loud and clear: 'I'm not getting into that thing!'

I could see the set of Brian's jaw and the look on his face, so I said: 'Later, Colonel. The people are very frightened. Give us a few minutes to calm them and then we'll follow you down in Father Gore's parish jeep.' The colonel could see that he would have to use force so he courteously agreed.

We spoke to the people for a few moments, telling them not to be afraid, that this was all part of being a disciple of Christ and that we were proud of them.

Indeed, I was proud of them because I had seen the barrio growing from the yearly Mass to many vibrant Christian communities, and I could sleep at night in peace knowing that no one would go hungry or sick without the caring hand of the community touching them – this being what discipleship is largely about. I knew, too, that the people were aware now of the causes of the deep injustices that had seeped into the mountains in recent years; that they were prepared to expose and oppose them non-violently; that they knew it was an essential part of being a Christian in a Christian community.

There are two routes to Kabankalan from Inapoy. We could go the long way down the left side of the river Ilog and cross it twenty-five miles further down at Talubangi Bridge, or we could go the way that I had gone twenty years before and cross the river into Brian's parish in the jeep. (Twenty years ago you could not cross the river in a jeep at this spot, but the massive forest cover of the mountains had been sawn away in Negros, as, indeed, all over the Philippines. Now rivers almost dry up in places in the dry season and bring disastrous floods in the wet season, resulting in great hardship to the farmers. This is certainly caused by a corrupt and negligent forestry policy.) To cross the river to Brian's parish would halve the journey, so we chose that route.

It was late afternoon when we crossed the river and the light was going from the sky. The track on the other side was a lonely one. Suddenly two dark green trucks rushed on us. Out jumped masked men in green fatigues with machine guns. Their balaclavas scared me.

I was so scared that I said to Brian, 'We're finished now.'

One man had no balaclava, only a handkerchief over his mouth against the dust, and Brian recognised him as Reynaldo, one of the ordinary Kabankalan police. Brian called out, 'Reynaldo!'

Major Yulo, the station commander of Kabankalan Integrated Police Force, jumped on our running board and ordered us to come with him.

One of the army vehicles went in front and one behind and they conveyed us to the town at high speed. The people in the hamlets we passed recognised the parish jeep and stopped and stared. They knew that a long-threatened event was finally taking place: we were being arrested on the charge of killing our mayor and his four companions. Army spokesmen had announced it to Reuters news agency some six months previously and so to the whole world. The local government-controlled media had been airing it ever since. We had lived for six months in anxious expectation that the axe would fall. And at last it had fallen.

Kabankalan is a large municipality in the south of the island of Negros. The population is over one hundred thousand. Apart from the parish

15

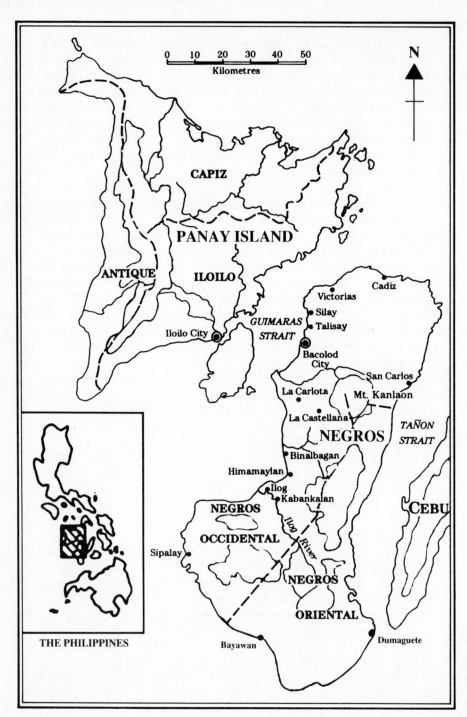

centred in the town proper, there are three outlying parishes within the boundaries of the municipality. These lie in the mountainous areas.

Father Brian Gore was parish priest of Oringao on the left side of the Ilog river which runs into Kabankalan. I was parish priest of Tabugon on the right-hand side of the river. Our people were poor settlers who had moved into the mountains in search of land to plant corn, rice and root crops. Hard as that life is, they prefer it to that of being semi-indentured labourers in the fertile cane-fields of the lowlands.

Concerned Christians were always dismayed about the plantation conditions in Negros and many a Nicodemus among the planters has tried to do something about it. Some notable farmers refuse to follow the absentee landlord pattern; they live and work on their land and attempt to make the conditions of their workers more tolerable. Their efforts are the exception which proves the rule.

The sugar industry has become so enmeshed in the larger export system that not only the workers but even the landowners have more and more become pawns in an international game. Of course, not all the Negros problems stem from the sugar industry. It has fishing and mining industries, and had a logging industry at one time, and all of these too have played their part in the general unhappy picture. However, our parishes were closer to the farming area.

Before World War II sugar farmers and employers generally tended to live close to their workers, and the consequent human contact, extended family network and daily closeness of living all worked in favour of the workers. However, when the Japanese invaded Negros, many big farmers took refuge in the city and others joined the guerrillas in the mountains. A great many family domains were burnt down, if not by the Japanese, by the guerrillas themselves. Thus, after the war many of the landowners never returned to their farms and their sons grew up receiving an income earned in part by a peasantry they were never to know. The gap between owner and labourer widened, with consequent alienation on both sides.

During the war the Philippines were utterly devastated and, in the general penury that followed, people struggled desperately to find their feet again. The constantly widening gap between the classes was not immediately apparent, but by the mid-60s, with the rising sugar prices, it was unmistakable.

The Church worried and decided to act.

In 1966, Monsignor Fortich was designated bishop-elect of Bacolod. 'The Holy Father is making you Bishop of Bacolod to do something for the poor of Negros,' he was told by a special emissary from the Nuncio. Pope Paul VI's encyclical *Populorum Progressio* was released in 1967 and it was a passionate appeal to Christians to take concrete, positive steps

Felixberta Moises ('Indan'), in white T-shirt, led a campaign on behalf of thirty-eight sugar workers to get the legal minimum wage – they were locked out for five months, and, after over fifteen hearings and a battle of a year and a half, many of the workers gave up because of starvation. *(Fr Brendan O'Connell)*

to help the down-trodden. Monsignor Fortich was ordained Bishop of Bacolod on 24 February 1967.

When he took up office, Bishop Fortich immediately set about implementing the encyclical's message and fulfilling the Holy Father's commission.

A stream of initiatives followed which were to transform the meaning of pastoral care for the people of Negros. The establishment of a social action office with a priest full-time in charge was quickly followed by the setting up of a social action council with broad-based representation from Negros society. Then came the rural congress, with its emphasis on development and the improvement of living conditions. An essential communication link with the broad mass of the people and the remote parishes was forged with a television and radio station geared to the education of the ordinary people and the spreading of the social gospel.

Nor would the work of inculcating social awareness, basic literacy and education fail for lack of practical example as far as Bishop Fortich was concerned: Church property was land-reformed to give an example of the type of reform generally required. The personal efforts of the bishop founded the Dacongcogon Sugar, Rice and Corn Co-operative. He carried his one-man campaign for economic and social reform to landowners, industrialists and politicians, while at the same time making extensive use of the Church-military liaison committee in an effort to protect the people in his care and bring about a climate of peace.

No one remembers Bishop Fortich taking a holiday or a day off.

Soon, his priests took up the cry and countless projects were started at parish level: animal dispersals, cottage industries, fishing and farming co-operatives, pump-boat dispersal, credit unions, schools for mechanics, and so on.

Two of the priests went full-time into labour-union work and helped to get the National Federation of Sugar Workers off the ground. Corrupt and weak unions were relentlessly criticised. A special organisation mobilised the ever-willing 'nun-power' workforce. The sisters went into *haciendas* (ranches) to instruct the people as to their rights. Even some *hacisenderos* were caught up in the new spirit pervading Negros and went so far as actually to extend invitations to the sisters.

The Federation of Free Farmers was given strong parish support and thrived. Injustices were roundly denounced and seminars on human development and human rights became commonplace. When the situation deteriorated, the Task Force Detainees saved many lives and kept the plight of prisoners and the occurrence of torture under surveillance and before the eyes of the public.

However, the permanent institutional parish expression of Pope Paul VI's 'integral evangelisation' made its appearance in the Basic Christian

Communities which sprang up throughout the diocese in the wake of the Holy Year, 1975. Latterly, these communities have joined non-violent protests and rallies against human rights violations – the more so as the noose of injustice tightens.

The guardians of the *status quo* felt threatened by projects and programmes which questioned the social system, supported labour unions and raised the awareness of the ordinary people. There were sporadic negative reactions from vested interests, in particular, certain associations of planters.

Attacks were broadcast on the radio; then a special television programme attacked the Church systematically, even attempting to malign Bishop Fortich personally. The social action director, Father Suplido, was libelled. The Columban Fathers were vilified: *'Nagkadto sila diri dala ang ila cuchara kag tinedor'* (They came here, knife and fork in hand!). Binalbagan Catholic College and La Salle College came in for attack. In fact, a boycott of La Salle was organised because they had dared to touch on the subject of justice in the Negros context. Some provincial newspapers joined the campaign, some of their columnists equating any call for justice with covert communism. Even the pope's talk at the reclamation area, when he came to Negros, caused anger and was a bone of contention. The magazine *Sugarlandia* answered the critics and 'exonerated' the pope ! Attempts were made to categorise the priests, some being labelled 'good' and others 'bad' – 'bad' meaning 'involved in social action'. It did not matter what a priest did or did not do, as long as he kept quiet on social justice issues, or at least kept references to them sufficiently abstract as to be innocuous.

There were many petty harassments and threats.

Sometimes, in a whole line of cars, the priest's would be the one to be stopped and searched. Father Brian Gore had hostile leaflets dropped on his parish from a specially chartered plane. At least two priests were physically assaulted. Some received threats. Many received warnings: 'You are on the list. Be careful!' Two priests were actually imprisoned, and several were detained. There was an attempt to sow dissension between the foreign and Filipino priests. A politician called for the sending home of white priests: 'I did not mean all of them, only some,' he explained – presumably the 'bad' ones. A prominent figure called on members of a Catholic organisation to report on sermons which were suspect. A scurrilous comic was printed at great expense and distributed free (with no acknowledgement of origin) with the express purpose of denigrating and discrediting the Church and the priests and, if possible, involving the bishop. It depicted priests as secret communist agents, financed by the bishop and helping the people in order to deceive them.

Such had been the Negros scene for the previous fifteen years.

But now things had come to a head because the powers of Negros had been consolidated. Financing, milling, buying, selling, shipping, security in the sugar industry, had gravitated into the hands of a few. A plan to discredit the emerging Church was afoot – a plan, in a word, to get the Church back into the sacristy.

The death of Mayor Sola and his companions offered the ideal opportunity to those unscrupulous enough to use it. Three priests, Fathers Brian Gore, Niall O'Brien and Vicente Dangan, were accused of having organised the killing, accompanying the killers and wielding an M16 armalite rifle.

We were accused for basically the same reason that the Church had been attacked during the previous fifteen years – because the work of the Church for justice rocked the social boat and endangered deep-rooted and long-standing vested interests. The tragic death of Mayor Sola had been callously used and shamelessly misrepresented in an effort to silence the Church.

But the Church could not remain silent. The Church could not turn its back on the scandal of the *sacada* (cane-cutter) system, the growing desperation of the landless peasants, the burgeoning urban slums, the hopelessness of so many sugar-cane workers, the cries heard from military outposts in the dead of night, and the infant coffins outside our churches.

The Gospel of Luke is clear. Our task is to

bring good news to the poor,
set the captives free,
bring sight to the blind,
liberate the oppressed,
and announce that the time has come
    when the Lord will save his people.

(Luke 4:16-19)

We must accompany the people in their search for life.

It was because of our attempt to accompany the poor in their search for life that Brian Gore and I, along with the lay leaders, were now careering down the mountain road, sandwiched between two military vehicles festooned with armed soldiers, to be delivered to the town hall, where we were formally handed warrants of arrest for the killing of Mayor Sola and his companions.

After a medical check-up we were driven to the town jail. A few more official signatures and we were ready to be locked up, but not before we were joined by Father Vicente Dangan of Cabacungan, La Castellana.

(While we were being collected by Major Yulo, another group of soldiers was picking him up to join us in the jail.)

Major Yulo approached me and said that he would give us (the priests, that is) his own office and an electric fan. It was only then that my 'cool' left me and I told him what he could do with his fan; and, for good measure, I added a few more remarks, which resulted in a slanging match between us – with me telling him not to get drunk as he usually did and him telling me that no one was going to tell him how to run his own prison.

Maybe it was good for both of us. It was certainly good for me as a warning reminder of the very real anger lying just below the surface.

I walked away into a corner trying to cool down.

Brian came over to me with a grin and said: 'I think I had better deal with Major Yulo in the future.' He was getting his own back, of course, because I had made a similar intervention between him and Colonel Agudon when he had refused to shake Agudon's hand half an hour earlier.

Anyway, from then on Major Yulo and I conversed with the utmost courtesy, neither of us wanting a repeat performance.

All documents were signed. We were formally admitted. The bishop, priests, lay people and ordinary onlookers, along with the press, withdrew. The gates clanged.

The keys were turned.

TWO

Behind Bars

Kabankalan prison is brand new. It has four cells, a shower-room and a toilet of sorts, but no water. The shower-room had been converted into a cell for a prisoner who had gone out of his mind and, the water situation apart, everyone was wary of approaching it. If we wanted to get out of our cell to use the facilities – such as they were – or if we needed to call the guard, this was achieved by rattling the gate. The outer gate would be unlocked first and then our own cell gate. The cell had no seats or table; it was simply a small cement-walled room about five paces by five, one window high up, and a door, both with grills – and there were nine of us.

We were too exhausted from the day's events to start discussing the future, so the nine of us sat on the floor in a circle praying, reciting the psalms, and reading from the scriptures. I read a poem from a book of Irish poetry that I had in my bag. We sang a song or two and then lay down.

Lying down was not that easy, as there was barely room for us to stretch our legs without putting a foot in somebody else's mouth. Some Kabankalan people had sent in plywood and cardboard boxes which we flattened out, so they provided a modicum of insulation for our backs against the cold, cement floor. I also had a towel that someone else had sent in and I swopped it with Father Dangan for a pillow.

Vicente Dangan – his nickname was Itik – had had a long battle to the priesthood. To finish his schooling he had to study by day and work by night as a security guard. That, and many other vicissitudes of life, meant that he was not ordained until he was in his mid-thirties. His early years in an orphanage and his time earning his seminary tuition gave him an unswerving desire to serve the poor. He had chosen a parish far into the mountains, where he lived in a small shack, growing his own food and struggling to start small Christian communities.

I was the last to sleep. I lay thinking in the fetid heat, careful not to move to either side too much. A deep peace had come over me. I did not worry about the morning and I may even have slept for a couple of hours.

We awoke around four. Our first task was to try to get water to wash and to clean out the toilet. Although there was no water in the taps we learned that water could be got by paying prisoners who were called 'living-out prisoners': they lived outside the four cells and slept on tables and benches in the police office and ran errands for the police. We quickly learned that if we set up the gate-rattle, the guard would let one of us out. I negotiated the buying of the water with the living-out prisoners. They brought the water in for us in buckets and poured it into an oil drum. We scooped it out and poured it over ourselves; but the problem now was that the drum leaked, so that speed was of the essence when it came to scooping.

During these washing sorties at the drum, we had a chance to look in on the other three cells and talk with their prisoners. These cells were chock-a-block. My diary for this first morning in prison reads:

> We bought water to get our first wash in two days. Those in Cell 1 haven't washed for a week. There's a deranged man in the empty shower room (his cell!). There's a man in for drugs on the floor of the corridor. A child of twelve, apprehended for stealing, is put in

23

Cell 4 with six people accused of murder. I said to him: 'Don't be amazed that you are in here. There are three priests in here also.' He laughed and I'm happy to see him laughing, though the 'murderers' don't seem so bad.

Back in our cell we prayed together for a short while, picking a psalm and a reading. Then I got to know Brian's lay leaders better.

First, there was Conrado, a community organiser. Conrado had been a teacher in the Kabankalan College but had given it up to prepare for the priesthood. He had not continued in the seminary and had joined Brian in his work of building small Christian communities. He was married with one child. I can best describe him as a lay assistant parish priest.

Next came Geronimo, who ran the barefoot doctor programme in Brian's parish of Oringao. He had helped me in building a community farm in the mountains some years before and had moved from there to work in Brian's barefoot doctor programme. He was married to Gina and had three children.

Next came Ernesto, the guitar-player; although all the leaders could make a good fist of the guitar, Ernesto was exceptionally good. He was also the unofficial jester and he shot out his jokes one after the other. In the parish of Oringao, Ernesto was a community organiser. He was as tough as old boot leather and his impetuosity was fortunately tempered by his magnificent sense of humour. He had four small boys, facsimiles of himself.

Wide-eyed Peter came next. Married, with several very small children, he had been working with Brian for years on various agricultural projects and was now in charge of the vermiculture programme. Brian had introduced this programme for rejuvenating the soil in the parish. The land had become sterile from excessive use of fertilisers, pesticides and herbicides. The worms, so necessary for soil aeration and the building of humus, had been exterminated. Brian had embarked on an ambitious plan of breeding worms. Their castings make the best natural fertiliser in the world and he was able to sell this fertiliser at a high price to help finance the parish, which would otherwise have been too poor to support many of the programmes. Counting, sorting and distributing the worms was a full-time occupation and gave work to many young people in the parish. Brian's aim was to introduce the technology of vermiculture and to share and spread it among the small farmers so that they could make a little money themselves, while simultaneously rejuvenating their own bits of land. It was working well and Peter, with his degree in agriculture, had been put in charge of it.

The Negros Nine, from left, Jesus Arzaga, Fr Niall O'Brien, Peter Cuales, Lydio ('Boy')
Mangao, Fr Brian Gore, Geronimo Perez, Fr Vicente Dangan, Ernesto Tajunes
and Conrado Muhal at Bacolod.

Next came Siting – 'Siting' is a nickname for the name Jesus, a very common name in the Philippines as, indeed, in all countries with a Spanish cultural heritage. Siting was in charge of the parish farm – a tract of land for growing corn to support the parish projects. Like all the other lay leaders he shared his knowledge in the many seminars offered to the members of the Christian communities.

And, lastly, Lydio – easy-going, good-looking and talented. He was in charge of the young people in the Christian communities. As the only unmarried one of the six lay leaders, he came in for much banter at the amount of post he received, as well as various visits from the fairer sex, as the time in prison lengthened.

Light came around six. We had each set up the gate-rattle and managed to get out to wash and use the toilets, such as they were. We prayed, seeking guidance and strength for the day ahead.

As light came, throngs of people from the town of Kabankalan streamed into the prison yard, bringing us food, clothes, good wishes and prayers.

One very touching act was that of a woman landowner who had had a head-on collision with Brian, as he had provided Church lawyers for her tenants in their battle with her. She arrived at the prison, was granted permission to come into our cell; then she herself spread a tablecloth on the cell floor and laid out a meal for all of us. It was the first of many such acts of reconciliation which were to take place during that coming year and, indeed, the very considerable giving of unselfish support from the people of Kabankalan stretched right across the class spectrum.

On the morning of 7 May, other priests began to visit us. Mark Kavanagh, parish priest of Kabankalan, came and told us that there were rumours of our being put under house arrest. Apparently there was also talk of all the Masses in Negros Occidental being called off and one big protest Mass taking place on Sunday in Kabankalan, and possibly of a march to the jail.

The nine of us held a meeting. By that I mean we sat down in a circle and formally discussed the topic. This was to be a simple tool which we were to use throughout the year ahead of us.

We cell-mates had the advantage of considerable experience in using group consensus. Each of the lay leaders had been involved, at one time or another, in setting up consensus-making groups, so the techniques were known to us. We were frequently capable of quick decision-making and quick action.

We discussed the intention of our captors to put us under house arrest. Our unanimous and adamant decision was not to accept it. A letter was drafted to Father Mark Kavanagh. We wanted him to transmit its content to the Church authorities in Manila, where negotiations were now going on.

Later on in the day, various priests came in and we spoke of our decision and the content of the letter.

Generally speaking, our fellow priests would hear of nothing but getting us out of prison immediately, whereas we felt that it would be giving the army a way out and would also allow them to proscrastinate – as usual. It would commit us to an eternal wait for legal action.

The day wore on, by no means slowly. We were to discover that two of our fellow prisoners had been in prison and on remand for two years and, as yet, did not even have lawyers. They had had twenty-seven court hearings for stealing 120 pesos (c. £10), yet no judgement had been given. This did not come as a surprise to us because, of course, we had been living with this sort of 'justice' for a very long time.

Our lunch was brought to us by the people of the town. We shared the food with the other prisoners and with the guards, and gradually the relationship with our captors improved. They were ordinary fellows who meant no harm to us and were carrying out their orders.

The Legion of Mary also came in and got permission to say the Rosary outside our cell door. Later on we were to learn that the bishop was suspending the celebration of Mass in Negros that Sunday. The demonstration was going to go ahead.

THREE

Painful Separation

At five-thirty in the afternoon, Major Juanito Yulo, the Kabankalan station commander, came in to say that Colonel Agudon and Bishop Fortich were coming to put us under house arrest! We were polite, but did not answer him. We were also shocked and immediately conferred as to what we should do.

Major Yulo came back to say that Captain Salim, a Muslim from the Hinigaran station command (next above Kabankalan) wanted to speak to us. We refused.

Later, Yulo returned once more, saying that the President of the Philippines was offering us house arrest, laying down three conditions, but that the six lay leaders were not included. We not only refused the

27

house arrest, but also said that we would discuss nothing until such time as Bishop Fortich himself came. We signed a document only to say that we had heard the message of the president read to us.

After that we conferred again, and my diary summarises our conclusions:

> We will not come out without our six lay leaders.
> We want bail and a quick trial.
> House arrest is too dangerous. We would be deported immediately as the rules are too stringent.

We were by now deeply worried. The first hope of a diocesan protest seemed to have evaporated or else to have been used by the bishop as a bargaining counter in gaining house arrest for us. Our message that we did not want house arrest seemed not to have reached Manila.

News had got out that we priests were adamant about not leaving without the lay leaders.

At eleven o'clock at night Father Nicholas Murray, a Galway man who was our Columban superior in Manila, and Father Michael Martin, our Negros superior, arrived along with Father Romeo Empestan, a diocesan priest with an unquestionable allegiance to the poor. I felt certain that they were a 'softening up' team coming in to prepare the way for the bishop.

They joined us sitting in a circle on the cell floor and began to argue the case for accepting house arrest. The meeting was tense – all the more so because of the friendship between us all. Their arguments were that:

1. the bishop and cardinal had fought for us; to refuse now would be to cause them great embarrassment, and possibly something even more than embarrassment;
2. the fact that the president had not given the lay leaders the same privilege was not their fault;
3. we might divide the Church, which was at the moment united and fully behind us;
4. when all was said and done, the only reason we were working in the diocese was that the bishop had accepted us; in fact, he could easily have prevented the return of Father Brian Gore, if he had wanted to, but he had not done so;
5. now where would you find a more reasonable man?

Our arguments were that:

1. it would be wrong to leave the lay leaders behind and to come out ourselves;
2. it would increase the danger to the lives of the lay leaders if we were

28

not with them;

3. our coming out would take the army off the hook, but certainly not us.

While we were arguing, the bishop had arrived and was waiting with many priests and reporters. Finally, our visitors withdrew and the bishop entered our cell.

Bishop Antonio Fortich is tall and handsome; the kindness of the inner man radiates out, lending an aura which epitomises a true father figure. But now we were going to have to battle with him – the man for whom we had such a very deep and real affection. Yet we felt that there was no way in which we could accept house arrest. He was obviously coming to try to persuade us to the contrary.

Somebody got a chair from the guards' quarters and the bishop sat down, wearily. It was by now midnight and he had travelled a thousand miles or so by land and air in the previous two days, quite apart from the endless negotiations in which he had taken part.

Once more, we found ourselves sitting in a circle on the cell floor, but this time around the bishop. Somehow his threadbare soutane seemed to heighten his weariness. He did not speak immediately, but simply sat for a moment, exhausted, his skull cap just slightly askew.

When he spoke, it was quietly and with concern. He said: 'Give me a chance to explain. You are all in for multiple murder. This is an unbailable crime. There's no way that bail can be got for such a crime, but if I can get three of you out and under house arrest, then that will make it clear to the world that no one takes the crimes seriously – which will undermine the very unbailability of the crime. They can't refuse bail then and, in fact, we could institute the bail hearings within ten days.'

We discussed the matter. The bishop had a point.

'But what of the safety of the lay leaders? Won't they be in greater danger without us beside them?'

The bishop remained silent. Then he spoke slowly and with great deliberation: 'If anything happens to the lay leaders, then I will resign as Bishop of Bacolod.'

He had made no mention of a divided Church, or an embarrassment to the hierarchy should we priests refuse what he and the cardinal had negotiated in Manila. (We were to learn later that the cardinal had even threatened President Marcos with the suspension of all Masses in the Philippines.)

We looked at each other, and finally I said: 'Monsignor, we'll do nothing that might humiliate you, but maybe it should be left to the lay leaders to make the decision.'

Brian and Vicente nodded in agreement and all eyes were turned towards Conrado and the five others. They looked at one another and the answer was clearly recognisable on their faces.

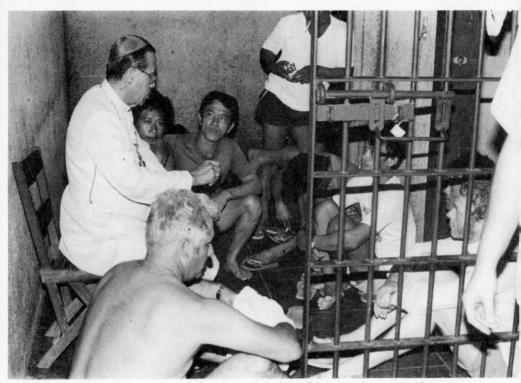

Bishop Fortich talks to the Nine at Kabankalan Prison in order to persuade them that the three priests should accept house arrest. *(Fr Brendan O'Connell)*

'*Sigue* (Okay), Monsignor,' they said. 'We accept.'

Suddenly, all the tense faces relaxed and were wreathed in smiles. We stood up, with the bishop clapping us on the back. Television cameras appeared from nowhere.

The bishop then said to us: 'Tomorrow, I'll come back to Kabankalan and you'll join me in concelebrating Mass and I will personally explain to the people why we have taken this decision.'

Was this decision right or wrong?

Very often, what seems to be right at a given time proves, with hindsight, to have been erroneous. Basically, what was happening here was the postponement of a decision until such time as our fellow-priests and the bishop could accept it.

Much was to happen in the next few months which gradually changed the minds of the presbyterate, the bishop and the cardinal. So the decision to leave our six lay leaders behind in jail was not irrevocable and, in fact, was to allow the necessary time to reflect on events and then to change. But it was to cause some very bitter moments, in particular for Father Brian Gore, as the next morning was to show.

FOUR

Buried Alive

I awoke the following morning in time to hear the BBC World Service announce that we were still in prison refusing to leave because of the six lay leaders. We set out for Kabankalan, where the bishop celebrated Mass for a full church, explaining to the congregation the reason why he had asked us to come out ahead of the lay leaders. However, this was only the first Mass.

The second Mass had a bigger congregation including many of those who had heard that the Mass in their own parish had been cancelled, but had not received the news that we had left the jail. The wives and families of the six lay leaders also arrived for this second Mass, and Brian went to meet them. He immediately saw the hurt on their faces, and to his anguish one of them said straight out, '*Dlin ang imo mga bata?*' (Where your children?), referring to the six.

The wives and children were not aware of the anguish and agony of the previous day's endless discussion which culminated in the decision

31

on the part of us priests to come out of jail under the conditions of house arrest, leaving the lay leaders behind us.

The bishop had already left. Brian himself celebrated the second Mass. In his sermon he said something which some were to criticise later, but which can be fully understood in the light of what he had been through.

He said: 'We are out of prison in order to facilitate the release of our lay leaders; but if they are not let out, I'll join them, even if it means committing an illegal act to do so.'

His point was taken by the families, all of whom were very close to Brian.

After the Mass a large part of the congregation went in procession to the Kabankalan prison to bring Communion to the leaders. It was an emotional procession and armed guards watched us suspiciously.

What we now faced were the bail hearings, and our legal counsel set about fixing a date immediately. These hearings were to take place in the town of Kabankalan where all of us had been working.

Kabankalan is a fine town, although none of its present buildings dates back much before 1935, as the wooden structures of Spanish times have not survived, except for one old house. Bacolod is the capital of Negros Occidental, but Kabankalan, 'the place of the bankal trees', comes second in importance. It has a large mountain hinterland with a population of over one hundred thousand and has two sugar factories – sugar cane being the main crop. The Columban missionaries have been working there since 1950. The town *plaza* in Spanish style is surrounded by the school, the church and the town hall, or *municipio* as it is called in Spanish. The second floor of the *municipio* is the courtroom where the bail hearings were to take place. To our dismay, we heard that there had been a complete rearrangement of the legal system and that there was a newly appointed judge in charge of Kabankalan Regional Trial Court, the court which was to host our case.

The judge, Emilio Legaspi, was a smooth-faced, good-looking man with a winning, if inscrutable, smile. Whenever I think of him I am reminded of Rouault's famous painting 'The Judge'. The first thing Judge Legaspi did was send his new gavel over to the church to have it blessed; Father Eddie Allen blessed it and, with a glint in his eye, told the emissary that the blessing would cease if any perverse decisions were made with the gavel. I presume that the bearer did not report the message to the owner.

Without any prior warning and to our dismay, Judge Legaspi had the lay leaders removed from Kabankalan by issuing a remittance order, transferring them to Bacolod Provincial Jail. This document was to prove vital later on, but for the moment it filled us with alarm. Father Mark

Kavanagh had Kabankalan prison under constant surveillance, so as soon as he had news of the transfer of the lay leaders, he telephoned the message through to Bacolod.

The journey from Kabankalan to Bacolod along the coast road is about sixty miles, so that by the time the handcuffed lay leaders reached Bacolod Provincial Jail a large crowd of sisters and lay people had gathered there. The unspoken tale this was to tell the jail authorities was that these prisoners had friends in Bacolod. This was going to be proved necessary, as several attempts were made to intimidate the six leaders in the months that followed.

In the meantime, of course, we priests were now under house arrest.

However, let me leave the lay leaders in Cell 8 in Bacolod Provincial Jail and the three priests under house arrest in their parishes – all waiting for the bail hearings to begin – and put you in the picture about the killing of Mayor Sola, a reluctant mayor.

I can still recall, as a curate in Kabankalan nearly twenty years previously, how he had to be dragooned into running for mayor. Basically he was a sugar farmer, a rancher and a pig rearer. His heart was in farming and he was eager to innovate. He was not an absentee landlord.

As a curate of his parish, my relationship with him was always cordial. His political speeches were short and to the point. His opponents claimed that he was a tough man with all the connotations toughness implies. I had no way of verifying the stories that were told against him.

At one time I used to help in giving retreats. The mayor was persuaded to go on one of these. I can say that he made a sincere attempt to put his life to rights and I was called in to help in his family relationships. Looking back now on those retreats which we gave in the sixties – retreats which were, in fact, short courses in Christianity – I feel that the emphasis was more on personal conversion than on social reform, although a true conversion must of course involve both aspects equally; they cannot be separated and one without the other is a sure formula for failure.

I moved on from the retreat movement after several years and eventually ended up in a parish in the mountains of Kabankalan which was still in the jurisdiction of Mayor Sola, although I in fact rarely saw him during the succeeding years. And these were years of great change.

President Marcos, knowing that he could not have a third term in office as president, since it was against the constitution, solved the problem by declaring martial law on 23 September 1972 (just a year before his term in office came to a close). He also changed the constitution to its present amalgam of confusing and contradictory provisions allowing him, Marcos, to be president or prime minister, or both, or neither, depending on the amended articles involved. Mayor Sola did not go along with this, but he was 'squeezed' by the simple means of being himself imprisoned; thus he switched from his traditional Liberal Party allegiance to President Marcos's New Society Party.

Martial law affected various parts of the Philippines in different ways. It was ushered in with a great blowing of trumpets regarding land-reform, anti-pornographic laws, anti-drug laws, and more besides. A Chinese businessman was executed by musketry for being a drug-pusher; young people were often stopped at road blocks to have their long hair shorn by officious military men; and discipline, law and order were the slogans of the day. However, the sugar lands of Negros were exempted from the land-reform, and the new military presence drove the students' protest underground and into the mountains. In fact, in a few years, martial law had given birth to a fully fledged armed peasant revolt with student leaders – something which certainly did not exist when martial law was first declared.

The military presence in Negros became very oppressive and went from bad to worse. Liquidation squads, under the euphemistic title of 'task forces', were stationed throughout the island. One of these groups, the Long Range Patrol, was stationed in Kabankalan, purporting to keep law and order. The threat to law and order was supposed to arise from a group of people known as the *salvatores*. The appearance of *salvatores* in the Visayas (the central group of islands in the Philippine archipelago), and, indeed, in the whole of the Philippines, has been a recurring phenomenon since the Spanish set an effective foot in the Philippines in 1565.

In all mission work there is a continual temptation to use the sword as the back-up to the Cross. Wherever this happens, there is likely to be a reversion to animistic ways. So every now and again throughout Philippine history, particularly in times of heightened oppression, there have been revolts which look back to old pre-Christian beliefs for inspiration, although they are well mixed with beliefs and symbols of the new creed – a sort of syncretism.

In the mountains of Kabankalan this has happened several times during the last hundred years – ever since General Sarabia marched into the mountains with his men in the 1850s and massacred the people. The form that it took in the 1970s was that of bands of men (*salvatores*) who went around on what they saw as a 'Robin Hood' mission of protecting the weak. They got their strength from the belief that they could not be penetrated by bullets. They wore certain talismans and charms and said certain prayers; these things were provided, at a cost of course, by their particular leaders. They saw themselves as being people doing good, but in fact they declined, sooner rather than later, into robbery, rapine and vengeance-killings.

Father Brian Gore and his small Christian communities opposed the *salvatores* staunchly, yet non-violently, and he also tried to educate them and to change them, as their main base was in his parish on the left-hand side of the river, looking up-river from Kabankalan, rather than in my parish which was on the right-hand side of the river.

To complicate matters, in another part of the Kabankalan mountains the New People's Army (NPA) of the anti-Marcos rebels was entrenched, and some of the officials in Kabankalan felt doubly threatened by these two groups. This was one good reason for the presence of the Long Range Patrol.

The Long Range Patrol itself was not above blaming the excesses of the *salvatores* on the NPA; nor had it any scruples in ascribing its own atrocities to the NPA, if it thought it could get away with it.

Others were saying that the Long Range Patrol also had another purpose: that of clearing the way for mining rights in the mountains for certain people. There is no conclusive proof of this.

In the month of March 1980, Brian and his Christian community arranged a massive meeting to complain about the many abuses by government officials in their parish. The mayor was invited to attend and was to be a speaker.

The format of the meeting was first to give the people a microphone by which they could air minor complaints, and then build up to the major military abuses. The first part would, naturally, concern the proper running of the municipality of Kabankalan. This was to be merely a lead-in. The second part – the most important and truly grim part – was to name and denounce military atrocities.

To the chagrin of the Long Range Patrol and other military personnel, who were there in force, some ten thousand people attended the meeting. Anyone with some knowledge of gathering crowds must realise that the gathering of ten thousand people on a mountainside like Oringao – or, for that matter, anywhere – for a protest is indicative of a fairly strong infrastructure of organisations, education and awareness. The army was stunned. The mayor was taken aback.

As luck would have it, the minor-complaints session about the town officials and the indirect criticism of the mayor's administration was all that there was time for before the heavens opened and the rest of the meeting was awash.

The mayor left the meeting feeling that the whole thing was a political exercise against himself. Self-appointed advisers found that it suited their purpose to feed this line to him. These advisers have a lot to answer for. Most people in a position of authority are, to a great extent, vitally dependent on the information and atmosphere which advisers convey to them. It can be very difficult to break through the circle of one's advisers and get to the people themselves – and if you do, it is just possible that the ordinary people will be unwilling to be themselves when it comes to talking. Short of disguising himself, and perhaps living among the people for a few weeks, someone in authority is, to a greater or lesser extent, at the mercy of advisers. And this, let me add, goes for us priests as well.

In the next few days or weeks two events occurred which were to form an essential part in the understanding of the whole murder case that was to follow.

The first was the mysterious disappearance of Alex Garsales and Herman Muleta. Both had been leaders in the Christian community; both had had conflicts with the Kabankalan municipal authorities; and both had taken part in the Easter ceremonies of that year. In fact, Alex had played the part of Christ in their Passion play and he used the occasion to make a personal statement of his faith which we still have. It is as follows:

> My Brothers: I, Alexander Garsales, of Barrio Tan-awan, do promise to be faithful to continue teaching the people. I offer myself to defend the poor and the oppressed, to stand for my brothers who are falsely condemned. I offer my life so that peace would prevail in this place in Tan-awan. And I will bear all sufferings so that you, leaders, will not be cowed by threats. I have experienced many sufferings, yet I was not shaken nor discouraged. You made me Christ whom we are now celebrating and all should stand for the truth like Christ did in the past, so that everyone would have faith. The Lord Jesus suffered yet he overcame evil. Though accused of evil doings, he was still made a King and a figure for us to follow here on earth.

That was on Holy Thursday. As if some evil person had taken up the challenge of those words, Alex and Herman disappeared on Easter Monday and their mangled bodies were found three weeks later. To say that the Christian communities all over the mountains were shocked to the core, would be an understatement. But worse was to come.

In April we were celebrating a requiem Mass for Father John Brazil who had worked in Oringao parish with Father Gore and who had died suddenly. Bishop Fortich was present at the Mass and preached a wonderful sermon encouraging the Christian communities and their thrust for justice. Towards the end of the Mass, a group of seven distressed women came and asked to see the bishop urgently. These women were from the border of Oringao parish and their husbands had disappeared.

36

A few weeks later, under Captain Baliscao of the Hinigaran Army Headquarters, the bodies of these men were dug up on the farm of Mayor Sola. An autopsy was to find that the men had been badly beaten; they had then been shot, and some of them had apparently been buried while they were still alive.

The widows had come to the bishop because he was a friend of the mayor (he is still a friend of the family). After the discovery of the bodies he felt that he was in duty bound to push the government to act. So he and Colonel Agudon initiated the prosecution of Mayor Sola, who was charged with the murder of these seven men.

The trial must have been a most harrowing event for the mayor's family, most of whom I knew. One of the lawyers for the prosecution was Francisco Cruz of the Diocesan Legal Aid Office and one of the chief witnesses called by the prosecution was the mayor's own cook. By a strange irony, when we went on trial a couple of years later for multiple murder, the lawyer for our defence was Francisco Cruz, and *my* cook was to be a key witness for the prosecution.

The mayor and his companions were still on trial when Pope John Paul II arrived in the Philippines in February 1981. The pope's coming to the diocese of Bacolod was a direct result of negotiations carried out by Bishop Fortich. The bishop's diocesan team gave special seminars to the people throughout the diocese so that the visit would bring about a renewed understanding of discipleship.

In the mountain parish of Tabugon, where I was parish priest, all our Christian communities took part in the seminars. Then they pooled together whatever money they had to travel the seventy miles to Bacolod city, capital of Negros Occidental to hear the pope, who was to speak in a vast open reclaimed area near the sea.

I was filled with apprehension. The people's hopes had been raised by the seminars. We had presented discipleship to them in the words of the prophet Micah: 'To live justly, to love tenderly and to walk humbly with your God' (Micah 6:8). If in this acutely unjust situation of Negros, the pope were to soft-pedal when it came to the matter of justice, it seemed to me at the time that the visit could do more harm than good.

Newsweek magazine had timed an article on Negros to coincide with the pope's visit. The title of the article was 'An Island of Fear'. Using Bishop Fortich's description of Negros as a 'social volcano', the magazine described in brutal detail the death with torture that had been visited upon Alex Garsales and Herman Muleta in the previous April and the fear among landowners that a strong human-rights sermon from the pontiff could lead to a challenge to their feudal domination on Negros island.

As the crowd awaited the arrival of the pope, who should drive up to the centre of the reclamation area but the Honourable Imelda Marcos, wife of the President, First Lady of the Philippines, Governor of Metromanila, and Minister of Human Settlements.

She went straight to the microphone prepared for the pope, and began to speak: 'Negros is not an island of fear, it is an island of love. . .'

She then disappeared quite as suddenly as she had appeared. She was gone almost before the people knew she had been there. There was no applause. Just puzzlement. It was quite obvious that the *Newsweek* article had made an impact; it had touched a tender spot to such an extent that the military commander of Negros filed a multi-million-peso suit against *Newsweek*.

All still awaited the pope. I will never forget the apprehension with which I awaited the talk of His Holiness, as I sat with the priests on the platform from which he was to speak. I could see my own people in the crowd with their banners – pathetic things made from old sacks.

The people were thirsty, hungry and tired, but bright-eyed with hope and expectation. The previous night they had slept on the grass in the open air. Tonight they would start the long trek home to Tabugon and their thatched shacks in the mountains.

Would the pope let us down? Would he give out social platitudes?

His Holiness arrived and started to speak in a strong, clear voice. After the opening sentences, I sat back in my chair and let them flow over me; I was no longer listening to each word. It was a ringing call for justice, banishing my fears.

'The Church,' he said, 'will not hesitate to take up the cause of the poor. She will be the voice of those who are not heard, not only when they demand charity, but when they ask for justice.'

'Not hesitate'! What a world we would have, if Christians all over the world were to follow these words. That night our bishop did not join the pope's entourage but stayed back in Bacolod to give a party for us priests in his own home. It was a personal little affair of shared joy. Bishop Fortich had pulled it off again. The pope had come. Nothing had gone wrong, no accident or assassination, no rudeness or breakdown, and, into the bargain, that magnificent talk which had surpassed our greatest expectations – surely the best he had given in the Philippines and clearly underlining the Church's non-negotiable commitment to the poor.

Quite suddenly the telephone rang and the bishop was called away. His expression changed. It was a sugar magnate, a leader in the political and economic world of sugar-land. His message was sharp and clear: 'Who prepared the pope's talk? If that is his message, then there will be war in Negros. . . and to think we footed the bill for all those decorations!'

The bishop hung up and then just sat there, the mood of celebration suddenly gone. We knew his policy well. He regarded us as his over-enthusiastic sons and thought we were in need of a pull on the reins every now and again, since he felt that we were a bit too hard on the planters. They too were his flock. He knew them all personally, and had been bending over backwards in an attempt to get them to see the need for reform, and for a change in the social structures. Now this message from 'number one' seemed to have torpedoed his delicate policy of even-handedness.

We gathered around him and began to sing. We sang all sorts of songs, trying to cheer him up a bit, and finally we sang 'We shall overcome': 'We'll walk hand in hand someday!' His good spirits returned and he began to share with us the inside story of the visit: his struggle to get Negros included in the first place; his verbal battles with Archbishop Marcinkus; his pride that the pope had written the talk himself in his own hand. In that unusual moment of intimacy and unity the spectre of threatening oligarchs seemed to recede. He had found his real strength.

One of the side-effects of the pope's visit was that article in *Newsweek*, as a result of which Mayor Sola was imprisoned, so that the antinomy between Church and local government was given a new fillip.

The court case against the mayor continued until finally he was released on bail and returned for a famous entry into his own town of Kabankalan, a town where, when elections were free, he had always won by a landslide. However, a great number of events had occurred since the halcyon days of his early years and now he found it more prudent to live in Bacolod and visit Kabankalan from there. It was on one of these visits that he was to come to grief.

On 10 March 1982 Mayor Sola was visiting his farm, Santa Isabel, in Kabankalan; he had taken a driver and three guards with him in a red pick-up. At about two o'clock he left the farm to go further up into the hills to have a look at his ranch. It was when he was coming back from his ranch at five-thirty in the evening, as the sky was already dulling with the approaching sunset, that he and his companions were ambushed.

The position of the ambushers had been very carefully chosen because they were invisible right up to the very last moment. Just as the red pick-up crested a small rise in the road, the firing broke out from both sides. In a matter of minutes the mayor and his four companions were dead. There was some evidence, also, that one of the guards who had been riding in the back of the pick-up had flung himself underneath the vehicle but was finished off by a close-range shot by one of the attackers.

The people in the little hamlet nearby, called Bayhaw, heard the shots and ran up to a knoll to see what had happened. They could not make out the faces, but they counted some seventeen armed attackers, who then set off in the direction of the hills. They all wore balaclavas.

It was not very long before the local police from the town of Kabankalan arrived under the chief of police Captain Malvas. They immediately began to investigate the matter and were joined, after some time, by Captain Mendoza, the intelligence officer of the Task Force Kanlaon (the successor of the notorious Long Range Patrol), which was stationed at Sonedco less than two miles away from the site of the ambush and much closer to it, indeed, than the police. All Sonedco heard the shots; why the task force arrived so late we do not know.

In the succeeding days, the provincial commander of Negros Occidental himself, Colonel Deinla, came to Kabankalan and, as a result of his investigation, issued a statement to the *Visayan Times* stating clearly that his investigations showed that Mayor Sola and his companions had been killed by the New People's Army. The report, published on 15 March 1982, read:

> Negros Occidental's provincial commander, Colonel Rohilio Deinla, attributed to the New People's Army (NPA) the ambush and killing of Kabankalan Mayor Pablo Sola and four others on 10 March last. The provincial commander blamed the NPA for perpetrating the ambush, following the results of preliminary investigations conducted by constabulary operatives.

On 28 March the NPA produced a revolutionary newspaper called *Paghimakas* which claimed that the NPA had done the deed and gave the reasons why, together with diagrams showing how they had done it. On 21 July, the *Visayan Times* issued another army statement – this time coming from Task Force Kanlaon – saying that they had captured two NPA hit-men who had admitted participation in the ambush.

To all intents and purposes, the mayor's death had been solved, though a large number of townspeople, particularly those of the more prosperous families, secretly felt and said that they thought it was the army who had committed the crime. Indeed, they were able to show all sorts of motivations, not the least being, they said, that some army people feared that the mayor would give evidence to show that ultimately it was the Long Range Patrol who had killed the seven peasants.

All that was nothing but sheer speculation. Meanwhile, the case was closed, so that people like me whose memories were fresh and who had many documents to prove my absence from Kabankalan when the crime had been committed never dreamt of preserving those documents or recording events that would have proved very useful to all of us later on.

Now, fourteen months later, we were suddenly faced with a court case in which an elaborate and carefully stitched accusation was being levelled against us. This case was to begin in a few days.

To start with, it was almost impossible to recall, in detail, what one had been doing on that fateful day of 10 March 1982, fourteen or fifteen months before, and our efforts to follow up the documents were severely hampered by the fact that we three priests were now under house arrest in our own parishes at considerable distances from one another and that the six lay leaders had been transferred to Bacolod Provincial Jail, about sixty miles from Kabankalan.

Meanwhile, the government-controlled press, radio and television had it all their own way and the ordinary man-in-the-street was beginning to get confused. A brief look at the concocted plot shows that in parts it was a masterly piece of work and was obviously composed by experts. The nub of the government accusation against us was that on 10 March 1982 at two a.m. we (Fathers Gore, O'Brien and Dangan) had accompanied a group of armed men from Father Gore's *convento* (parish community house) in Oringao to my *convento* in Tabugon. From there to the site of the murder, outside the hamlet of Bayhaw on the outskirts of Kabankalan, Brian had driven, I had been in the vehicle, Father Dangan had held an M16 rifle and accompanied the killers; then Brian and I had driven away again at six a.m. leaving the others to commit the murder.

There was a lot more to the indictment than that – such as three previous conspiratorial planning meetings – but if one were to look into the heart of the matter for a moment, one would see immediately that Brian and I would have considerable difficulty in finding alibis for ourselves between the hours of two and six on the morning of 10 March. These are the hours when the world is sleeping, particularly in the Philippines where late-night customs do not exist.

Who could a priest get to witness that he had been fast asleep in his bed? There could be no doubt that those who had thought up the plot were professionals and, what was more, we knew that they had seventeen so-called witnesses to hand, because the eighteenth had actually escaped and had told us that he had seen the affidavits of the other seventeen. He had also seen, to our amazement, that the seventeenth witness was none other than my own erstwhile cook, who now claimed to have accompanied us and taken part in the ambush and the killing of the mayor.

What had at first appeared ludicrous had taken on a deadly earnestness.

FIVE

We Ask for Bail

Courts and all their trappings are designed to inspire awe, respect and even fear. In them the guilty are those for whom the fear is intended, but in reality any human being feels intimidated in a court of law, except, of course, the judge and lawyers who are as at home there as either you or I in our kitchen. It is a great advantage and is presumably to be used for the sake of law and order; but if the courts are corrupt, if the judges are venal, and if the lawyers are self-serving, then all this can be used as part of a great instrument to bludgeon the innocent or the merely ignorant. And the unkindest cut of all is that it all appears to be fair.

Long before the court opened for business on the morning of 17 May 1983, the crowds had begun to gather from all over the island of Negros. Though members of the Christian communities coming from Oringao, Brian's parish, were harassed by the military on the way, the total number of people outside the court eventually reached some two thousand. They sang and prayed and waved banners. Inside, the court was so packed that people had literally climbed up the walls and were clinging to various fittings. Pictures of previous mayors of Kabankalan going back to the last century, though high up, were knocked askew. Hundreds of people, including many priests and nuns, were in the packed *sala*, as the courtroom is called in the Philippines. By the time the lawyers for both sides arrived in their *barongs* (mandarin-collared embroidered shirts which hang outside the trousers),the atmosphere was one of great tension.

Finally, the judge himself entered on the dot – suave, collected, inscrutable. He smiled and gave a little allocution; the theme, then as later, was that he looked to God for guidance in all that he did. It was not overdone – just enough, quietly unassuming, relaxing. And we all did relax.

Then the bail hearings began. We had envisioned bail hearings as taking a couple of hours, and they normally do not take more than a matter of minutes. However, it was not long before we were to learn that we were in for a long haul because, to our amazement, the prosecution, after some tedious legalistic sparring on matters of procedure, began to call on the doctors and other witnesses to prove that the mayor had actually been killed. It was to no avail that our lawyers pointed out that we did not dispute this.

Top - Fr Niall O'Brien under cross-examination during the bail hearings at Kabankalan. *Above* - Onlookers crowd into the courtroom, down the stairs and onto the street outside – at Kabankalan during one of the hearings. *(Far East)*

It was quite evident from the start that delaying tactics were to be the order of the day. For some reason we had all relaxed. It took a long time for the penny to drop. For the next two months, witness after well-trained witness was brought in to tell the public that among others they saw the three priests and six laymen at the scene of the crime or that they actually took part in the preparations for it.

During all this time the press was allowed full access to the court. The weeks dragged on and every session became a useless battle to have the hearings held daily, or at least more frequently. Again and again the prosecution argued for later starting, longer breaks, early finishing and delayed hearings. They nearly always managed to gain the delay they sought.

We were feeling completely frustrated. But frustration was not our only feeling. Emotions ran high several times in the court, for instance when Sofronio Manila, a man from the mountains in Father Gore's parish, claimed that the actual planning of the death of Mayor Sola and his companions had taken place in the church at Oringao.

At this point Attorney Johnny Hagad, our chief defence lawyer, stood up and said to Manila: 'Do you mean to tell the court that the three priests sat between the altar and the confessional box, in front of the Blessed Sacrament, and planned to murder the mayor and his companions in cold blood?'

The interpreter, a quiet and devout man whose own brother is a priest, began to translate into Ilongo for Manila. But as he translated, the shocking impact of the words bore in on him and, to the amazement of the court, he broke down and wept. In fact, most of us in the court were deeply moved and it was not the first time that the session had to be halted on this account.

As each witness against us was called upon to take the stand, he had to identify us. This was easy because we were all in the dock, not in the crowd, and no attempt at a mixed identification parade had been carried out. It was just a matter of studying our photographs, which were now, of course, in every newspaper, and getting our names right. So the witnesses pointed us out with impeccable accuracy, except for poor old Lucio Raboy. Lucio, from the moment he took the stand, looked hunted.

My heart went out to Lucio. He admitted later under questioning in open court that he had been told that if he refused to act as a witness against us, he would himself be implicated in the crime! However, when the time came to identify us, we had managed to slip Father Eugene McGeough in beside me in the dock.

Eugene is from Kildare and is the parish priest of the nearby parish of Isio. It was obvious that Lucio had been warned that I was the difficult one to recognise, because there was another priest beside me who was a bit like me in appearance and also because I had shaved off my sidelocks. So, with great intensity, he pointed me out, much to my disappointment. Then, just as he came to point out Brian Gore, a doubt overcame him and, to the surprise of all of us, he swung around and pointed to Father Michael Martin from Carrickmore, Co. Tyrone, our superior in Negros, naming him as Father Brian Gore.

There was a roar from the gallery and, though delighted myself for any break, my heart went out to this man, Lucio, who looked like a trapped rabbit – trapped between his relentless military custodians and the crowd in the court, who must by now have seemed to him like a threatening mob. I could not help thinking how much evil lay behind this case, how the witnesses were even more victimised than we were, and I wondered what was going to happen to them when all this was over. Could they be left around to tell the tale?

The endless delays and postponements were very wearying. Frequently, we would arrive at the court to be told that the next witness was sick or indisposed, or to be given some other excuse. One must remember that getting to the court was quite an achievement, as some of our lawyers had to travel sixty miles down to Kabankalan. With Solomon-like deliberation, the judge listened carefully to each plea for a delay. He weighed the arguments on both sides with great gravity. . . and usually came down in favour of a delay of one sort or another.

On one classic occasion, the prosecutor asked for a break of thirty minutes. It was ten o'clock in the morning and the defence said there was no need for a break. However, with great solemnity the judge said that he would give fifteen minutes; he banged his gavel and dismissed the court 'until eleven o'clock' – an hour! Sometimes we felt that these breaks were vital for the prosecution, especially if a witness was beginning to crack or some of his story had to be patched up.

The bail hearings ran all the way into July. By that time the people who had to travel down the mountains to attend the court were exhausted. For a subsistence-level farmer, one day away from food-seeking is a heavy burden. The praying and singing crowds had diminished. The court was still full, but the early days of the hearings were gone, when a murmur from our supporters in the courtroom would spill out over the balcony and be re-echoed by the crowd in the *plaza* below.

Against the twelve witnesses for the prosecution, we would only produce one. This one was to be me, and my testimony was to be devastating. I took the stand and after a few preliminary questions, my lawyer, Francisco Cruz, asked me: 'Father O'Brien, where were you on 10 March 1982?'

'I was on the island of Luzon in the city in Manila.'

'When did you leave for Manila?'

'On 8 February 1982.'

'When did you return from Manila?'

'On 22 March 1982.'

'Did you at any time during those dates return to Negros?'

'No.'

It was obviously a sharp blow to the prosecution. If I had been in Negros at the time of the killing, it would have been impossible for me to find a witness to guarantee that they had been with me between the hours of two and six a.m. on 10 March 1982, but since I had been in Manila, all I had to do was to have witnesses to the effect that they had seen me in Manila on 9 March after the last flight had left for Negros, about three hundred miles away across the islands and seas of the archipelago.

Then my lawyer showed the court the testimony of my stay in Manila, comprising numerous documents, hospital records, seminar print-outs with my name on them, receipts for articles bought and invoices of money withdrawn.

I was still on the stand three weeks later and under cross-examination from the prosecutor, when my evidence was brought to an abrupt end by a dramatic scene in the court.

The prosecutor (or *fiscal* as he is called in the Philippine courts) lost his temper for once, when Attorney Cruz requested him to 'ask sensible questions', implying, rightly, that the questions were all off the point (he had been trying to prove that I was connected in some way with the IRA – merely part of the delaying tactics). The *fiscal* exploded, challenging Attorney Cruz to fisticuffs downstairs. He was not held in contempt of court, but he did not appear at the next hearing on 17 July 1983, at which both sides closed their case and the judge retired to make his decision.

We presumed that the decision would come in a matter of days. After all, the judge had heard every word of the case and had his own notes. But we presumed wrong. The six-month comedy of the stenographic notes was only beginning. The prosecution asked for time for the stenographic notes to be finished. For some mysterious reasons these same stenographic notes took months and months, and although I often visited the stenographer with my guard and heard her various explanations, they appeared to me to be quite unconvincing and the whole case began to take on an even more sinister note.

I refer here to my guard, because as soon as we three priests were let out of prison, we were assigned our personal guards under the system of house arrest, which I will now outline in detail.

SIX

House Arrest

The document containing the terms of our being put under house arrest has been lost, but to the best of my recollection there were five conditions:
1. each of us was to be accompanied, at all times, by two armed guards;
2. at no time were we to leave our *convento*;
3. no visitors were to be received;
4. there was to be no talking to the press or any other media;
5. only sacramental ministry was to be engaged in.
Of course, the terms were unacceptable and full of contradictions, but Brian, Vicente and I made sure to sign nothing. We also, rightly, banked on the basic Filipino humanity, which interprets all laws broadly and with a great amount of common sense.

Our first few days with our guards were ones of great confusion. No one had made any provision to feed them, so they frequently had to eat with us. They themselves had received no instructions and were visibly afraid that they might be knocked off in an ambush attack made on us – possibly by the army! They had their own various family problems to attend to and from time to time they asked our permission to be absent. Hence, each of us developed his own *modus vivendi*.

The station commander could spare only one guard for me. His name was Boy Negro and he was a gentleman. May he rest in peace. Boy exhibited typical Filipino courtesy and delicacy, never causing any problems. He had his rice farm to attend to, so he often left me on my own. That created problems, because when I wanted to travel I would have to go to his rice farm looking for him. Going to Bacolod was always a hassle. I was compelled to have a radiogram from the provincial commander in Bacolod to the station commander of Kabankalan giving the necessary permission. Brian had the same problem. However, Itik's chief of police did not follow that rule, but then Itik had two guards, not just one!

On one occasion, I was laid low in Bacolod with a bout of dysentery which required admission to hospital for a couple of days. Boy Negro slept in the bed next to mine, with his gun under his pillow. When the doctor came around the next morning, he had to attend to both of us – to me for dysentery and Boy Negro for high blood-pressure.

We were back in our parishes – Brian in Oringao and I in Tabugon, with the Ilog river dividing the two, and Itik in Cabacungan in the mountains of La Castellana. This is the ridge of mountains which forms the backbone of Negros island and divides Occidental Negros from Oriental. Itik was further north than we were, and nearer Bacolod.

Father Dangan had taken over Cabacungan as the first priest to live there. He lived in a small shack, had no real church, and grew his own food. Most of the time he ate out with parishioners, and slept out at times too. He feared the possibility of an ambush on his own home. At the same time, the situation was eased somewhat for him, because the son of one of his guards was also the sacristan of his church; indeed, the guards seemed to become part of Itik's extended family. Good-natured, placid, able to rough it, Itik's appearance would have made him a natural for the role of Friar Tuck in a more benign age. (But appearances can be deceptive, and he epitomised the old adage 'still waters run deep'. He has that unshakable determination to make that preferential option for the poor which Pope John Paul II had called for on his visit to Bacolod.)

Brian was back in Oringao, lost in his work of building small Christian communities, which was made more difficult now that all his lay leaders were in prison in Bacolod. It was the lay leaders' wives, under Brian's direction, who were gradually taking over the various activities of the parish. He had his worm projects in full swing. But Brian and his people were suffering constant harassment from the local military detachment. His attempts to get permission to go to Bacolod were frequently frustrated, with the result that I was to see very little of him – or, for that matter, of Itik.

My parish problem was somewhat different from the others'. I was going back to Tabugon to take my leave, eventually, leaving Father Terry Bennett from Omagh, Co. Tyrone, to take over as parish priest. This arrangement had been made before my arrest, as at that time I was about to take my home leave in Ireland. It was only the night before my arrest that Terry had arrived, and we both agreed that it would be a good idea, now that I was under house arrest, if I were to stay on for a few months with him, to introduce him to the small Christian communities, to which he had a full commitment.

Theologically the small Christian communities draw their inspiration from the pastoral model of Church found particularly in the Acts of the Apostles: 'All the believers continued together in close fellowship and shared their belongings with one another. . . They had their meals together in their homes, eating the food with glad and joyful hearts, praising God and enjoying the good will of all the people' (Acts 2:44-47). Sociologically the emphasis is on smallness of scale. Individual communities should never be so big that members cannot know all the others personally – 'face-to-face' community with self-reliance being an important ingredient. The methodology necessarily relies heavily on reflection on the Scriptures, so that Gospel values can be applied to the daily life and problems of the communities.

In Tabugon and Oringao we had many small Christian communities and we had organised groups of these into mini-parishes. As a community all were expected to be involved in the works of mercy and in the defence of the rights of the poor. In this light the sacraments were essential armaments in the struggle to serve, not a superstitious dressing on a secular life. The Eucharist was not an escape from the cares of the world, but a commitment to change it with Christ. I would say that attendance at Sunday liturgy increased tenfold in Tabugon over a few years due to this approach.

Father Bennett also wanted to learn about the barefoot doctor programme, into which I had put a lot of work. Anyway, both of us had agreed that it was best for the outgoing parish priest to spend a period with the incoming one so that, even if he were going to change procedures, he would at least know why the procedures that he might wish to change were introduced in the first place. Knowing this, of course, would put him on his guard. There were all sorts of minor matters to be cleared up. By no means the least of these was that I had adopted, in a manner of speaking, two small children.

My 'adopted' children arrived in the following way: Mario Suarez came into the *convento* one day. He was from the Christian communities of Inapoy, and was the chairman of our justice and peace committee, covering thirteen small Christian communities in his area. He held in his hand a typed report and a drawing. The drawing was of a small child with arrows pointing out injury marks all over his body. The report consisted of a list of details as to how a child named Boy and his little brother Roney had been maltreated by two aunts with whom the children had been left by their mother. It came as a shock to me because, in twenty years in the Philippines, I had almost never come across cruelty to children, nor, indeed, to animals.

My parish was divided into sixty small Christian communities, and groups of these communities were formed into a sort of mini-parish. We

49

tried to get these mini-parishes to develop some degree of self-reliance, which is an essential key to human dignity. I hit the ball firmly back into Mario's court, saying that it was a very good report, that I thought the committee had done a fine job, and that he ought to convene the core group of the mini-parish and ask them what they thought should be done about it.

Mario agreed. As he went away, I congratulated myself for the way in which I had handled the case. A few years previously I would, no doubt, have been the one to try to solve the whole matter.

Some days later I heard a commotion outside the *convento*. Quite a crowd had gathered there. The leaders from Inapoy mini-parish, one of the notorious aunts, and two small children, aged four and six respectively, were also there. Mario stepped forward, explaining that they wanted me to speak to the aunt and that the children had said that they wanted to stay with the priest!

I knew that that would not be possible. The *convento* was surely no place for two little fellows that size, and, anyway, another parish priest would soon be taking over and I wondered just how he would feel about it.

I called the elder child to one side. His hair had been shorn, and gashes and cigarette burns were visible all over his skull and body. I was immediately thrown off balance at the sight of the tininess of the little fellow and all those scars.

'Where do you want to stay?' I asked him.

'With you, Pads.' Where he got the word 'Pads' I will never know; it is a diminutive of 'Padre', meaning 'Father', and is sometimes used by seminarians, but it tickled me no end.

'How do you know me? Have you ever seen me before?' I asked him.

'Oh, yes. When you say Mass in our chapel.'

I quizzed him over again. He was adamant. And, into the bargain, he began to show me all his wounds.

My short interview with the young aunt confirmed my guess: shortage of food, children being foisted on her, and her resentment being taken out on the children. It was quite obvious that the children could not go back to her.

Finally I capitulated and agreed to take the children until such time as their mother or some other relative could be found for them. I was almost certain that some of their relatives would turn up, because in the Philippines children are never abandoned.

I explained the temporary nature of my acceptance to the group, so as not to set a precedent. I did not want to undermine their sense of responsibility within their own community or give them a way out when it came to solving their own problems. As soon as the crowd had dispersed, Boy and Roney leaped into the *convento* like rabbits scuttling back to their burrows. They made themselves at home immediately and began to charge around the place examining everything. They showed everyone in the house the marks on their bodies – knife marks, cigarette burns, finger- and toe-nails crushed by a hammer. It seems that on one occasion, because they had eaten peanuts intended for seed, they had been forced by the aunt to eat the husks as well!

When they began to show their wounds like this, I felt uneasy, but finally realised that it was better this way than being reticent and secretive about what had happened. I felt that, for cathartic reasons, it was better to talk the thing out.

When suppertime came, Roney was too tiny to sit up on a chair, so he sat on the floor with his plate, while Boy sat on a stool with his head barely reaching the edge of the table. They took three helpings of rice and wolfed them down with great gusto and energy. It gave me great pleasure to watch them both, talking and babbling to each other and to us.

It was soon apparent that there was a big difference between the two of them. Boy was open and affectionate, but Roney was aggressive and kept his little fists tightly shut and ready to defend himself all the time. It was a frightening reminder of what he had been through.

One night Roney asked to sleep with me. It happened like this. Everyone was out, so that Roney and I were alone in the *convento*. He had begun to cry petulantly. Normally at times like this someone picked him up and rocked him in their arms. I was engrossed in writing an article on the small Christian communities – partly for Terry, to help to introduce him to them when he arrived. However, the crying was so insistent that I had to put down my pen and take Roney in my arms, rocking him until he fell asleep. Or so I thought. However, as soon as I went to put him down again, he started to cry. This happened several times. Finally he spoke: 'I want to sleep with you.'

There was nothing for it but to bring him into my room, lay him on my bed beside my desk, and keep writing away, one eye on the page and the other eye on Roney. He, for his part, stopped crying, but kept an ever-vigilant eye on *me*, waiting for the moment when I would lie down beside him and he could cuddle in.

When I eventually lay down, I could not help reflecting on the depth of the great hunger of many abandoned children for love and tenderness. I hardly slept a wink, for fear of crushing the little fellow. The bed was very narrow – a bamboo shelf, really – but at least Roney was on the inside where he would not fall off.

It was to become a great joy for me to remember to bring home little gifts for the two little fellows, Boy and Roney, but I never stopped wondering what on earth was going to happen to them as my arrest loomed large and Terry's expected date of arrival was imminent. In the event, the arrest was so sudden, taking place the day after Terry's arrival, that I had little chance to explain anything.

Back now in the parish I was able to explain to Terry how I had come to accept the children. In my absence he had grown fond of them so it really presented no problem.

But one day their mother appeared. News reached her somewhere in the north of the island of what had happened to Boy and Roney. She arrived unexpectedly during *siesta* time carrying a new addition to the family. Boy and Roney greeted her with some diffidence as if they were aware that she had in some way abandoned them – but they felt no diffidence towards their new little sister.

The mother decided to visit her own village, collect a few things, get the full story of what had happened, and come back next day to collect the children. It gave all of us the time we needed to prepare to say goodbye, because, as Terry and I admitted to each other later, we both felt a deep ambivalence over the parting.

Next day she returned and Boy and Roney greeted her this time with affection. I can still see them clinging with one hand to her dress, the other desperately holding onto a green plastic army car which I had got for them (and over which there had been much squabbling), riding away in the back of the parish jeep.

It was time for me to go too and leave Tabugon to its new parish priest.

SEVEN

To Leave or Not to Leave

With permission from the Kabankalan Chief of Police I moved now to Himamaylan, the next town northwards towards Bacolod. I was now partly under the Himamaylan Chief of Police and he gave me a new guard, Leon by name. My position now left me freer to move about on my new work as I had been appointed Vocations Director for our seminary which was to open in the coming June. If Leon was willing, I could visit the surrounding schools; I would also be able to follow up the mysterious delays in the stenographic notes without which we were told there would be no bail decision – though no one had heard of a legal precedent for such a thing. My new guard turned out to be a good-humoured, talkative six-footer who was determined not to let me out of his sight; but he was also a friend and he often helped me in getting permission to go to Bacolod city to visit the lay leaders. This was becoming more important as pressure on them grew. They had recently been visited by Captain Mendoza, the official army investigator, who now threatened them with another murder case – the killing of Jimmy Jaena.

Jimmy had been a *salvatore*. Everyone knew this! He recruited in the lonelier parts of my parish and Brian's parish and in particular he recruited a simpleton named Juanito Roa. With Jimmy's backing Juanito terrorised all that part of the parish, so one day we decided on a classic non-violent tactic and a thousand of us arrived out at his little house to confront him. We celebrated Mass but I refused him Communion and told him it was because of the killings he had done and that he could not be part of the Christian community until he changed. It was an excommunication. Like a lamb he submitted to us, and a sack of knives, talismans and charms was collected from his followers there and then.

Juanito returned with us to the *convento* and the people returned to their houses, to sleep peacefully for the first time in months. Juanito promised to leave the area and start a new life. He could not go immediately as his wife had to sell the pig. That was a fatal delay for him, because that very night a hundred yards from the *convento* a terrible murder took place: a young couple and their child were strangled.

The Kabankalan police came to investigate and insisted on taking Juanito with them. Now it was clear that Juanito had been involved in murders and had terrorised the people, but it was equally clear that he had had nothing to do with this murder, and the police knew this. However, having made the long journey to Tabugon, the police did not want to return empty-handed. I asked them to promise me three things: that they would not torture Juanito or beat him up; that they would release him if they had no evidence; and that they would arrest Jimmy Jaena, who was behind Juanito's mountain activity. They agreed, and they did fulfil their promise to arrest Jimmy.

As a result of army investigations Juanito was charged and sent to prison in Bacolod. Jimmy was not only released but also enrolled as a sort of army intelligence operative.

Juanito told me afterwards that he had strongly denied anything to do with the murders which took place near the *convento* but had admitted to some of the crimes ascribed to him, including enrolling people in the '*Salvatore*-NPA', but that these documents of enrolment were prepared and written out by none other than Jimmy Jaena. Juanito's argument was simple: 'How could I prepare these documents when I am not able to read or write?' Jimmy was cornered but he responded bravely and said, Yes, well, he had written the incriminating documents which he had previously denied writing but he had done this, he said, under the direction of Father O'Brien! This was patently ludicrous even to the military, but the outcome was that Juanito was remanded to Bacolod Provincial Jail and Jimmy was made an army agent and released back to the mountains to continue organising the *salvatores*. It seems likely that some military men had a vested interest in *salvatore* unrest; maybe it gave them the justification they wanted for military incursions into the mountains.

Part of Jimmy's act was to start *salvatore* groups. Basically, he had no other purpose than that of making money. He sold them the amulets, the charms, and their membership forms for what he called the '*Salvatore*-NPA'. Jimmy did all the scribing of the documents, as the sort of people he inveigled into the loose movement were normally illiterate.

The NPA of course was not amused at Jimmy using its name on his spurious documents. Anyway Jimmy was now in three groups at once. And one day someone knifed him to death. Who, we will never know. However, Captain Mendoza not only was now accusing the lay leaders but even brought in a would-be false witness to look at them in preparation for a repeat of the previous month's identification charade which had taken place at the bail hearings.

Having brought his 'witness' to look at them, Mendoza then said ominously, 'You know you could get the electric chair for this.' Then he added with concern, 'If you are tortured, just write to me at my office.' The message was clear: the screw was to be turned, but if they wanted some let-up then Mendoza was the key; contact him.

Meantime there was no sign of the stenographic notes being finished and no sign of the judge's decision on bail.

In August the bishop called a meeting. The bail case seemed to have gone into limbo; the pressure on the six was alarming; and knowledge of an attempt on Brian's life and a possible blackmail case against me had come to the bishop. We met solemnly in a room in Batang, our head house at Himamaylan: we three priests, our acting superior Father Mark Kavanagh, Father Terry Bennett, Bishop Fortich himself, his secretary Baby Gordoncillo who was also the Social Action director, and one of our lawyers, Attorney Frank Cruz.

The meeting opened with the bishop saying quite simply that the time had come to take a long, hard look at what was happening.

'I am prepared to back you all to the end, even if it means years and years, but there have been some ominous new developments and I think we should discuss them with an open mind. Firstly, I have heard from a source I can't reveal that there may be an attempt on Brian's life. You are a young man, Brian, and I feel you have a lot of good work to do before you.'

Brian was silent.

Someone then mentioned the fact that maybe it would be a good thing to collect whatever winnings we had while we were still ahead. No one could judge what the army would do – moral principles did not enter into their calculations. If the priests would go home the bishop would personally deal with the authorities over the fate of the lay leaders. We all knew his powers of negotiation and diplomacy. Above all, we had to be realistic and not just feed our own egos. Families and lives were at stake.

Gordoncillo glanced at his notebook and said: 'I also hear, Niall, they have a plan to try blackmailing you with some theatrical scandal – that you have three children in your parish.'

There was a long silence. The bishop was being reasonable; he was only trying to look at all angles, to keep minds open.

Someone asked Attorney Cruz if we had a chance of winning the case in court. He thought not. Everything was stacked against us. We could not even get the stenographic notes typed.

There was another silence, the sort of silence which normally connotes a growing consent.

Then Baby Gordoncillo said to Itik, 'You have said nothing yet, Itik.'

Silence from Itik.

'Go on, Itik, give us your opinion.'

'Well, I'm prepared to follow the group.'

'No. Your own opinion.'

There was a long silence.

Then Itik spoke: 'I'm prepared to follow the group, but' – and now his voice changed – 'if you really ask me my opinion, I think we should follow Christ!'

Nobody stirred.

Then, after a long time, someone coughed and said, 'Well, Monsignor, perhaps we had better think a little more about this. I mean, if the other priests have not been party to our discussions here this morning they'll not see why we have come to this decision and that will divide us. Maybe we should discuss it with all the Columbans and see if we can get a group consensus.'

'That's a very good point,' said the bishop. 'That's a better way. Call all the priests to a meeting next Thursday and put these points to them.'

And so we broke up.

Not for the last time, Itik had saved the day.

August 9 came, and twenty-one priests arrived. It was one of those great discussions, so rare in life, when fellows notorious for dragging red herrings across the trail miraculously controlled themselves. Difficult questions were put and answered.

For example, Brian was asked straight out why he had come back from his holidays if he suspected that he was going to be accused.

Brian said: 'If I hadn't come back the accusers would've had all the more reason to say I ran away because I did it. Also, it's often jibed at us that we missionaries start fires and then bail out ourselves. How could I go off to start small Christian communities in another country and tell people to stand up for their rights, knowing that when things got rough I had bailed out before?'

'But, Brian, have you accepted the fact that there is a real danger to your life?' The question was put quietly and reluctantly. No one wanted to be melodramatic.

'Listen, lads, I don't mind admitting I'm afraid – not to be afraid would be foolhardy – but precisely for that reason I'm taking precautions. I don't travel at night. We have lights on around the house all night and groups from our communities come on a rotation basis to sleep with us at night. But, let's face it, our people are in constant danger to their lives. When they work for us they are in even more danger. Many people have told Nelson, my driver, that he is foolish to work for me, that he's in danger of being killed. I'm not in more danger than Nelson, and, of course,' and here he smiled, 'all of us here *hope* don't we? And I too hope that I'll get through. . .'

Someone wheeled a blackboard into the room and we wrote up on it the options:
1. negotiate now;
2. no negotiations ever;
3. decide after we get bail.

The whole question was batted around and finally we took a secret ballot. The result came out as follows: 1. negotiate now – one vote; 2. no negotiations ever – two votes; 3. decide after we get bail – eighteen votes. The three made it clear that they would back the eighteen.

In my diary for that day I have written:

> At night we were very happy with our unanimity. I feel that the process is almost more important than the product – to have a united process.

For me it was a great moment because at the back of my head I had further hopes: this marked the first slight turn of the tide in the direction of those hopes.

Meanwhile Father Mark Kavanagh had to face Bishop Fortich with

After the concelebrated Mass with the three priests who had been released under house arrest, Frs Cullen and Dangan bring Communion to the six lay leaders in Kabankalan Prison, 8 May 1984.

the news that the meeting had decided against his suggestion. The bishop was stern at first and very disappointed, but as the day wore on he changed and eventually accepted that the decision was probably for the best. The tide had turned. It is his ability to listen and to change his mind which has made Antonio Y. Fortich a great bishop.

EIGHT

The Doña Cassandra

The Columbans were founded in 1918 in Ireland to engage in the mission of christianising China. The success of the communist revolution of Mao Tse-tung in 1949 led to the expulsion of the society from China. The choice for continued missionary activity for the society, which by now had spread to Australia and America, lay between Korea and the Philippines. Unlike Korea, English was relatively widespread in the Philippines, a legacy of American colonialism, and this made for an easier transition across the South China Sea. The Philippines rapidly became the society's largest mission field and today more than two hundred Columbans are active throughout the scattered archipelago.

My vocations job, entrusted to me pending the outcome of the bail application, delighted me. With a thaw coming in China in recent times we may yet see the day when Columbans will be allowed back. Who better to take up again the dialogue with that great culture than Filipinos, with their magnificent powers of adaptability, and their generosity, patience and strong faith?

I persuaded my guard to accompany me to the surrounding schools. He chatted up the female teachers while I spoke to the students, inviting them to come to a live-in seminar on vocations which I planned to hold when they were interested enough.

We made an unusual pair on the vocation work, and on one occasion I asked him to accompany me to a school in a nearby town.

'I will go to any other town, but not that one, Father.'

'Why?'

'Well, like yourself I am also accused of murder and the accusers live in that town, and frankly I don't think I would return alive.'

No wonder he was so understanding of my situation!

Life was by no means dull under house arrest, what with daily visits to the schools with Leon, the continual battle to get permission for me and Leon to go to Bacolod to visit the lay leaders, and the constant attempt to move the stenographic notes along. And as if that was not enough my mother now said that she was coming out to the Philippines to visit me. My father had visited a few years before and that had been a great success, but I worried that my mother might be too frail and would not be able to withstand the tropical heat. I was to be proved wrong.

The time for the live-in vocations seminar approached. I asked Brian and Father Eddie Allen and some sisters to help me. Brian pulled no punches in his talk and did not promise any 'rose garden' to the boys – so much so that when question-time came I began to feel that maybe we had overdone it, because one typical question was, 'If we're killed will our parents be told?'

I had never given a vocations live-in before and I thought of telling them the old story of Leonardo da Vinci and how when he was painting the Last Supper he looked for someone to model for Christ. He then looked for models for the other apostles, but the painting took him a long time and it was many years before he got someone to model for Judas. He found him in a prison. When he had finished the painting, the Judas model said: 'That's the second time you've painted me. Ten years ago you asked me to be Christ.' It is a great story to emphasise the pivotal point in a young man's life and how he has the choice as to which road he will take. 'It's up to you': that is the point of the story. However, I decided not to tell it. I felt on reflection that the story was a little outlandish; it was probably not historical and must have been developed by some zealous retreat master.

Then the very next day I had permission to go to the prison in Bacolod to see the six. In the prison yard I was approached by a man of about thirty years of age.

'Do you know me, Father?'

I temporised: 'Well, you're from my parish, aren't you?' I was thinking furiously: where had I seen him before? I asked, 'What are you in for?'

He answered: 'Murder. I killed a man. But don't you remember me, Father?'

Silence from me.

He continued: 'In the parish pageant I was Christ at the Last Supper and the Crucifixion.'

I suddenly remembered.

He had changed. Next time I held a vocations live-in I did tell the Leonardo story!

It was at this time that Benigno Aquino was due back from the United States. He was the only viable opposition figure with across-the-board support. Though coming from the ascendancy class, he had learned adversity and come to understand the hardship of people during the seven years of his imprisonment (two of them in solitary confinement). Many said that he had undergone a true conversion of heart while in prison. He had been allowed to go to the United States to have a by-pass operation. Once there, Marcos would not let him return as he posed a special threat to the régime. However, he was determined to come back. On 21 August he landed at Manila International Airport and was immediately surrounded by government soldiers, who escorted him off the plane. His foot had hardly touched the tarmac when a shot rang out and he was dead – less than sixty seconds after leaving the plane. The message was loud and clear: no opposition would be tolerated.

But the people responded magnificently and the protests spread to the whole country. The crowd which turned out for the funeral was the largest ever recorded in Philippine history. When the government-controlled press ignored all this, the people in desperation defied the laws, and the streets were soon covered with what came to be called the 'alternative press'. In this alternative press lay a hope for us, too, because they began fearlessly to print what was happening around the country. Sales of the government-controlled press plummeted so much that they in turn had to loosen up and not lie so blatantly, lest they lose their customers altogether.

Demonstrations broke out all over the country, not least in Bacolod, and yellow, which had been the colour of welcome for Aquino, became instead the colour of protest and defiance. One of the young Filipino priests asked my mother, who had arrived to visit me in the Philippines, if she would speak on World Human Rights Day at a rally. I had already been apprehensive of her coming to the Philippines, but she had been determined. I was doubly apprehensive of her speaking now, but she made up her own mind again and stood up before fifty thousand people in the *plaza* in Bacolod city. She was one of many speakers. I was in the crowd with my guard, Leon, who had made good friends with Mom. We had not told him she would speak, so he was quite taken aback when she appeared on the platform wearing a yellow rosette, and especially when she managed a few words in Philippino. I, of course, was in agony, my innards were writhing again, wondering if she would collapse, or fall off the stand, or forget the lines. To my surprise she sailed through it. The ceremonies and speakers had a long way to go yet, so I made sure to send out a glass of cola to the daïs where she sat. I laced it with a little something to help her through the ordeal.

News had come that Captain Mendoza was up to more tricks. Through my ex-cook, Pancho, he had begun to contact students from Tabugon (the parish I had just left) to see if any of them would agree to be witnesses. Rewards were being offered openly.

Then in November some shocking news arrived. A great friend of mine, Sister Nanette, a Dutch Carmelite sister, who had been a leading light in the barefoot doctor programme on the island of Mindanao and had visited me personally in the parish, had set out with her lay leaders from the island of Samar for the island of Cebu on a boat ominously called the *Doña Cassandra*. The *Doña Cassandra*, like so many other passenger boats in the Philippines, was purchased from Japan in a run-down condition but was considered good enough for the transportation of passengers between the islands. Before the boat left there had been indications that it would be a rough journey. Some priest friends asked Nanette to leave the boat and go with them by plane. She declined, explaining that she did not want to leave her lay leaders to go it alone. Shortly after departure from Samar, the ship took in a good deal of water through a hole in the hold, so that the cargo began to shift, according to several witnesses. People began to panic, but they got no instructions on how to save themselves. In fact, when they began to put on life-jackets the crew members told them to take them off, with the result that when the boat finally turned on its side many people had to jump into the churning waters without life-jackets. Many others were trapped inside the boat and went down with it. Hundreds were drowned, among them my two dear friends, Boy (a lay leader) and Sister Nanette. Exactly a year earlier she had written the following words: 'Recently I renewed my religious vows at the funeral of Diego, a young pastoral worker who was killed. I stood near his dead body and, crying from anger and sorrow because of such brutal killing, I prayed, "My God, I want to go with these suffering people all the way in their struggle, whatever may happen to me."'

I was stunned when I got the news. I could hardly believe that I would not see Nanette or Boy again, but the circumstances of their death seemed to revive with urgency my own growing conviction that we should be with our lay leaders. I wrote to Brian and Itik and arranged a meeting. We met and immediately agreed that the time had come. We agreed to surrender the privilege of house arrest to President Marcos and return to prison with the lay leaders.

However, this was not as easy as it seemed. How were we to do it? We made the following plans: 1. write to our fellow priests, explaining why we were going back; 2. write to the cardinal; 3. simultaneously telegraph President Marcos to the effect that we were surrendering our privilege of house arrest; 4. radio Brigadier General De Guzman and radio the colonel; 5. inform the bishop so that he would not be blamed for, as it were, instigating this, but so that he should at least know.

You can imagine the discussions as to precisely how the above should be done, but finally we fixed a day. It was to be 5 January in the new year.

The following is the letter we wrote to our fellow-priests:

> It is now eight months since the three of us (Brian, Itik, Niall) left Kabankalan Prison – leaving our six co-workers behind. We did so in order to facilitate their release. . . in the hope that our being out would undermine the so-called unbailability of the crime. There were other reasons, too, such as not embarrassing those who at so much personal cost had arranged the house arrest.
>
> Our being under house arrest has not facilitated the release of the six: in fact it has had the opposite effect; it has in some way clouded the ludicrousness of the false accusation and removed the urgency of releasing the whole nine and an outright dismissal of the case; it may, in our opinion, even place the six in a very special danger. . . But even more cogent than all this is the conviction which we, the nine, hold that it is not right that we priests should (without proven advantage to all) go free while the six remain in prison.
>
> It is clear to all that the six lay leaders find themselves in their present predicament precisely because they followed the Christian call which we their priests proclaimed to them. This, more than anything else, compels us to make a move which no one else can make for us. Frankly, the greatest agony of our last year has not been arrest, has not been internment, has not been harassment, or false accusations. . . it has been the fact that we were separated from our co-workers at the very moment when solidarity with them meant so much to us and was a necessary witness that all we preached about Christian brotherhood and solidarity were not just empty words to be abandoned when the crunch comes.
>
> As priests we found this anguishing but accepted it for the reasons mentioned above. We feel now that these reasons no longer obtain, so we have decided to respectfully surrender to the appropriate authorities the privilege of house arrest. . .
>
> During the last fourteen months it has sometimes been tempting to view the harassments the Church had undergone as distractions from the work of building up God's Kingdom. Somehow we felt that if only these events were over we could go back to our parishes, do useful study, continue our development projects, etc. But as the months went on and we prayed and dialogued together, one thing became clearer to us and that is that this is a grace-filled moment and that Christ's Kingdom is coming about precisely through the

patience and endurance of this time. This patience, endurance and struggle of the whole Church in Negros *is* the good news.

We would like to thank each one of you for the support you have given us. We thank you too for your prayers, group actions, sermons and fasts. We know that this has been an added burden to the work you are already doing. In life the struggle to know what to do is often more severe than the sacrifice in actually doing it.

My God bless us all and guide us as we struggle together to bring about his Kingdom.

NINE

Decision

During the days leading up to 5 January I spent many a night on the balcony of our central house in Batang, Himamaylan, sounding out the other priests to see how they felt about the decision. I visited the Filipino priests to get their reaction also. I was surprised at how much their attitude had changed. They now felt that the stenographic notes and the bail delay were a ludicrous charade and that the time had come to do something. This decision was ours, but we could see that although they would not push us they would back us.

We celebrated Mass together on the morning of 5 January; the news was gradually leaking out and many older visiting priests were present. We could see that they warmly supported us and that meant a lot. But first we wrote a letter to Cardinal Sin, who had worked so hard with Bishop Fortich to get us house arrest:

Pinalangga namon nga Cardinal [Our Dear Cardinal],

We are writing to you to thank you for all you have done for us in the last year and specifically for facilitating our house arrest. We know that no one has more work and problems than you and that is what makes us especially grateful.

For some time we have been meeting together, praying and dialoguing and evaluating the case with the six lay leaders and with our fellow priests and we are now convinced that our being separated from our lay leaders is now being used against us quite effectively. We feel that with the changed circumstances it is no longer right

for us to remain separated from them, so we have decided to respectfully surrender this privilege of house arrest to the appropriate
authorities. This may in turn facilitate the speedier resolution of the
case but above all we are doing it because we feel it is a matter of
conscience.

Your talk in Bacolod gave hope to many and it was greatly
appreciated. May God guide you in all you are doing. You are in
our prayers as we know we are in yours.

In Christ,

Father Vicente Dangan,

Father Brian Gore,

Father Niall O'Brien.

Father Murray, our overall superior, said he would deliver the letter
personally to Cardinal Sin, but he would prefer that we first receive the
approval of Bishop Fortich.

The three of us set out for Bacolod with warm farewells from the
others. But first we had to telegraph President Marcos. The radio man
at the telegram office was an old friend from the days when I gave retreats
in Binalbagan. I told him the telegram must go immediately. He looked
at it and at me knowingly, and he promised. Off we went to our next
destination, which was Bishop Fortich. Now this would surely be harder
than anything else.

I was driving and as I drove the bishop's face kept coming up before
me: smiling and fatherly, laughing, stern, angry. Which one would it
be? For me, there is nothing harder in the world than to hurt or go
against someone whom you care for and who so obviously cares for you,
and this is how we felt about Bishop Fortich. We had worked together
for twenty years, and he had been a faithful guide and father all that
time. What would his reaction to our decision be? We decided that Itik
would be the one to tell him.

We arrived outside his door in the palace, which is the old *convento*
built by the parish priest of Bacolod in Spanish times before the revolution. The bishop was not yet up from his *siesta*. We paced up and down
outside the door like agitated animals in a cage. We shooed away pros-
pective visitors, unceremoniously telling them that we were first and
had to speak to the bishop alone. They must have been surprised, to
say the least. Every now and again one of us would put his ear to the
door and listen to hear if the shower had been turned on or if there were
any signs of movement. After what seemed an age, we heard movement.
We knocked immediately. The bishop opened the door.

'Welcome. I suppose you know today begins the Chinese New Year?
It's the year of the rat,' he said with a chuckle. We laughed too, but a

bit too loudly. 'Well, what can I do for you?' he said, sitting down.

We pulled up three chairs around the desk. There was a silence.

Itik began: 'Well, Monsignor, we came to see you because we want to talk to you – and that's why we are here and have come, because – well – we would like to talk to you, so here we are' – silence '– in order to speak to you and. . .' My innards were in bits and I swore I would never get Itik to deliver a message like this again, because it just would not come out of his mouth.

Even so, after what seemed another age, he finally said, 'You see, Monsignor, we are going back to jail.'

The bishop's placid face gradually broke into a smile. 'You're probably doing the right thing.'

He could not say more, because we had leapt from our chairs and thrown our arms around him. We were in tears.

'You know, Monsignor, we are so ashamed to have our lay leaders in and us out. We have sent the telegram to President Marcos.'

While the others were talking to him I rushed back to the door, where I had a messenger waiting outside. I told him: 'Rush to the plane – it's about to take off – and tell Father Nicholas Murray, who is about to get on, that he can bring the letter to Cardinal Sin. It's okay with Fortich!'

'But have you informed Cardinal Sin?' Bishop Fortich was saying as I returned to the trio.

'Yes, Monsignor, the letter is on its way,' I said, breathless. 'It will be delivered personally by our superior.'

We all began to relax and the bishop offered us a drink.

As we walked out of the bishop's room, who should pass us going in but none other than the chief provincial prosecutor. He gave us a stiff smile, and in he went. Little did we know that he carried with him another 'deal': that we should leave the country and ask, if you don't mind, for house arrest for the six lay leaders! His secret weapon was a small innocuous notice which had just appeared in that day's paper, reading: 'Judge Emilio Legaspi will be absent indefinitely for health reasons.' So the true nature of the bail hearings was finally visible: there would be no bail – it was a deal or nothing. We had made the right decision, even if it was only five minutes before the bell! But more excitement awaited us that night.

The Philippine Constabulary Headquarters of Negros Occidental lies a little north of Bacolod city, and that is where we now headed. Since I still had my guard with me, we passed the armed gates without query and made our way to the inner compound where the provincial colonel lived. The colonel's personal house-guards were a little bewildered at the number of guests we had with us – lawyers and media people.

I dismissed my own guard, Leon, at the door, telling him I would now be in custody and he would not be needed. He was nonplussed, but at least he would not be blamed for abandoning us: he had been with us up to the end.

Finally the colonel arrived in his crowded office. He was obviously unaware of what was brewing and was taken aback when we told him that we had respectfully informed the president and Brigadier General De Guzman of the surrender of our house arrest and that we were now in his custody. His first reaction was to go into his room and produce a bottle of Fundador brandy – not as a celebration by any means, but as a normal gesture of hospitality and as a help to all of us to get through what he knew would be a heavy discussion. He explained, as he poured liberal glasses of brandy for all of us, that he could not accept us. We replied that it was too late, we had no guards. The conditions of house arrest were no longer being kept by us, so we automatically returned to our previous state of detention and, what was more, we had no intention of keeping the conditions from now on.

That bottle of Fundador was consumed rapidly in the ensuing verbal battle and when it was all over the colonel stood up and said, 'Well, you will stay with me until I get further orders.'

The crowd dispersed, the media people rushing back to catch their deadlines, leaving us alone with the colonel and his guards.

'This is a bachelor's household, you know, so I have no food in. We'll have to go out to supper,' said the colonel.

We looked at each other and nodded. So we got into his armed jeep, walkie-talkies blaring, guards running hither and thither, and a second, well-armed jeep accompanying us. We arrived soon at some night club. We were very early and the band was playing to empty tables. The woman in charge of the establishment came over to attend to us. She soon had food dishes coming our way and the colonel bellowed out his song requests to the band and we had the place all to ourselves, except of course for the armed retinue all around us.

More Fundador arrived, and the colonel told us a little of his own life-story. He was a poor boy when he left his provincial barrio in his bare feet. 'When I came back I was a fully fledged major and I was wearing Florsheim shoes: the first thing I did was to buy back the bit of land my father once owned.' I was touched by the little anecdote, although it disturbed my set image of him.

All through the meal, messages kept coming through walkie-talkies to the officers and guards who accompanied us, though never at any stage did they join in the conversation except to laugh at the appropriate times.

Finally, the colonel stood up and we were off to a new destination.

We did not know where and he did not tell us. We arrived at a beautiful house. The colonel walked straight in with the three of us in tow behind him. At the table was a group of congressmen, that is, members of the rubber-stamp assembly called the *Batasan* which Marcos has cobbled together to take the place of the old senate and congress. There must have been a sort of caucus in session because it was a more or less exclusive group, but all stood to attention as the colonel came in. I was relieved to see Jun Gustilo there, one of 'God's gentlemen', a man universally respected for being able to rise above the human circumstances in which he has to live. Although they were about to sit down to a well-laden table, the colonel called them away to a little meeting and told them about us. It was obvious he was displaying us as sort of trophies.

Bottles passed around again and again, and there was an air of slightly over-done courtesy mixed with a little tension. It was shattered, however, when a police station commander from Cadiz, who was drinking too much, rounded on Father Dangan and said, 'I'll kill you.'

Itik answered calmly, *'Tilawi,'* which means 'You just try!'

The tension heightened and amid a certain amount of shuffling and coughing, the colonel rose. 'Two hundred bucks,' he said, holding out his hand to a congressman.

The congressman rummaged through his pockets and produced the cash.

The colonel did the rounds getting money from each. Then he looked at the cash and said, 'That's not extortion, Father Gore.'

'No,' said Brian. 'I'd just call it friendly persuasion, Colonel.'

'Well, we're off,' said the colonel, and it was clear that we were on our way back to the night club where things would be livening up. We knew there would be more to this than met the eye, and Brian and I were agreed that the idea was to fill us with drink and photograph us in compromising situations! Part of the colonel's propaganda war. Quick thinking was called for. So I said, looking at my watch with slight alarm, 'Bishop Fortich likes us to be in bed before twelve, Colonel.' One of the congressmen raised an unbelieving eyebrow as if to say, 'You could have fooled us.'

But the colonel, who never pretended to be a religious man, was observant where taboos and such-like were concerned. If priests were supposed to be in bed by twelve he was not going to have the wrath of God on him for thwarting this. He piled us into the jeeps and at break-neck speed delivered us back to headquarters before the hour of twelve struck and some spell was broken.

We were put in the room of his helicopter pilot, who had to find somewhere else to sleep until the colonel could find proper accommodation, as he called it, for us. The door was closed and we were on our own.

It had been a long day, full of event, ending with this bizarre night with all its tensions. And yet it had all come off as planned. We sat down and prayed our Vespers together, which is the Church's prayer of thanksgiving – thanksgiving not just for our safety, not just for the day, but for the privilege of being allowed to partake in the banquet of life.

TEN

The Philippine Constabulary HQ

Friday, 6 January 1984

We awoke early, and whom should we see in the garden but Boholano Senior, one of the witnesses against us – in fact, one of those who claimed he had killed the mayor with us! – watering the grass, poor fellow.

The first day in the army headquarters was eventful. It was Brian's fortieth birthday and the colonel planned a birthday party! The press were going to be present, including the television, and I was a bit apprehensive. It was clear that the colonel was going to use the press for his own purposes. Meantime, he took us to our new room, a guest room in a building just opposite his own well-sandbagged house. He explained to us with an enigmatic smile that Mayor Sola had been confined in this very room when he was accused of murder.

That night there was a party for Brian as promised. The colonel produced good whiskey and food and invited Channel 8, Bacolod's most docile channel, along to give a gleeful picture of the whole event. This went all over the world.

It is interesting to note that from the start the introduction of the media to the event came from the military. The announcement to Reuters news agency in November 1982 of our guilt and the up-coming trial came directly from them. The full use of cameras in the court continued during the bail hearings while most of the stuff coming out was evidence *against* us, but cameras were later cut out from the court when the evidence began to go the other way. At the birthday party he threw for Brian, the colonel took every opportunity to show media people how comfortable our quarters were. The three of us lived in this small air-conditioned room with its own bathroom, so we could not deny that it was quite all right.

During the day we were asked to sign several papers, but we declined because our lawyers were not present, we said.

Loud shots began to ring out outside our window and we soon discovered we were beside the firing range and that businessmen and landowners came there during the day to practise firing. We noticed most of them had walkie-talkies in their cars, a sort of élite militia. Preparing for what? Only the colonel knew, because the firing range was his baby. What amazed us was that instead of using bull's eyes they were using human shapes as targets for practising what looked like street warfare.

One night we were awoken around midnight by firing outside. Standing on a chair I could see out through the high bathroom window without being seen. There was the colonel, seated below at the firing range, glass of whiskey in one hand and smoking gun in the other. Around him were attendant officers with ice bucket and whiskey bottle. I watched. Several times, after a particularly intimidating barrage of fire, the colonel turned around, grinned at the others, and looked meaningfully back at our room just ten yards behind. I remembered his well-known nickname 'Colonel Hotshot' and wondered what he really meant by his oft-repeated line, 'There are no snakes in *my* forest.'

Among the visitors to the birthday party was Mrs Socorro Tubilla. Mrs Tubilla is a valiant woman. Her husband has a high position in the Philippine navy but this has never stopped her from denouncing government abuses on all occasions. It happened that she had been in the local provincial hospital that same afternoon and had found soldiers in need of medicine and blood. She herself had supplied the needful, and since she met the colonel at the birthday party she took the opportunity to tell him that his men were being neglected.

The colonel was furious, but controlled himself. 'Mrs Tubilla, you will be reimbursed immediately.'

She looked him calmly but directly in the eye and said: 'No, Colonel, I don't want the money. I just want you to take more care of your men.'

Coming from Mrs Tubilla this was too much. He just managed to control himself, but as soon as the visitors had gone he lined up all the soldiers and officers at full attention and with arm outstretched and forefinger almost touching their noses he went up and down the line roaring at them. They never blinked, and I slipped away, not wanting to add to their embarrassment. It was bad enough that two of his men had been killed that day and three wounded in an NPA ambush up in the Kabankalan mountains, the very place the three priests came from, but to have this woman, an obvious sympathiser with subversive types like Dangan, Gore and O'Brien, telling him that he was neglecting the wounded, well this was too much. When he had finished, he roared away in a jeep for solace in the city. His office was abandoned. I slipped over and made a call to my mother, who was now safely at home in Ireland.

When I called I often asked if particular events which had happened to us in Negros had reached the Irish media. Frequently her answer was No. I knew they were reaching the Australian media because NBC and ABC television were often present and we heard mention of developments on Radio Australia. As far as I could see, we were not getting the same coverage from the Irish media.

I wrote to my father and asked him to send me the telephone numbers of the main Irish newspapers. I could not understand why, during the six months of house arrest, they had not picked up the telephone and contacted us. I felt public opinion was going to be vital if we were going to be extricated at all. I could not understand how what was going out on Australian television had not reached Ireland, because when I quizzed Australian television men they told me that anyone could get it from them without much difficulty. We had held a meeting on how to get the Irish and the national Philippine media in on the case. The death of Aquino had loosened up the control of national Philippine media, and it was up to us to give them the information.

To our chagrin and surprise, the birthday party scene, which the colonel had deliberately set up and invited the media to, reached the Irish media. It was therefore clear that the authorities were using the media for propaganda purposes.

At our meeting we had appointed Father Brendan O'Connell from Galway to make regular press releases and we set up a chain of communications between us and Manila and the Columban headquarters at Navan, where first Father Michael O'Neill and later Father Sean Rainey got the information and could give it out to the press. The Irish media could now get fresh information by telephoning Dalgan Park. But it still did not strike them that they could get more immediate and fresher news if they telephoned Kabankalan, where they could easily contact us. Meanwhile, we could hardly keep the Aussies off the Kabankalan phone.

We were able to use the telephone in the colonel's office at certain times when he was out on the town. We also managed to write down the history and background of what had happened and collate the various statements we had made; we had two thousand copies of this printed, so that when visitors came we gave them copies. At the bottom of each page was written in bold type, 'Please help us by multiplying and distributing this.' Thus the perennial question of visitors as to how they could help was answered in practical terms.

My diary reads:

> Surprise, surprise, the woman who washes the clothes of the colonel – we meet her daily – turns out to be the wife of Indiape, the first witness to appear against us in the bail hearings and, more surprising, who should be having breakfast in the colonel's kitchen yesterday but Vicente Pancho, my erstwhile cook. As he left the kitchen, I suggested he visit us in our quarters, but he said he was afraid the colonel would see him. We took the chance to tell him that we held no ill-will against him – after all, the poor fellow was more a victim than anything else. I asked one of the staff why Pancho had visited. They said he worked at the house of one of the officers and he was coming to pay money back which he owed to the colonel's batman – very interesting!
>
> One night the guard on duty turned out to be the guard who at times guarded the witnesses against us. According to him, they were all billeted in quarters just opposite the gate of the constabulary headquarters under strict guard.

About this time talk of hunger strike began. Before Christmas the six lay leaders had done a nine-day fast. It was a protest, a spiritual protest, and limited. It got a great amount of publicity. Now it was being suggested that maybe we should do the same. I opposed it all the way. I felt that neither Australians nor Filipinos knew just what the implications of a hunger strike are in Ireland. It is a very ancient thing. In Celtic times an injured man would go on hunger strike to show he had been wronged. On the face of it, it was non-violent, but one thing about the hunger strike in the Irish situation was that once embarked upon it must be carried through; there is no turning back until the aim is achieved. Looking back on the discussion now, I think that maybe I was not really listening to Brian's side. I saw hunger strikes only in Irish terms, but of course there can be many variations on the theme. My attitude was also coloured by the fact that I have always had a very bad stomach, so that for me a hunger strike would only be a desperate last resort.

Finally I said to Brian: 'Look, Brian, if you lads go on hunger strike I'm willing to be your public relations officer. Now this would be very embarrassing for me, but I am prepared to do it.'

Brian laughed, I laughed and we all laughed, and gradually the idea of a hunger strike died out.

In the meantime we were keeping up contact with the six in Bacolod

Provincial Jail. My mother had given them a present of a tape-recorder before she left and now they were putting it to good use. They discussed everything together in their cell and taped the discussions, putting questions to us and giving us the news. The tape was smuggled to us, and we replied, putting our questions and doubts to them. This was to prove vital for later developments.

Some of their news was disturbing. My diary for Saturday, 14 January, reads:

> News from the jail. This morning the warden called out four of them [the lay leaders], and who should be there but a certain well-known plantation owner. He gave them coffee and then told them that he had seen us (he had not) and that we lived in an air-conditioned room, well off, and not thinking of them. He suggested they turn State's witness and then said that if they did they could get out and be okay. Then he raised his hand and made a circle of two fingers, giving them the money sign. Then he said, 'I have a bit of liquidation of my own to do, but it is not any of you six.' Who then?

Each morning we celebrated our Mass together around the table. We chose readings from Saint Paul's Captivity Epistles and shared the homily, by which I mean that we each commented on what the particular reading was saying to us and answered each other. We also prayed our Vespers together, using the little Ilongo *Evening Prayer Book* which I had had made for our lay leaders.

We gradually learned that we were not the only prisoners in the headquarters. There were other political prisoners. We caught glimpses of them at times; that was all. One night we heard shots. The following morning we discovered that one of our co-detainees had been shot dead. 'Trying to escape' was the answer we got when we asked one of the officers why. But the other staff told us that he was naked when he was shot; in fact, he was in the rafters of the house, so the 'trying to escape' explanation did not seem to hold water. It was ominous. I dreamt that night that soldiers burst into our room and gunned us down. In my dream I was torn between saving myself and saving the others.

By this time we had a steady stream of visitors and our 'Information–Out' machine was beginning to tick over, although Ireland had still not caught on in the same way as Australia. We had the great advantage of being able to assess continually what we were doing. We realised we must join the six sooner or later in Bacolod Provincial Jail. They were being put under various pressures. They were being told that we were living in the lap of luxury. Although they did not believe this or that we wanted it that way, the same information was going out on the local media.

On the smuggled tapes we received a frank answer to a frank question: they told us they would prefer us to be with them. In fact, they said one of the prisoners in the cell next to them had 'escaped'. This prisoner had been visited recently by the military who held us. The strange thing was that no search had been made for the escaped prisoner. The six felt he had been allowed to escape to do a 'hit job' and that we could be the target. The military would just shoot the man later, killing the culprit and the evidence with one bullet – an Aquino-type job! They felt we would be safer with them in the civil prison where all the prisoners would be on our side. They themselves would certainly be safer with the press around. Anyway, all over the world we were accused of common murder, not a political crime, so why were we here in the constabulary headquarters? And now this sudden killing. We were determined to move, but how?

We discussed many possibilities, but two problems faced us: 1. what legal basis had we for changing prisons? 2. granted a sound legal basis, how would we do it, because, if asked, the authorities would just not allow it, since they had too much to lose?

One day I practically shouted, 'Eureka!'

'I've got it,' I said to Brian and Itik. 'Do you remember that remittance order that the judge pulled on us when he suddenly shifted the six to Bacolod Provincial Jail? Well now, that was probably planned before Cardinal Sin twisted President Marcos's arm by threatening to call off the Masses and so got us out on house arrest. So that remittance order *probably* contains *all* of our names. If it does, then legally at this moment we should be in Bacolod Provincial Jail.'

We contacted Baby Gordoncillo, the Social Action Director, and he immediately made the journey to Kabankalan where he went quietly through the court records. Then he returned to Bacolod and burst into our room brandishing the original remittance order. 'Your names are on it,' he said exultantly. We danced around the room. We had our legal basis at last.

But how to get out of the provincial headquarters and into the Bacolod Provincial Jail? It could be dangerous. We decided to sleep on it.

ELEVEN

Escape into Prison

We had decided to get out of the constabulary headquarters and move to Bacolod Provincial Jail and were still arguing about the details.

We laid our plans carefully. Thursday 26 January at four in the afternoon was chosen as the moment. Many priests would come to visit us at three o'clock that day in the van with the smoked windows. The van would park with its doors facing away from the colonel's house. The lads would get out and in the mêlée we would get in. The van would appear to drive off on some errands, as it often did, to come back later. We would drive straight to the provincial jail. The six would have all the prisoners warned: we would be ushered in to 'visit' the six; our passage would be smoothed in. At that very moment our lawyers, the Social Action Director Baby Gordoncillo and our acting superior Des Quinn would arrive at the warden's office. They would not show the remittance order, but would claim that we should be in this jail; when the warden pleaded, 'There is no remittance order,' only *then* would it be produced – after the warden had made it quite clear that it was the remittance order which would do the trick. The lawyers would then leave.

So went the plans, but they went wrong, as we shall see later.

Now our acting superior, Des Quinn, was in favour of postponing things. He and his council felt that the bail decision would arrive and would undoubtedly be in our favour. In fact, the news at the moment was that the judge was actually on his way back to grant it. 'Let's wait and see,' he said. Six and a half months had elapsed since the hearing had ended.

However, the dust of his car had hardly settled when a telephone call came from Kabankalan. I took it. It was Mark Kavanagh. Someone had seen the long-awaited bail decision being typed: bail was denied. It was denied, that is, to the eight of us, but a fifty-thousand-peso bail was given to Itik – Itik who, according to the 'evidence', was actually carrying an armalite. What was more, the judge dismissed my evidence as uncorroborated, self-serving and unauthenticated! So much for all my documents. But the worst was to come. The judge had gratuitously added a sinister paragraph which read: 'By and large, capital punishment may well be justified.' The death penalty – like footsteps coming after us in a dark passage. Stunned, I brought the news to the other two.

Itik's reaction was immediate: 'I will not accept bail. The bailability of one is the bailability of all.'

We were discussing what to do when a knock came on our door. It was seven-thirty in the evening, and I quote from my diary:

> There was a knock on the door. I opened it slightly and saw the colonel and the prosecutor. I told them to wait. Brian did not want me to speak to them, but I insisted that we must be courteous. When I went out to them they looked super-solemn; they handed me a sheet of paper with the word ORDER in capitals written on the top of it, and I made as if I didn't know what it was (it had to be the bail decision, of course). They asked me if Brian had seen it. I said no. They indicated that the judge had decided against us. Then I said to them – and frankly I don't know what came over me, but this is what I said:
>
> 'When all this is over, the truth will come out. God knows who killed Mayor Sola and who helped to cover it up. Those who have taken part in the deceit and have been involved in torture, bribery and destruction of the lives of the so-called witnesses will have to sleep with that knowledge all their lives. And it will rankle in them like acid and they will have to look their children in the face, knowing what they have done. As for myself, I hold no rancour against those who did it. Thank you, Colonel, for bringing this order personally.'

As soon as the bail decision broke, the media were on the trail. Brian was on three different radio programmes next morning directly from the colonel's office. It seems that Mr Hayden, the Australian Foreign Minister, was now getting interested and he was due to visit the Philippines in February 1984 (that is, the following month). Newspapers of all sorts came in to ask our reaction. I decided to allow myself to be sad; I did not want to put on false gaiety and alienate myself from my true feelings. I felt that that would be bad for me.

Extracts from my diary:

> Myself and Itik had lunch with a silent colonel. You could hear a pin drop.
>
> The colonel said, 'What's the name of this fish?'
>
> '*Dalinoan*,' said Itik.
>
> And that was all the conversation.
>
> Brian didn't join us because he knew he would blow his top.
>
> Reporters all day. I was too 'down' to make a statement. All I said was, 'God knows who killed Mayor Sola.'
>
> We agreed on our strategy. Baby Gordoncillo goes to Bacolod

prison now today and 'tests the water', makes appointment with warden (it wouldn't help if we arrived and the warden wasn't there and some underling said he wouldn't be back). When we go tomorrow we do not show the remittance order till the warden complains that we haven't got one. Then we produce it. We prepared all our information papers for distribution, the ones we had printed, and then we got ready for the morning.

O Holy Spirit, guide us tomorrow to be successful in our endeavour, and may our case be joyfully concluded. We ask this through Christ our Lord. Amen.

D Day. Thursday, 26 January
Somewhat fitful sleep as dawn approached. Spectres of possible calamities.

We celebrated Mass and read the last words of Matthew's Gospel: 'The eleven disciples went to the hill in Galilee were Jesus had told them to go. When they saw him, they worshipped him, even though some of them doubted. Jesus drew near and said to them, "I have been given all authority in heaven and on earth. Go, then, to all people everywhere and make them my disciples; baptise them in the name of the Father and of the Son and of the Holy Spirit, and teach them to obey everything I have commanded you. And I will be with you always, to the end of the age."'

We went over each detail again. The lads were to arrive at three p.m. We were to be gone and at the prison at four p.m. Australian television men kept coming in the middle of this planning. Then the colonel himself came over to our 'guest house', completely unaware of what was going on. He met Brian and offered him a beer. Brian refused, saying that we were fighting for our lives and he could not see how we could be friends. Then the colonel went off in high dudgeon and telephoned the bishop. Since he could not get hold of the bishop, he got Baby Gordoncillo.

Baby came over immediately and after seeing the colonel came to see us.

'The colonel is in a rage,' said Baby. 'He is deeply hurt, he says, by Brian saying "We're not friends."'

Brian and Itik and I did not know whether to laugh or be angry.

'It's not so funny,' said Baby. 'He is determined to see the bishop today to have all your privileges curtailed. He's talking of no phone calls and no visitors, etc.'

How would this affect our plans to escape?

Before he left, Baby's last words, with that enigmatic smile of his, were, 'Don't fail to come to our appointment.'

Well, things began to go wrong from there. The priests never arrived at three p.m. We could only surmise that Baby's fears had been fulfilled and that new restrictions had been introduced.

We decided to walk to the outer gate, one by one, as if rambling unobtrusively.

When we got there we found the van stalled there, with all the lads. No visitors allowed to the inner compound.

What to do? Does the colonel know of our plan? Or are these just new restrictions? If he knows, then are we being watched? A car with tinted glass and a driver, was parked just beside our van. Who was that? Should we ask the colonel's permission to visit the bishop and use that as our exit permit? Would the guard let us pass?

Finally it was simply solved by one man who said little but seemed instinctively to know the right thing to do: Itik. He went over to the van quietly and got in, screened by the visitors. I followed eventually, then Brian followed after further discussions. Then we were joined by Des Quinn, who sat up front with Frankie Connon and Rolando the driver. We crouched in the back seat . But who was the man in the car with the tinted windows?

'Close the door – for God's sake, start.' The other lads were milling around in groups unconcernedly, covering our entry to the van. Continuing from my diary:

> We noticed a car in front of us. Dark windows. Two-way radio. Man at wheel seemingly looking at us. Was he placed there by the colonel?
>
> 'Hurry up, Rolando, start.' He started. It seemed hours. The other priests hung around us as if nothing. . . Our van made for the gate. One of the Aussie TV men had been asked to get the guard at the gate into conversation.
>
> The gate seemed to be closed. 'Stop, Rolando, stop.' 'Keep going, you'll make it.'
>
> Rolando sped through the half-open gate by a hair's breadth. (He didn't acknowledge the guard, who was in conversation with the Aussie media man.) We held our breath (the three of us were crouched down on the seats). Through the gate, turn right; like an hour – a hundred years, no one spoke.
>
> Then Des said, 'Well, no shots in the air, lads,' and we relaxed and smiled.
>
> Then: 'Put your foot on the gas. . . Go through the market. . . No, keep going. Take off your hat. . . Put it on. . ' Until we got to the prison.

When we got to the prison the six had 'friends' waiting to usher the three of us straight in to 'visit'. (The prison guards at first thought we were just more foreign visitors.) Then we entered the cell and closed the gate. A guard came in after us and queried. We told him we were having a meeting. He went to the warden to report. He came back to say we must have our meeting outside the cell. We told him it was too late, the meeting was over, and the meeting had agreed that we stay *in* the cell. They could not accept this. Our lawyers then presented the remittance order.

From the cell we asked Des Quinn to go to the warden and say: 1. it is better to have us come quietly like this; 2. it is legal; 3. we will not leave unless there is a legal document telling us to do so which is stronger than the remittance order; and 4. Brian added for good measure, 'I won't go back to the army headquarters!'

So, what with the lawyers, the *fait accompli*, the reasonableness of the case, and Brian's ultimatum, the warden agreed to accept us as 'guests'. All this time the international media were present – newspaper reporters, photographers, television cameramen.

When the crowd moved away (the media people to meet their deadlines), the warden called us to his office. As a safeguard we decided that only seven would go; Peter and I would remain behind in case it was a ruse. It was not. The warden was just plain nervous. He was a pleasant man; English was not his first language.

> He wants us to call ourselves 'guests'. His wife is nervous. She does not want him involved. Our lawyers have walked off precisely so that we can say we won't do anything without our lawyers. We have told him this.

Back at the constabulary headquarters at Kamingawan a comedy of sorts was taking place, which explains why there was no hot pursuit. It appears that just at the time we were taking our leave, the bishop himself was arriving. He was immediately closeted with the colonel, who had called him urgently. The colonel had a serious complaint to make against his priest 'guests'; he was hurt by Father Gore's deliberate rejection of friendship. He now presented the bishop with new regulations: no more telephone calls, no more guests except at the gate house, and so on.

Bishop Fortich fought the new regulations all the way: 'Now, Colonel, say if Father O'Brien's mother is sick and she wants to contact him. How would you feel if your mother was sick and couldn't contact you?' The argument went on and on.

The colonel then relented on various aspects and the bishop managed to have the new regulations whittled down. They were duly written out and the bishop offered to deliver them himself to the priests in the 'guest room', opposite the colonel's house. Some captains and majors accompanied the bishop.

We had left Donie Hogan in our ex-room precisely to deal with such an eventuality. The bishop knocked solemnly on the door. When Donie, and not one of the notorious three, answered the door the bishop showed no surprise. He just began to read out the new regulations. The army men stood beside the bishop, and Donie kept the door only partly open. It must have seemed a little bizarre that the priests did not invite their own bishop into the room but just listened to him through a partly open door.

'Well, those are the new regulations, and the colonel and myself are both agreed.' With that he turned on his heel, Donie closed the door and turned the key in the lock, the bishop got into his car and drove away – fast!

The captains were soon back, hammering on the door. Donie opened it with wide-eyed surprise. 'Yes?'

'Where's Father Gore?' 'Where's Father Dangan?' 'Where's Father O'Brien?' they said excitedly.

Donie: 'I don't know where they are.'

'Where are they?'

'Oh, they've gone out.'

'Gone out where?'

'I think they've gone to the provincial jail.'

No tape-recording exists of the colonel's reaction when his men brought the news, and even if it did, I would probably not be able to include it here. However, it seems the colonel went straight to the governor's house after that, and we did get a report of that discussion because, as it happened, one of our new co-prisoners had been detailed to sweep the floors in the governor's residence and he happened to be doing just that when the colonel arrived. He took inordinate glee in repeating it to all back in the prison.

By the time the colonel telephoned the warden all had been decided and we were no longer under military jurisdiction. We were under the civil jurisdiction of Bacolod Provincial Jail with incontrovertible documents, and outside the jurisdiction of the colonel. It seems the colonel's telephone call to the warden was not one hundred percent coherent.

Radio Bombo [local radio] announced at 8.30 p.m. that we are illegally in jail. We reckon that if we are illegally in jail then we should be punished with jail – so the more illegal the more legal!

We were so exhausted that we couldn't eat or speak, we just sat there on the edge of the double-decker wooden beds, breathing heavily.

TWELVE

'They Asked for It'

Friday morning, 27 January

I arise at five a.m. and our gate is open. I got into the inner yard and jogged around in the dark, only to come a cropper by falling over a pipe I didn't see in the dark. I washed the wound carefully with soap and water and wrapped a clean handkerchief around my foot. I poured water over myself and sat outside the cell. I noticed the hot sun is going to be shining in here in the afternoon (bad news for *siesta!*). We don't get the morning sun, which would be a gentle and welcome blessing.

Guess who's here! My old friend, Juanito Roa. I am indirectly responsible for him being here, although I have tried hard to get him out by supplying him with a lawyer. He came to visit me in my cell. I told him long ago when I used to visit him, 'Some day I'll be in there with you.' For a man who has such a gruesome record he certainly has a very gentle smile.

'Tell me,' I said to Juanito (we were alone and equals now), 'did you kill the second man?'

'No. It was the group.'

'Did you really cut off their ears and eat them? There were many witnesses, you know.'

'No, I didn't.'

'You just like that story to get around, eh?'

He nodded with a very special and sheepish grin.

'And the fellow you said would be your twenty-seventh victim – that's not true?'

Juanito: 'No.'

'I knew that, but you had the whole area terrorised.'

I had been trying hard to get Juanito out because I knew he had gone through a genuine change of heart. It happened the night he stayed in the *convento*. We had a huge wall-picture eight feet long of Christ being scourged. In mediaeval style the artist had introduced, around the central scourging picture, events of life in Negros, such as land-grabbing, army atrocities, property speculation, usury, unfair wages, religious hypocrisy, robbery and rape; there was something for everyone. The night that Juanito stayed with us we each took time to talk to him gently about the dignity of human life and what it means to take another person's life. The following morning he spoke spontaneously for the first time. He led me over to the large picture of the scourging and, pointing at one of the soldiers with the whip, said, 'That's me.'

The large crowd of ordinary men, women and children coming to his house to protest, the refusal to give him Communion, fear, the little talks in the night alone: his heart was genuinely touched, and when the police did take him away I hoped he did not think I had planned that.

I tried to follow up his children, but I myself was in difficulties in the succeeding months with my own case.

I was happy that I was with Juanito now and that any cloud of suspicion he had about me had been lifted. To my surprise he had taken up the unlikely job of tailor – and all sewing jobs in the prison, including my own, were being brought to him!

> Today is plebiscite day in the Philippines. The people are to vote on whether they want a vice-president or not. They do, but there are a few other things thrown in in package-form (as always). So far the plebiscite is going badly. All over the prison, little transistors are on and the prisoners are tallying boycott numbers with exuberance. My cut foot has made me a half-invalid, so I move about more slowly. My arm is also sprained.
>
> The anti-plebiscite people picnicked in the *plaza* in front of the cathedral, and when they felt that they had a victory they have just marched now to the jail (five thousand?) and shouted outside. We eventually had to be allowed to speak to the crowd through the outside gate, as the guards were getting worried that otherwise they wouldn't go away and might even break in.
>
> Arm and body aching all day.

Saturday, 28 January
I slept badly with terrible pain (I'm a complainer). I carefully bandaged my cuts so as to avoid infection, using soap and water and disinfectant. The other prisoners are getting much less food than us, which is embarrassing. They get five tiny fish like sardines for the whole day and some fourth-grade rice. Friends send us in extra food apart from our ration, which is otherwise the same as theirs. Later we will complain on their behalf. They also get a sort of soup. Well, it is a huge vat of hot water with the shell heads of prawns and the claws of hens floating in it; they call it 'Helmet and Adidas Soup'!

We are ten in our cell and it is tiny and we can hardly move. My arm is aching. The sisters of the La Consolation School came and

Above - Fr Niall O'Brien baptising an infant born in Bacolod Jail.

Right - Living conditions in the jail – an inmate eats dinner. *(Fr Shay Cullen)*

told us that on Monday they would bring the theology class for a talk on vocations!

I visited Cell 6. It suddenly struck me that one thing we must do here is to give them hope. They all sat around me on the floor and I told them the story of Emmaus. As I came to the part where the two strangers suddenly realise that Christ is not dead but alive – 'They only realised he was present when he was gone' – I was suddenly very moved myself, and we were all moved because I suppose what I was saying is that he is alive and here with us in the cell now. . .

Now the wives have arrived it will be an emotional day. We have listened to many prisoners' stories, and have many visitors. We have plans for many changes in the prison and may start an organisation called 'Friends of the Prisoners'.

We killed a rat in our cell. Cell number one took it, skinned it, cooked it and ate it immediately.

Papers reported an eighty percent turnout for the plebiscite. We know Bacolod had a fifteen percent turnout, because the prisoners tallied it carefully as it came off the radio. The official report seems like lies.

The big news this morning: last night *News Watch* – which is the national TV's 'controlled' news – announced that our house arrest has been revoked. One of the more sycophantic of the national papers, *The Manila Times*, has a headline: 'They asked for it and they got it.'

John Bowman of Radio Telefís Éireann got through to me on the telephone. It was the breakthrough with the Irish media that I had been so anxiously awaiting. From that Bowman interview which was broadcast over Radio Éireann came a surge of Irish media interest which helped inform Irish people of the real situation in the Philippines. John Bowman mentioned the call from our superior in the Philippines, Father Martin, to the Irish government to send out a representative to investigate our case, and I had the opportunity to welcome such a move and add my opinion that a person-to-person approach was more significant than any bureaucratic approach in a country where human relationships are so important.

At the end of this call, which I had taken in the warden's office, I felt that at last the Irish media had been called into play and that, if properly informed, they could do as much to inform public opinion in the northern hemisphere as Australian television, radio and newspapers were already doing in the southern hemisphere. It was a source of reassurance in the growing tension leading up to the trial. And, in any event, I could now look Brian in the eye on the 'information' front!

My diary records the position we had reached:

> We now know where we stand and we can plan. Our plans go like this: 1. our primary aim is a speedy trial; 2. mobilise all public opinion to this end; 3. Foreign Minister Hayden is arriving in February – that should help increase pressure; 4. if it doesn't, we have planned a long march from the end of Negros to Bacolod to coincide with the anniversary of our arrest; 5. if we don't get out by the election of 12 May, then we could be here for a long time; 6. after that date the only hope is Reagan's visit to Ireland.

The levers of Philippine power lie ultimately not in Manila but in Washington, but before I say any more about this, let me give you a general picture of the high security quarters.

THIRTEEN

The High Security Section

Enter the large iron gate on Gatuslao Street, Bacolod city; pass quickly through the straggling yards and 'living-out' prisoners; do not look to either side; keep your head down and do not heed the many calls of the inmates, or you'll be swamped long before you get to the top-security section of Bacolod Provincial Jail.

Pass through another guarded gate into the high, dark, visitors' hall; keep going until you get to the gate at the other end of the hall. Look through the bars: before you is the closed quadrangle containing the prisoners locked into ten cells which look out on the quadrangle, each through the eyes of its own iron gate.

Here two hundred prisoners live, the large cells with thirty inmates and the small cells with ten. (Apart from this there is a sort of black hole where recalciltrant prisoners are punished.) Inside the cells the prisoners sleep on mats on the cement floor.

In one corner of each cell is a hole in the ground leading to a sewer; this area is loosely surrounded by a screen of old sacks, and serves as the toilet. In another corner a charcoal fire burns and acts as the kitchen. A single glaring electric bulb remains on night and day so that the guards can count the prisoners at any time.

Sometimes an electric ring burns; its wires have been hooked precariously to a bared patch on the electric light wire. Over the electric ring prisoners are boiling glue, which they will use in the intricate marquetry at which they work away in the gloom. The smell of glue pervades the cell.

But come in, the guard at the quadrangle gate is not too strict today. You are going to visit Cell 7. We started in Cell 8 but it is small, and with nine of us in it you couldn't swing a cat. We thought of changing with Cell 7. They anticipated our needs and offered to change, the offer being made by their *bosio* (leader).

We said we would prefer it if all of them sat down and dialogued about it so that the decision would be a genuine consensus – because this was the way we made decisions in the Basic Christian Communities. So they met and it seems for various reasons they liked the idea.

A group of very industrious ones who hoped to be out soon and wanted to concentrate on their artifacts and avoid trouble opted to go to our cell, while others went to cells where they had friends.

So now we are in Cell 7 and as a consequence we are able to celebrate Mass.

So, come across the quadrangle to Cell 7, but step gingerly; on your right is a jet of water spurting out of the wall, low down. This is the only source of water, so the two hundred prisoners must wash here in public. The jet of water is so low down on the wall that you must squat down on your hunkers to use it.

Just beside the jet a lazier flow of water pours from a hole in the wall; this is 'used water' from the guards' washing quarters and it flows almost on top of those washing in the quadrangle. Five inches away is a thin jet of drinking water. These three flows create a mini-lake of stagnant water in which you stand as you wash. Step carefully because there is an open sewer with human faeces from Cell 10 (which has more than thirty prisoners) passing along it. Many ducks are feeding at this sewer. These ducks belong to the wife of one of the guards, so step doubly carefully as their droppings are all over the yard.

You have now reached Cell 7. Look through the gate. Five wooden pallets on the right and four on the left. The sacking screen indicates the toilet in the left corner; a table borrowed from a guard is in the centre. There are three narrow barred slits for windows, a charcoal fire burns against the back wall for cooking, and there are nine of us scattered about the room, eyes a little watery from the smoke, doing this and that.

Sorry I had to bring you through these details, but I had to set the scene. In the daytime the prison quadrangle looks like a scene from *Midnight Express,* but in the evening when the sun sets and only the silhouette of the old Spanish jail is visible in the dimming light, with the rounded arches of the cell gateways picked out by the glow from within them, it could well be the set from the opening scene of *Carmen*.

I gaze up at the dying sky; it seems to reflect the waters of Bacolod Bay, which are only some five hundred yards from here. My thoughts fly away to another bay where as a boy, sitting on the grassy banks at Maretimo, I gazed across to Howth on many a summer's day and watched the gentle approach of evening over the water. As I remember dear friends, I am filled with gratitude that I was given such happiness then so that now it can be my strength.

At six o'clock in the morning the gates to our quadrangle open and a 'live-out' prisoner, called a 'trustee', claps his hands to announce that the first batch will be allowed into the yard to wash. The huge pots of rice have arrived, and the five sardines apiece ration for the day is about to be distributed.

First the counting of the prisoners. Then the gate of one cell is opened and a group comes out to wash. They run across the square to be first to the water, but they do not push each other around. They carry plastic gallon oil containers to collect water in. Others take their time. Most are wearing just shorts and briefs, which they wash and change. Though the water facilities are meagre, every prisoner is careful about personal cleanliness. Nobody is unwashed; if they are, they are sick.

Prisoners are some twenty to a cell, but sometimes it increases to forty. Each has a rolled sleeping mat and keeps his few belongings rolled up very carefully in that mat. At New Year many burned their mats in a strange mixture of helplessness and hope. Some felt that nothing mattered; they could not be worse off, so to hell with it – burn the mat and sleep on the cement. Others may have burned their mats in the hope that soon they would not need them. Our lay leaders kept their mats, but burned newspapers instead to show solidarity with the other prisoners.

But back to the cell. There is a marked difference between cells. Some are proud of their cleanliness and leave their rubber flipflops at the cell door when they come in, and then proceed in their bare feet. Some cells have a higher division of labour than others, and have teams sweeping and washing the floors and fetching water. Some are into gambling. Some are busy making handicrafts from plywood and the stems of the sugar-cane flower called *bilaho*.

The most popular work is a large Last Supper done in a sort of marquetry; the colouring is achieved by burning the *bilaho*, from light brown through speckled to black as required. There is also a picture of Our Lady of Mount Carmel, and the stiffness of the marquetry lines accentuates the iconesque appearance to good effect. Desk hold-alls, calendars and trinket boxes are made; a lot of the day is spent in traipsing back and forth for the little bits and pieces of felt, glue and metal needed to finish the items well.

Most prisoners are not involved in these handicrafts. They just sit around lethargically and hopelessly in a sort of suspended animation. At ten-thirty in the morning the rice ration arrives again, but the fish allowance is not repeated; it has already been given in the morning.

At night-time two of the cells say the Rosary. In one cell they all kneel formally before a painting of Our Lady which they painted themselves on the wall. They pray and sing. Strange, isn't it, how one cell differs from another? Why, I wonder? I feel that in the answer to this question lies the key to many human problems here at the provincial jail.

Our cell is number seven (*celda siete*). It is about ten paces by seven. The floor is of broken cement and light comes in through the door (which is an iron gate facing on to the quadrangle) and through a six-inch barred' slit in the opposite wall. Compared with *celdo ocho* which we came from, it is almost luxury. And this week we celebrated Mass for the first time inside our cell.

The walls are blackened with the cooking and bear the macabre messages of generations of inmates. Our lay leaders solved the problem of the mouldering plaster by pasting newspapers over the walls. There is no fear of being bored by a monotonous pattern, everywhere you look yesterday's news and advertisements stare back at you. Recently we have divided ourselves into three teams, one priest and two lay leaders in each, and by turn we do the cooking, the cleaning and our daily liturgy.

From early morning till closing-down time visitors come: sometimes old friends who break down in tears; sometimes eager nuns who are anxious to show their students what is happening and troop in with a whole class. All come to inspect our quarters. Many bring food gifts and thoughtful items like germicidal soap, Lysol, mosquito killer, or even a pack of cards. Then there are reporters and camera crews; the administration so far has been patient with them all, basically because that is the Filipino way, but more so because no one in prison believes we killed the mayor.

In the evening we have our Mass together around our table with a shared homily as we struggle to see God's hand in all that is happening to us. Sometimes we have Vespers or Evening Prayer and the psalms seem as if they were written just for us.

After our liturgy we sometimes have a formal meeting, planning various angles of our case, or how to get the best value from the visits of guests and reporters, or what to do for our fellow-prisoners. Sometimes we have meetings with our lawyers.

So far our cell has been left open at night – maybe the warden feels the pressure of the people – so we are able to take the opportunity of the deserted yard and wash at the jet of water. Other prisoners call to us from their cells, and we do errands across the yard, such as buying a cigarette or taking some medicine from one cell to another or fetching water.

Now midnight has come it is time for the changing of the guard. The gates are rattled open one by one and we are counted. Most are asleep, and I am putting the last touches to my diary.

Every morning each cell is allowed into the quadrangle for a short while for what is called in prison language 'shunning' (which I think is an amalgam of sunning and shining). Anyway, after the long dark hours inside the cell the prisoners sit against the wall on a ledge and let the morning sun, still not too strong, fall upon them.

I slip out then also with my breviary, but as soon as I start the psalms someone is bound to come up to me: 'My case has been five years without a hearing, Father,' or 'It's three years since my lawyer visited me,' and another and another. I begin to get irritable. I had hoped to slip away from the babble of the cell and be on my own. Somehow I have to establish a time for being alone.

I take the easy way out and say, 'Write the details down for me,' but that is unfair. Many cannot write, and anyway paper and ballpoint pens are just not around, and then again writing a case down is a discipline which needs practice. Finally I make a compromise: 'Tonight I'll come to your cell and discuss it.' And I hope they will continue not locking our cell gate at night.

A prisoner calls from Cell 1. His name is Lynel and his court case hearing is tomorrow. Can I give him some pocket-money for his big day out? I do not want to fall into the hand-out system. It would put us above the others and injure their dignity. Anyway, it would be impossible to carry through and would end up in ill-will. I have been through this before.

'Lynel, you draw, don't you? Will you draw my cell?'

'Yes, but I'm too busy now doing patterns for the marquetry. Father Dangan has two orders.'

'All right, do it when you've finished and I'll give you this as an advance.'

His dignity has been respected and I have a picture for my letters. If there is one thing I have learned in the last twenty years it is that hand-outs destroy the recipients and frequently turn them into beggars, while giving a temporary relief of conscience to the giver. And if there is another thing I have learned it is that this rule must be broken sometimes, or your humanity will be in peril. The anguish and irritation caused by the borderline cases is something we must live with.

However, such a policy of no hand-outs obviously must be accompanied by a positive and aggressive attempt to solve the problems underlying the widespread poverty. It is precisely in tackling the cause of the disease rather than the symptoms that we run into trouble.

Basically this is one of the reasons why we are in prison. Each one of our parishes had many land problems because of land-grabbing by the powerful, and we always made the 'machine' of the parish available to the poor to help them hold on to their little pieces of land.

I recall eleven families in my parish who by the rarely implemented rules of land reform had the right to own the little bit of land they were tilling as share-croppers. Now the land was foreclosed on by the bank, so the tillers applied for the land under the law; but a rich neighbour with a large tract of land himself also had his eye on this land and did a quick 'deal' with the bank – I say 'deal' because in actual fact no money changed hands. We got the diocesan lawyer to help and fought the case at the land reform office. We won, *mirabile dictu*. But the landowner's relative is married to a very influential military man in Negros. So naturally one thing leads to another. The military are more and more involved in local commercial life in Negros.

The day Father Vicente Dangan signed his subpoena, a friend of mine happened to be at a party attended by the military. The latter were 'in their cups' and they were rejoicing that Father Dangan had finally been brought to book because they said he was encouraging the peasants not to move from a place called Masulog in his parish. They themselves had an interest in this land, although it is in fact public land. Father Dangan had no alternative but to side with the people if he wanted to be faithful to his calling. I am proud to be his companion in here in *celda siete*.

In Father Brian Gore's case there were so many land cases in which he and Father John Brazil, now deceased, took the side of the poor people that it would be impossible to mention them all. The largest involved thousands of acres which belonged legally to the government agricultural school. Two groups had encroached on it. Hundreds of peasants with nowhere to go had squatted there, planting a few vegetables and a bit of corn, and then a small group of large landowners had extended their sugar-cane fields into this territory, each taking large swathes of land.

When the local government came to clamp down they began to oust the little people but not the big ones. Hence came a clash with Brian and John, who provided the use of diocesan lawyers for the sqatters. If John Brazil had lived he would probably be here in Cell 7 with us tonight.

FOURTEEN

Prisoners 30855, -6 and -7

Leaves from the diary that I kept throughout my stay in prison reveal both the turmoil and the torment of the time. First there was the coming to terms as a group with the restrictions and unpleasantness of prison life. Then there was the endless, frustrating uncertainty of waiting for trial, which affected us each individually at the oddest of moments. The worst anxiety was caused by the continual raising of false hopes, caused by rumours that the case against us would be dropped. Rumours and alarms became commonplace, adding to the gnawing unease. And all the time there was the knowledge that out there beyond the prison walls there were powerful and evil forces, and that the conduct of the trial was largely in their hands. Had we done the right thing? Would people understand?

However, these bouts of fear and false hopes were interlaced with the busy routine of our new-found prison 'parish' with its five hundred inmates, visits from fellow-priests, parishioners and the media, and planning sessions. The media visits take up a major part of my diary: we had several Australian television stations in almost continual attendance, not to mention Irish and Philippine television people; all the major Australian and Irish newspapers and radio stations were in constant contact with us; in fact, the media people played a central role, even to the point of deep personal involvement.

Monday, 30 January
A bit of sunning in the morning. The food is atrocious – National Grains Authority rice – but it doesn't bother me. We need a whole supply of medicines. Needless to say, the various forms of dhobi's itch and TB are the most common diseases.

We had an important meeting among ourselves:
1. We fixed a rota system as to who will do what work in the cell and when: Geronimo, Peter and I will cook and clean and look after the liturgy on Mondays and Thursdays; Brian, Lydio and Conrado on Tuesdays and Fridays; Itik will be with Siting and Ernesto on Wednesdays and Saturdays; on Sundays we will each prepare a meal.
2. We decided to go ahead and print a book, making the documents of the case available for everyone.
3. We decided to postpone organising the prisoners until we get

our act together a bit better. We have to prepare for the court case . . .

Later, in Cell 8 (the one we vacated), I met a boy called Diomedes. He was tortured personally by a certain colonel, not our fellow. Among other acts of torture, a catheter was put up his penis. It seems he was involved in some stealing. The colonel had it in for him, because several years before the colonel wanted him to be part of some athletic team and he refused. We haven't heard the colonel's side, naturally, but I have come across so much torture that I am inclined to believe.

While I was in the cell a fellow came around wanting to pawn his trousers for ten pesos to some other prisoner. Since 'supper' is at four-thirty in the afternoon, by ten at night everyone is very hungry and clothes are pawned for next to nothing to get a few pesos to buy food in the store. The store is run by the wife of one of the guards, and remains open most of the time because one of the trustees (living-out prisoners) watches it. Everyone, even visitors, complains about the high prices in the store. The same lady who owns the store owns a great number of ducks which are loose in the yard; they feed off the open sewer and leave droppings everywhere, making the yard a real mess. We want to get rid of the ducks, but how? One cell, it seems, keeps a dog – to be eaten on some special occasion. . .

Tuesday, 31 January
Long day. Many visitors. I slept well on the wood. Alfredo Talatala came to visit. He wept bitterly when he saw me. It was the first time we had met in ten years: a fine lad, he now has three boys. I was deeply moved, remembering that he was my altar-boy when I first came twenty years ago and one of my first friends here. We gave him documents to distribute. (In fact, we are giving documents to all our visitors.)

The sun shines into the cell all day, they say it is the hottest cell. No wonder the lads were willing to swop! Channel 10, Bacolod Television, came. We spoke hard, all of us. I was a little worried about the *sub judice* aspects, but we are all so disgusted with the judge.

The '*Tres Marias*' (three Marys) arrived: that's the name we have given to Nena Deleon, Momie Paz Torres and Rosita Montanez – a businesswoman, the chief nurse in the local hospital, and a well-known sugar farmer, respectively. They are wonderful women and have bravely come out openly in favour of our innocence from the very beginning, though it has cost them some friends.

We held another meeting and decided: 1. if our lawyers agree, we will invite Senator José Diokno to be a consultant in our case; 2. we need an investigator; 3. when Foreign Minister Hayden of Australia comes, our chief request will be to have a speedy trial.

Wednesday, 1 February
It seems that Hayden's being on the horizon has helped. Today we were asked to fill in a *sub poena* (a legal document giving notification of a forthcoming court case) for 7 and 9 February, which means the trial proper is going to open or appear to open while Hayden is coming.

Thursday, 2 February
Today is the Feast of Candlemas. The people have been walking through the streets since before dawn in solemn silent procession with candles and flying banners. At five a.m. they arrived at the prison gates; it was very impressive, the silent procession. . .

The warden called us to his office. It seems that finally we are fully fledged prisoners and the news report that the president has withdrawn our privilege of house arrest has finally filtered down through the bureaucracy to his level. We were finger-printed and our names written in a huge ledger, a relic from Spanish times, because the headings were in Spanish and English.

Then we were asked to fill in a form saying we would obey the rules of the prison, after which we were given our numbers. I am now prisoner number 30856. From now on we get a prison ration which will be food to the value of three pesos a day (about 10p). The guard, knowing that the people send in a continuous stream of food to us, suggested he would have our ration as it would be no loss to us. We vehemently refused and said we would take it each day so that we could give it as an extra to some inmates with tuberculosis.

This morning we were taken by surprise when the guard announced that visitors would no longer be allowed into our cell. We felt it was a quiet way of informing us of our change in status: no longer 'guests', we are here for real. Somewhere deep down in the pit of my stomach I felt a reaction, a foreboding, not unlike how I felt as a boy on my way to school when I had not done my homework.

This foreboding must be examined and faced and not left in the vague realms of fear. What am I afraid of? Many years wasted and lost? The endless futility of running on the bureaucratic treadmill of the court system, all leading nowhere? Not seeing my family for a long time? Being convicted?

I confess I have not dealt with all of these, but as regards the first I feel that with five hundred fellow-prisoners this place is parish enough for any priest, and by writing letters and diary I am giving a purpose to my day.

There is, as of now, only one bulb in the cell and, as we are all 'in', there is a lot of noise, but I've made the promise to myself to do this writing so I am forced to pull myself together and the effort gives a small sense of a job done.

As for the futility of the court system, it is frequently worse than futile, and can even be blasphemous. I use this word advisedly, because I believe that the whole legal system as it has developed up till now is a great instrument constructed by the human race against encroaching chaos. When there is no legal way (however creaking) of solving disputes, then violence is all that is left. Those who destroy the legal system by continually suborning it bring us to the edge of the abyss. They are the real subversives.

However, though convinced that the legal system has been destroyed for the most part, we have decided to carry our case forward, so that observers and the world will know the score, whatever the outcome of the case may be. And our defence will be on public record.

Incidentally, after the trouble to get the court stenographer to finish the bail hearings, the actual transcript turned out to be far from accurate in many places. For example, in an attempt to connect me with the IRA, the provincial *fiscal* asked me if I had ever volunteered for the army in Ireland, and I answered, roundly, No, whereas in the stenographer's record it has come out as Yes. . .

As for the interminable delays which surely await us, I see no escape from these and I think we must make a conscious and sustained effort to give purpose to our lives by working here in the prison as if it were our parish, to bring love and justice and forgiveness to those whose lives we share now – and, indeed, to learn from them. I say 'learn from them' because my experience of working in the Philippines has always been that I have received more than I gave.

As for the other fears, let me not try and solve everything in one go.

FIFTEEN

The Trial Re-Opens

Before I go any further I must introduce you to our lawyers. We have six. Our chief lawyer is Attorney Juan Hagad. His family has worked with the Church for a couple of generations, and he is a man of integrity. He and his wife Titay have spent thirty years working together on all the great Christian movements in Negros. Their two sons are lawyers: Andy, phlegmatic and perceptive, and Danny, fiery and openly outraged by injustice. Danny gets mad in court. This is great, because he carries some of the anger for us who are forced to be quiet in the dock. Then there is Frank (Francisco) Cruz, the lawyer of the Social Action Office of the diocese. He has put his life on the line by holding this job for many years now. His Spanish wife frequently accompanies him to court and supports him all the way, as indeed do the wives of all the other lawyers. With him are Archie Baribar and Romeo Subaldo of the Free Legal Aid Group (FLAG). Romeo is very gentle, but always makes his point effectively (not that making one's point has helped in this bizarre case). Archie is newly graduated and a decision to join the five means he has chosen one of the more difficult paths, a path few lawyers choose.

We often disagree with our lawyers. We have had many a tussle with them, but we hold no secrets from them because we trust them. And in all the ups and downs so far they have suffered and rejoiced with us. They are our dear friends. What more can I say?

At a meeting with our lawyers we have decided several things: 1. we will bear the Supreme Court in mind, and if we lose here in Negros we will carry our case to the Supreme Court; this means using all the witnesses we can; 2. we will ask for proper inspection of the site of the ambush after the prosecution finishes producing its witnesses; 3. our lawyers would like Senator Diokno to be a consultant. Senator Diokno is a leading opposition lawyer and spent several years in prison under the Marcos régime. He is a man of impeccable integrity and something of a genius. He is the leading criminal lawyer in the Philippines.

A telegram came from Cardinal Ó Fiaich. Very encouraging: prayers have been said in all the Irish churches on Sunday and Tuesday for·the re-opening of the case. The Australians continue to send their consul all the time; they have never missed, not even

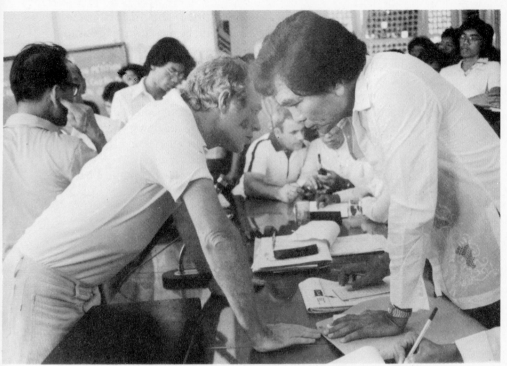
Fr Niall O'Brien confers with defence lawyer Frank Cruz.

once, since the very first case against Brian. Our Irish Honorary Consul is in continual contact with Dublin; he was down here during the bail hearings, but I have told him it is unnecessary to come in the meantime.

The wives of the five lay leaders arrived. We have come up with a new name for ourselves – The Negros Nine – and they have had it done out on T-shirts. It is a better name than 'Gore *et al.*', which has been our legal title and the one used by the newspapers up till now. It is also a improvement on 'the three priests and the six lay leaders', and helps to even out the emphasis a bit.

Brian has started putting the cell in order. He has put in a better light so that I can write at night.

Sunday, 5 February

There was a rally in the *plaza* asking for the dismantling of the state-sponsored body for sugar, called Nasutra – surely this is the first time the land-owners have rallied. Things seem to be moving.

We prepared a statement for many television and radio stations.

Lots of food around, which we shared with the other cells.

The sisters are going to make special vestments for us. We want the words '*No tengas miedo – soy yo*' (Be not afraid – it is I) on the stoles, because the day we arrived in the prison and were feeling apprehensive we found these words on a wall poster in our cell beside the picture of a sinking ship: they gave us great courage. On the stoles we have also put a design of a hand grasping barbed wire and a dove about to land on the hand – our symbol of active non-violence. The dove of peace can find 'space' to descend if human beings absorb some of the violence.

Monday, 6 February

We held Mass at dawn with the purpling sky visible through the bars. Many old friends came (we could hardly move, there were so many in the cell); there were even two whole classes of students from La Consolation College.

Channel 9 from Melbourne came in also this morning. UPI photographers (a bit pushy!). Bishop Myles McKeon of Bunbury in Australia (the bishop who ordained Brian) has arrived as a representative of the Australian bishops. Graham West, Australian Consul; Michael McCluskey, Irish Deputy Ambassador; Charlie Bird from RTE; Channel 10; plus Channel 7 from Melbourne; Bob Wurth of ABC; Bruce Dover, Australian journalist . . . And who should arrive in the midst of all this to visit us but Myrna, the daughter of the colonel. We had got to know her and her children while under army custody. She shared the guest house with us, and Itik had grown very close to her children (he has a way with children). The visit took us by surprise; I am sure her father would not approve. Filipinos insist on being human, and we were delighted to see her.

Many phone calls from Ireland and Australia. These phone calls will save Brian's life yet: since the phone is two hundred yards away, they give him the only exercise he gets, and he sorely needs it. (He can't do the calisthenics in which I indulge in the mornings, because he injured his knee playing Australian football.)

At the moment we have decided to ask Attorney Cruz to make a formal request to the judge that the prosecutor should not put the answers into his witnesses' mouths. The prosecutor has been doing this shamelessly, and with impunity, up till now – but some people say that this is a lawyer's job!

People come to the prison looking for blood, which seems to be a common practice. Four prisoners went to the hospital to give blood. They will get some money, a small amount, with the rest probably going to those who arranged the deal (the guards). I inquired about this, and it is the normal practice. There is a trade in blood here, especially from prisoners. For a while blood was even being exported from the Philippines. I read in *Business Day* (a very reliable business magazine of the *Financial Times* type) that exports of blood from the Philippines are now forbidden.

Charlie Bird back at night busily doing his background research. Cell packed with people arriving for the case. Big television teams˙ during supper (we harden our faces and keep on eating). Phone keeps ringing from Ireland, and Australia.

We rose early the next morning and celebrated Mass in the dark at four-thirty for the success of our trial that day. At six o'clock we got into two Toyota land-cruisers, with a driver and two armed guards in each, to take us to the court in Kabankalan – about sixty miles away. One of these vehicles had been involved in a famous ambush two years before, in which a certain military officer had liquidated one of his subordinates as the latter was returning from his wedding. His wounded bride was one of the only survivors of the wedding party. The military man lost his post for a few months, but he was now back in the same position again. So he owes something to those who put him back!

Just as we were getting into the vehicle a man approached and said to Brian: 'Son of a bitch! If you're not killed, you'll be deported.' Then, as the vehicle pulled out, the same man lunged at a reporter who had given us the 'thumbs up' sign. He was obviously under the influence of drink. As we finally set off, the warden was shepherding the offender

– who was clearly a good friend of his – into his office.

Once out of Bacolod city the drivers drove so fast it was obvious that they shared our apprehension about the dangers of the journey. In fact, we went so fast that both vehicles eventually broke down, presumably from over-heating. Charlie Bird, who was following us at break-neck speed, leapt out of his pick-up and began interviewing everyone there before the vehicles were ready to move off again. Filipino priests who lived in parishes along the way arranged an escort for us, and they kept up with the Toyotas all the time.

When we reached Kabankalan the court was over-crowded, although our people had remained away and had instead filled the church of Saint Francis Xavier across the road from the court-house. The reason for the over-crowding was that farm-hands had been trucked in from the mayor's farm. They all wore little pieces of black material on their upper garments, and were supplied with soft drinks and food. Even in the dock where we were, there was hardly standing room.

The first surprise the judge sprang was that he had telegrammed Chief Justice Fernando to allow Lydia Equito to return as stenographer. She was the very stenographer who had been found guilty of contempt of court at the bail hearings for taking so long to finish the notes and whose gross inaccuracy had been used by the judge as one of the excuses for taking so long to reach his decision.

The next surprise was that the prosecution complained that the court was over-crowded and asked for a change of venue to Bacolod. We agreed, but our attempt to get the hearing to go on in the meantime was turned down by the judge. Apparently all the ballyhoo about having a speedy trial was just that!

Even after repeated requests, the judge refused to give any guarantee of a date for renewed hearings, by which the media people could set their calendars. I felt so angry at the cavalier way in which the whole thing was treated. Media people had come from all over, and the Irish representative had come from Canberra for no other purpose when the hearing date had been fixed at the instigation of the Chief Justice of the Supreme Court himself. And now it was postponed *sine die*. However, *is olc an ghaoth na séideann maith do dhuine éigeann* (It's an ill wind that blows no one some good). The shift to Bacolod was a positive thing in our favour, because more people would be able to witness the trial, which would serve as a conscientising factor for the people of Bacolod.

Meanwhile, Bishop Myles McKeon of Bunbury was addressing the people over in the church. As he was speaking, Brian walked in (the case had by now been adjourned). He walked right up the aisle to the ambo where the bishop was speaking. The bishop put his arm around Brian and said to the people that of all the priests he had ordained Brian had given him most joy. As he spoke he was moved to tears, and tears also streamed down the faces of many members of the congregation.

There was only one telephone in the *convento* in Kabankalan where Father Mark Kavanagh was parish priest, and correspondents were going wild trying to get their stories out.

I was feeling down. I just thought, 'Here we go again.' I also felt sad at seeing people from my former parish in Tabugon, who had come all the way down from the mountains specially for the occasion, which turned out to be yet another deception. I sorely missed the consolation of having my own parish and felt frustrated at not being able to meet with the people and thank them adequately for the sacrifices they had made.

At about two in the afternoon we got back into the Toyotas with our guards and started the race back to Bacolod. When we reached Bacolod we passed through the shopping areas and I could not help wondering when we would be free again to meander around, just enjoying the guileless occupation of window-shopping. When we got to the jail we felt somewhat as if the walls were closing in on us. We got out of the fume- and dust-filled Toyotas and, a bit depressed by the day's events, passed through the quadrangle and were greeted by our fellow-prisoners, who were happy to see us back. There was a genuine sense of welcome, as if they had been apprehensive lest our presence in the past weeks, with all that it meant, was only a seven-day wonder which might be taken away from them.

However, the day had a long way to go yet. No one was pleased with the morning's hearings. Charlie Bird and crowds of other media people were around the cell. Deputy Ambassador Michael McCluskey took me aside. He gave me a secret request from the Foreign Affairs Ministry in Manila. Before he did this, he made it quite clear that he was merely acting as a conduit: he had been asked to hand on this message and in no way did it reflect his view; it was just that he had been asked courteously to carry it and he felt that there was more to be lost by appearing boorish and refusing than by agreeing. Anyway, he knew I had my own opinion. I assured him that I thought that passing on messages like this was one of the functions of a man in his job and any sort of dialogue was a good thing. 'So what's the message, Michael?'

'Are you willing to go home?'

'No. Not because of my own reputation, but because of the seven Filipinos who would be left high and dry with the case hanging over them.'

Michael said he knew that this would be my answer, but in putting the question he was just fulfilling the promise he had made to the ministry.

Top - Posters hammered on the wall of Fr Gore's parish church at Oringao during the trial. *(Fr Frank Connon)*

Above - A state witness, Roberto Indiape, giving 'evidence' during the bail hearings at Kabankalan. *(Fr Frank Connon)*

Among the many visitors that day were two representatives of Law Asia who had come to monitor the case. They are an independent body of lawyers in the Philippines. They suggested that, instead of just repeating the slogan 'speedy trial', we should request the Minister for Justice, Mr Puno, to free the prosecutor for hearings three days a week, and Chief Justice Fernando should be asked to insist that Judge Legaspi hold hearings three days a week; anything less than three days a week is not a 'speedy trial', they said.

While I was writing my diary entry that evening, news came that a boy called Helmie Pabillar from Oringao, Brian's parish, had been tortured the day before, with a gun put into his mouth to make him say he was involved in the case. It was chilling to think that while the farce of a hearing had been going on, they had been torturing someone in the mountains to make more evidence. No wonder the case had to be postponed! It suddenly struck me that, although many people had been tortured in our case, we had never caught the military red-handed. How could we, when we only found out after it was all over? However, Helmie Pabillar was still in their custody, possibly with still visible marks. How could we get him released? The only answer was to bring out our big guns: ask Bishop Fortich himself to go south to Kabankalan with lawyers and media, and demand Helmie's release. I ran to the telephone and got straight through to the bishop: 'Monsignor, we have some important news. I don't want to tell it over the phone. Could you come over?'
'Yes, immediately.'
Then we sat there, waiting for his arrival.

SIXTEEN

Torture

While waiting in great excitement for the arrival of Bishop Fortich, my mind ran over a previous instance of torture which had been brought to my notice, that of Fernando Tanallon. In that case we had nearly been too late. If Helmie Pabillar was at this moment undergoing a similar experience – and I had little reason to think otherwise – then its exposure to the full glare of international publicity could do nothing but good.

Fernando Tanallon had been in military custody between 13 and 18

March 1983 and continually tortured to get him to implicate Brian Gore and myself in the murder of the mayor and in membership of the New People's Army. (At this time I was still in Tabugon parish.)

His distraught mother came to me to say her son was at army headquarters in Tabugon (this army detachment is supposed to be solely for engineering purposes) and was being tortured. When, through the help of Father Patrick Hurley, a Columban from Cork, we finally got him out, his wife, a close personal friend of mine (I had married the two of them), wrote out what had happened to him. As a consequence of the torture, he was himself physically unable to write, so he dictated his account to her, and I reproduce it here in its original form:

On 13th March 1983, at about 6.30 in the morning (Sunday) I, *Fernando D. Tanallon,* was picked up, together with my father-in-law *Leopoldo V. Florentino,* at the house of my father-in-law situated at Barrio Balicotoc, Municipality of Ilog, Province of Negros Occidental, by the members of the Engineering Battalion Philippine Army (PHILCAG) stationed at Barrio Tabugon, Kabankalan, Negros Occidental.

Upon arrival at their detachment at Brgy, Tabugon, Kabankalan, Negros Occidental, they immediately put me inside the empty water tank and exposed me to the burning heat of the sun the whole day. In the evening of that date, Lt. Lamayo started torturing me. Every time that I would not accept his implication that I am a member of the NPA, he would hammer my body with the butt of an armalite. He also twisted my head and banged it on the table many times.

He wanted me to list the names of the people in Barrio Balicotoc, Ilog, Negros Occidental, who are members of the NPA or those supporting the NPA, but every time I answered that I have no knowledge of what he was saying, he would bang my head against the table. He continued torturing me up to the time I was very weak, and then before leaving me that evening he ordered that I be chained in the leg with a padlock in the other end connected to a big iron bar outside the building. In the morning he would remove the chain but in the evening he would do it again.

The next morning Monday, 14th March 1983, he removed the chain from my leg and let me squat under the burning heat of the sun from morning up to noon, and sometimes would mimic by putting a pistol in my hand (empty of bullets) and would command me to shoot him. In the afternoon of that day he started hammering my feet with a stone and was about to put a lighted cigarette in my eye every time I could not meet his demand.

In the evening he let me stand in the corner of the room and let me inhale and exhale deeply while boxing my stomach, and he also would sometimes twist my head and bang it on the wall and on the table.

Tuesday morning, 15th March 1983, he again started manhandling me while interrogating by boxing me in the body and twisted my head time and again with a few minutes' break every time he was fed up of questioning me. On this date he wanted to pinpoint the Barrio Captain of Barrio Balicotoc as a member of the NPA and wanted me to sign a statement to that effect. I told him how could I because I had no knowledge about it. The questioning and manhandling continued up to late in the evening.

Wednesday, 16th March 1983, Lt. Lamayo wanted me to sign a statement that Fr Gore and Fr O'Brien (both Catholic priests) are the principal recruiters of the NPA. I told him that how could I sign the statement because I have no knowledge about it; but every time I refused to sign he would insert armalite bullets between my fingers and squeeze them. He would stop only when I would shout at him to shoot me or kill me so that I may suffer no more.

Sometimes he would command me to run away because his purpose is that if I run he would shoot me with his armalite. In the evening of the same date, he told me to dig a big hole at the back of the barrack because according to him this would become my grave if I would not sign the statement implicating Fr Gore and Fr O'Brien as recruiters of the NPA, and when I did not sign he placed me in that hole standing and covered my body up to the waist, pointing an armalite and demanding that if I would not sign I would die that very moment. In response I told him that it was better that he would shoot me because I could not suffer any longer but I would not sign the statement because I knew nothing about what he was saying. And that if he was afraid to fire a shot, because it would call attention, he could use his knife instead to end my life. He instead twisted my head and executed karate chops on my shoulders, and when he found out that I was already weak, he ordered his men to remove me from the hole and brought me to the barrack and again put a chain on my leg and locked me.

Thursday, 17th March 1983, at 2 p.m. more or less, Lt. Lamayo loaded me in their service jeep and brought me to Dancalan, Ilog, Negros Occidental, at the headquarters at Task Force Kanlaon. Again I was investigated in that office; however in the evening one of the guards again came to me and struck the side of my body with the end of the barrel of a gun.

Suddenly, at about 4.30 p.m. more or less, Fr Hurley appeared, together with my sister-in-law, together with another woman from another barrio who asked the help of Fr Hurley. So, at almost five in the afternoon I was released from the hands of the military and Fr Hurley accompanied me up to the town of Kabankalan, Negros Occidental.

(signed) Fernando D. Tanallon

Fernando had later escaped to the hills.

However, although we knew that the witnesses against us were undergoing various forms of persuasion and duress and were under constant guard, we were still not able to prove anything to the outside world.

The news was now that this lad Helmie Pabillar had not capitulated, and that he was still in their possession and had not run away. Now, with all the press still here, if the bishop could be got to guarantee his safety we could show the world what was going on. My diary reads:

Then the bishop arrived in our cell. He agreed to go down to Kabankalan and lend his authority. The lawyers are now making out a plea of *habeas corpus*. (*Habeas corpus* – literally, 'produce the body'– is a legal principle under which an arrested person can apply to a court for a writ instructing the police or prison governor holding the accused person to 'produce the body' before the court and show reason why that person is being held.) They are going to ask for Helmie Pabillar to be freed. All the press will go too. . .

Lawyers, bishop, media and Des Quinn, our acting superior, went to court in Kabankalan to try to free Pabillar. The arguing was close and tense. The military were determined to hold on to Pabillar, who at one point shocked our people by asking to go back into military custody. This would have totally undermined our plea.

The boy was obviously in a daze and filled with fear; the military have ways of doing this to people. Charlie Bird of Irish television leant over to Des Quinn and whispered, 'Get the boy's father to talk to him.' Des whispered the message to our lawyer, who asked the judge's permission. The judge could hardly refuse, so the father was allowed to speak to the boy and then after a moment of suspense the boy changed his request and he asked to go home with his father. It was a close shave.

The judge agreed to let Pabillar go, but would give no writ of *habeas corpus*. He said Pabillar had not been in custody but only undergoing 'tactical investigation'!

Pabillar is now with the bishop and at eight tonight he will give a press conference.

At the press conference Helmie told how he had been subjected to

Top - During a historic strike of sugar workers in March 1982, six hundred military intervened to try and break it up. The lorries are loaded with sugar cane to be processed at La Carlota Sugar Mill, Negros. The strike eventually collapsed. *(Fr Frank Connon)*
Above - Fr Donal Hogan SSC blesses the grave of Norberto Estimoso who was on his way to work when he was picked up, tortured, and shot by the Civilian Home Defence Force, 17 April 1983. *(Fr Sean Quigley)*

maltreatment and interrogation and how one of the military men had placed a knife to his throat, trying to make him admit that he took part in the ambush of Mayor Sola. He continued: 'They gave me food and after I'd eaten it they interrogated me again. During the interrogation Sgt. Esteban held me by the hair and put the barrel of a pistol into my mouth while a certain José Aguilar urged me to admit that I took part in the Sola ambush. When I could no longer stand it I "admitted" participation, and a statement was taken down.

'After staying two days at the military outpost in Oringao I was brought to the army headquarters at Dancalan. I was again interrogated, this time by a short fat man with glasses. My Oringao statement was typed. They asked me to sign the document, assuring me there was nothing wrong in signing it. I did. Then I was taken before a judge at what seemed to me to be Himamaylan, then back again to Dancalan.

'When news of the *habeas corpus* petition came, some officers instructed me to tell the court that I did not want to go home because I might be killed.'

At the conference Helmie denied any participation in the Sola ambush. He said he did not even know Fathers Gore, O'Brien and Dangan and had not even met them. Helmie is twenty-three years old, and a resident of Sitio Bayii, Himamaylan, Negros Occidental. He has not received any formal education beyond grade one.

When Charlie Bird examined Helmie he still had the burn marks of the ropes on his wrists.

The media got it out all over the world. It was the first time that this torturing had been so clearly documented in connection with our case. Although an Amnesty International report contains numerous carefully documented accounts of torture in the Philippines, some people just will not believe. 'Hearing they do not hear, and seeing they do not see.' The final part of the Amnesty report reads:

> The Amnesty International delegation has been presented with evidence on forty-nine cases in which serious allegations were made of abuses by members of the Armed Forces of the Philippines (AFP), the ICHDF, the Integrated National Police (INP) and irregular paramilitary units apparently operating with official sanction. These included allegations of: arbitrary killings; 'disappearances'; torture and other forms of ill-treatment; arbitrary arrest; and incommunicado detention.

It was precisely to the sort of acts documented and condemned by Amnesty International that the pope was referring when he told President Marcos, in his address to the diplomatic corps in Manila in February of that same year, that 'even in the exceptional circumstances that could sometimes arise, the violation of the fundamental dignity of the human person. . . can never be justified.'

The special drama of Helmie Pabillar's case, coming at the time it did, alerted the world to the wider negation of human rights in the Philippines and gave courage to many Filipinos risking their lives for these rights.

SEVENTEEN

Getting into Prison Life

Extracts from my diary:

Friday, 10 February
All the priests of the South Vicariate of Bacolod diocese arrived and celebrated Mass. Hundreds of students visited us, and each of us took them for a class, choosing different topics.

More phone calls from Ireland: they told us that four Irish delegates have filed our case to be discussed at the European Parliament.

The BBC held a long interview with me by phone for their World Service. Ilan Ziv, the Israeli who made the film called *Man Alive* about our case is back; the film has been issued in several languages – German, Dutch, French and English. He is making another film. He is deeply interested in the idea that God speaks to us through the poor, and has discussed this with us at length.

At night I distributed medicines. It is not the best way, but all we can do at present.

News has come that Channel 10 of Bacolod, which has lately been more courageous in covering our case, has received a telephone threat. Also, someone has fired a bullet from the roof, in an attempt to kill the news-reader; the bullet passed through the editing room. Someone didn't like the interview with us?!

Saturday, 11 February
News from Ireland today: Bishop Casey is coming to represent the Irish bishops. Tom Fawthrop of *The Irish Times/Guardian* was here, and I took him around the cells. He is more than a correspondent:

he has a deep personal concern for and knowledge of the Asian scene.

Several hundred students came and we took it in turns to tell them what is happening. Lynam of Australia Channel 7 was filming like mad, but his cameraman was overcome by nausea. *Asia Wall Street Journal* came up with a great cartoon by Hung Mo Gwai, who turns out to be a Dublinman. We will send him our documents because it is a very influential newspaper.

Crowds all day.

Sunday, 12 February
Visitors from early morning to late in the evening.

Father Joe Coyle of Derry arrived. He never misses a day; he brings us the daily papers, and some *calamansi* citrus fruit to prevent us getting scurvy.

Itik's witnesses came down from his parish in the mountains of La Castellana and reviewed their testimony. His alibi is unbeatable, because he had so much on during the fatal days. Even has a photo.

Brian Morrison, an Australian priest who has his own radio programme, has taken on our case full-time. Our Brian has talked live on the radio in Australia countless times now.

Brian and Itik and I have decided the only thing to do is to spell out in detail what a *speedy* trial means and push that through by all the means that we have at our disposal: 1. ask for a roster of stenographers, not just one; 2. ask for a five-day week (that is the only way we will get a three-day week!); and 3. ask for a courtroom which is free just for our case (until now, believe it or not, we have no courtroom fully assigned to our case).

We have had a strange visitor from X who asked us not to reveal his name or anything else about him. He was travelling on a boat to Samar when he met a military man who told him that he was Sgt. Y of the Task Force Kanlaon, a liquidation squad situated in the South of Negros at the time of the mayor's death. Sgt. Y said he was 'responsible' for the death of the mayor! I don't find the story convincing enough: the man telling it was scared and a bit incoherent. We'll see!

The judge has still not set a date for the case: he has to 'clear up his existing cases'. Maybe end of next week.

Tuesday, 14 February: Saint Valentine's Day
This is a big feast in the Philippines. Many visitors, including Des Mullan, *Irish Independent*; he is profoundly shocked by jail conditions.

The papers today say that the judge has been freed full-time for our case. Our pressure is working. The date is now fixed, it says, for an unfixed day at the end of next week.

We plan to print two thousand copies of a large poster to be posted around Negros: FREE THE NEGROS NINE – FREE ALL POLITICAL PRISONERS.

We had a meeting together and came to the following conclusions: 1. we will put our own lock on the cell, so that there will be two locks – ours and theirs; 2. we must push for five hearings a week; 3. reduce visiting hours – eight till eleven in the morning, and three till five in the afternoon. We are exhausted by the numbers. All the big schools are sending in the top classes. We try to give each a talk, but it is difficult. This has all been arranged by the Social Action Director, Baby Gordoncillo; 4. we will divide up the cells between us for work. Brian's team will take Cells 10 and 11. Itik and company will take 1, 3, and 4. I, and company, will take 6, 8 and 9, and the *bartolina* (a tiny, windowless, punishment cell); 5. we decided to start our own investigation teams to follow up the military man who was supposed to have something to do with the crime; to contact the 'witnesses' against us; to see if our investigators themselves have a past record. I am in charge of this.

At our Mass the topic, of course, was love. We read the first Epistle of Saint John because it is Saint Valentine's Day, then we shared the homily.

Conrado asked: 'How can we love those who are doing such things to us?'

Brian said, 'We must stand up for our rights.'

I said we love them by opposing them, as a parent opposes a child who is doing wrong. Any other course would be encouraging them in their wrongdoing.

Itik said, 'Saint Augustine says we must love the sinner but hate the sin.'

I added that we may feel anger but we should exclude hate.

We decided to sit down and write a sympathetic but firm letter to our principle antagonists, telling them with simplicity and directness that what they are doing is wrong and that we are praying for them. We sent three, each of them confidential.

Last night I was plagued by a strange headache. We are not allowed to turn off the light and it seemed to aggravate the headache. At about three a.m. I decided to turn it off, as the next counting of prisoners would not be until six, but someone else put it on again as the guards will complain if they find it off.

109

At five-thirty, I prepared the table with a wooden chalice, a paten and candles, and woke the others for Mass. I was the celebrant. We sat around the table, with me facing out towards the gate and looking through the bars at the sky which had just a shadow of pink in it.

The other day I heard that RTE's 'Today Tonight' team is coming, and I decided to get my hair cut. I was told that one of my fellow-prisoners is a barber. He lives out (that is, in the area outside the maximum security area, but inside the wall nonetheless). Unlike us in the quadrangle, who are, naturally enough, not allowed scissors or dinner-knife, he is allowed all the instruments of his trade.

He tied a white cloth around my neck and brandished an old-fashioned cut-throat, the type I remember lying around unused in our bathroom cabinet at home and which we would surreptitiously open and examine or sharpen a pencil with – when my father was out, of course.

'What are you in for?' I asked casually. (That's the way you ask the question here.)

'Homicide,' he said.

'What did you use?'

'A butcher's knife.'

'Well, as long as you didn't use that knife,' said I, nodding towards the cut-throat.

'No,' he said with a grin, and we both laughed.

I sat in the quadrangle as he worked away, and many comments came from inside the bars, with suggestions on how to go about the task, and the remarks were such that I could have been back in Dublin.

Gradually we are getting semi-permanent visitors in our cell. One is a little boy called Roney, who is thirteen but looks ten. He is in for murder. The story is that his father, who has only one arm, was attacked by a group of men. The little fellow ran to the aid of his father and apparently administered the fatal blow when he fired an Indian target (which is a long nail with an arrowhead point and is fired from a baby catapult). Roney did not plan to kill the man, but the victim died as a result of the wound a week later. Roney's father is in too, which leaves the mother and three younger sisters alone at home. Roney joins us for Mass and meals and he takes away food for his father. We are all very fond of him and he calls the lay leaders *manong*, which means 'elder brother'. In fact he has moved into our cell.

Another little fellow around our cell this week is Daryl, the son

110

of Geronimo, one of the lay leaders from Brian's parish. Daryl is called after Brian's elder brother. Every two weeks the wives and children come to visit the lay leaders. It is a great day for the families, and when the children leave the lay leaders are visibly depressed. This time Daryl stayed behind. Geronimo is teaching Daryl to write (he is five), and at night Daryl sleeps locked in Geronimo's arms on the wooden bed next to me. As I write I glance over at them and feel comforted at their affection. It is simple things like this that will stay with Daryl later on. Imprisonment is surely harder on the lay leaders than on us seasoned bachelors.

Geronimo has been working for many years in Brian's parish. He runs the health programme. This is a sort of barefoot doctor approach necessary in mountain areas where there are no doctors and the roads are so rough that they would knock the life out of any sick patient who dared attempt the long journey to the town of Kabankalan. Geronimo has mastered the art of therapeutic massage, acupressure (which is acupuncture without needles) and herbal medicines. He has trained a lot of others and supervises herb gardens in the various communities. He also gives seminars on the negative effects of the work of some multinational drug companies in many of their Third World activities. The programme tries to resist the huge bottle-feeding lobby of some of these companies; the basic thrust for the health programme is preventive hygiene, community sanitation, clean water and good food.

However, food in the mountains presupposes land; hence all of us have been actively involved in defending the mountain settlers' rights to the land they till, but there's the rub. Some people who already have plenty of land feel the need to expand and 'consolidate'. They have powerful backers, and hence the inevitable clash with the small Christian communities. This is another piece of the jigsaw in our case.

Bishop Casey is due to come tomorrow. We are looking forward to this. He was here before in '75 and came all the way up the mountain to visit the farming co-operative in which I am involved.

I hear that 'Today Tonight' will also arrive – headed by Joe Mulholland, with Joe Little as interviewer. Father Michael Martin, our superior, who has been on vacation in Ireland, will be coming back with them.

EIGHTEEN

Casey Arrives

The planes from Manila to Bacolod usually fly directly over the prison yard. At seven in the evening we saw and heard the BAC One-Eleven jet passing over. Our eyes followed it and we knew Bishop Casey would be on it, and probably the 'Today Tonight' team too. There would be lots of letters from home.

After arriving, visitors usually have their supper and go to bed, and then come to see us the next morning. However, Casey came straight from the airport. His arrival caused quite a stir, with camera crews running backwards in front of him and forwards after him. All the prisoners, and not only us, were excited. His whole bearing was of someone supremely concerned with our conditions. It was a great meeting, and the television crews got a good deal of footage. After meeting us he went 'home' to the Redemptorists, supposedly to get a bit to eat and a rest, but of course the discussions went on until two in the morning.

Next morning the bishop was back to make a proper visit to the prison and the cells and to consider the various cases. The Irish television team arrived in the morning and covered it all. Then Casey was away again, to go into conference with the bishop and meet the Filipino priests.

He asked for no media people to be at our Mass that night and it was a good idea, though at first I wondered how we could enforce this. They had been almost living in the cell for days. However, except for Frankie Connon of the Redemptorists, who took some shots, we had Mass on our own. We took the reading of the day and it turned out to be James 2:1-9. 'Do not try to combine faith in Jesus Christ, our glorified Lord, with the making of distinctions between classes of people.' On the other hand the reading also said: 'It was those who are poor according to the world that God chose to be rich in faith and to be the bearers of the Kingdom which he promised to those who love him.'

The bishop ate with us and we were all greatly encouraged, especially the lay leaders, because he represented the whole Irish hierarchy. The lay leaders felt his concern strongly and told us so.

However, the bishop was off again in the morning, this time to visit the celebrated Karl Gaspar. I mention Karl here because he is a wonderful person and a typical Filipino, and also a personal friend. Karl is one of the best-known Filipinos internationally, particularly in the

Visitor from Ireland, Bishop Eamonn Casey, representing Trócaire, with Fr Niall
O'Brien in Bacolod Jail. *(Fr Frank Connon)*

field of human rights. He is a poet and a theologian and a man of most gentle disposition, coupled with quiet courage, opposed to violence. Trócaire had invited him to take part in their tenth anniversary celebrations, but his arrest had intervened. Casey left us to try and see him in Davao.

We had just received a letter from Karl, and we sent a reply with Tony Meade of Trócaire, who was with Bishop Casey. Karl's letter had been to all nine of us, and it was handed round and read again and again, and served to uplift our spirits. It was dated 14 February 1984. The basic reason for his arrest had been his documenting of military abuses on the island of Mindanao. He wrote:

> I write you from behind our own prison bars and barbed wire here. Knowing that this will be read behind your own prison bars and barbed wire in the provincial jail there, fills me with a sense of solidarity. But on the other hand it emphasizes the extent of repression in our country, for the prison bars have engulfed all corners of this archipelago. Even those outside the detention centers aren't quite sure whether they are any freer than us, given the death of freedom in this land. . .
>
> Your example of fortitude and strength in the face of tremendous pressure is a source of encouragement for us who also must face and bear our own cross. Since we are all pawns in this national security game, the outcome of your case could have important implications on all those who are victims of the lies perpetrated by the repressive state. If truth is vindicated in the end (for who could believe that you are capable of those crimes for which you have been charged in court?) then the forces of evil would have crumbled under the mighty light of righteousness! However, it is realistic to expect that, despite the pressure coming from all over the world, the truth will not be allowed to surface. After all, this régime can only find its legitimacy in the lies that have become 'truth' in the course of their own self-fulfilling prophecy.
>
> Whatever happens, you have made a prophetic statement. You have shown that you will not be crushed by the intimidating power of your captors. You have inspired us by your sense of community among yourselves, with those who have access to privileges forsaking these in favor of protecting each other's rights. Your attempt to stick to each other, to share your common anguish, to be together in your struggle for freedom – all these make us more sensitive to our own co-detainees as we seek to deepen our compassion for those who are less privileged. In the words of Martin Luther King, writing from a prison cell in Birmingham: 'You have carved a tunnel of

hope through the dark mountain of disappointment.' Your hope is our hope. . .

Karl Gaspar is still under arrest as I write this book.

NINETEEN

Sniper on the Roof?

The Majestic Night Club was across Gatislao Street, exactly opposite the gate of Bacolod Provincial Jail. It had a distinctive horseshoe-shaped doorway, and when night came there was always a crowd milling around there with a certain amount of raucous bargaining over possible favours. The prison guards slipped over there, and there was a good relationship between the two institutions. We got to know something about it because a prisoner in Cell 6 had been a bouncer there and was now in for killing two of the patrons. This same prisoner was sometimes allowed out to act as bodyguard to a certain rich land-owner, especially when the latter was going to the casino. Who actually allowed him out I am not too sure, but I do know that the land-owner was a friend of the warden. As I was saying, sometimes the prison guards slipped over for some light entertainment – in fact it was said that on one occasion the guard on the gate left the prison gate to a reliable prisoner! If that prisoner had recently killed two Majestic patrons, then I suppose he would have felt safer inside the prison than out and would have been less likely to want to escape.

On the evening of Monday, 21 February, the news came in that the Majestic had been closed down. This seemed strange, and I could not help feeling it was sinister. To a certain extent I felt that the Majestic, with its comings and goings all night, kept its own unconscious watch on the activities around the prison compound, which was not necessarily a bad thing. Anyway, I put it out of my head and was the last to go to bed.

At around one in the morning, before I lay down, a man appeared outside the cell and lit a fire to heat some water in an old billy-can. He was a prisoner called Claudio from the non-security part of the prison and his wife was visiting him with their two children. He told me that she was sick and that one of the children had a cold, so I got two aspirins for her and some Vicks for the child. The man looked absolutely forlorn;

115

all he had was warm water to offer his sick family who were sleeping on a table in the visiting room.

After this, I pulled our cell gate closed, lay down on the wooden bed and went to sleep.

At about five a.m. I was suddenly woken by something strange. I heard muffled voices talking about people on the roof. Now, if you looked out through the rungs of the cell gate there was a spot on the roof where the parapet was unfinished and which looked at right angles toward Cell 7. It seemed to have been planned long ago as a watching-post, but it was unused and only accessible from the guards' quarters. Two men had appeared right there behind the parapet, one with a garand 30-calibre rifle, the type used for picking off people. Claudio, who had remained up all night, noticed them, and so did several others. When they realised they had been spotted, the armed men ran away over the roof. Maybe it was the noise of the running that had woken me.

All day we tried to find out what it meant. The only access to that part of the roof was from the guards' quarters, and even then it would be a very difficult climb.

No amount of investigation ever revealed who had been up on the roof, but the general excuse given was that they had been chasing an escaping prisoner, which was very unlikely, since it would be the best route to take in order to fail in an escape. (It is also interesting that the escaped prisoner was later caught, but he told us that he had escaped over the outer wall of the compound and not come near the roof of the cells.)

That night we changed our sleeping arrangements.

The Majestic never reopened. People said it had not looked good with all the visitors coming to the provincial jail, so whoever owned it had to shift somewhere else. In a way I missed the music that used to come from it until the early hours of the morning and warm the night with the sense of human presence outside the walls. At the time of the incident we thought that the closing of the Majestic was ominous and might have been ordered so as to remove night witnesses to any untoward incident at the prison.

Wednesday, 22 February
Excitement rises as Australian journalists expect strong outcome of visit of Australian Foreign Minister Hayden. Irish Foreign Minister Peter Barry on the phone promised to put the Irish position; also promised to push for hearings five days a week, and to keep up the pressure about our security.

Thursday, 23 February
Court hearings reopen today in Capitol (Provincial Government Headquarters), starting at nine a.m. (clearly to impress Hayden that the case is moving!).

Rise at four-thirty a.m. and prepare altar for Mass together. I preside. Channel 9 from Australia present. Then we walked to the court – many cameras, etc.

Morning session: the bereaved relatives of the victims of the Sola ambush were on the stand. The prosecution are laying the ground for a massive civil damages case – surely millions of pesos. Mrs Sola, widow of the mayor, took the stand; she held herself with dignity and answered quietly and sincerely. In answer to Attorney John Hagad's question about me, she told the court that I was a family friend and adviser. She is a woman who has suffered greatly. Afterwards Itik and I went to her and thanked her for speaking the truth.

Dermot Kinlen, representing the International Jurists, is present, and cuts a formidable figure. He is accompanied by Rob O'Regan, who is an observer from the Australian Law Association. They are both to be neutral observers. We all feel that outside observers are essential.

Newsweek magazine arrived and we were also visited by Lydia De Vega, the Philippine Asian Games champion runner! Visitors, phone calls, letters; diplomats, press, superiors and relatives of lay leaders – the cell is packed like a sardine-can. When at last in the evening we tried to assess the court hearings we felt bad because, in spite of all the talk of a speedy trial, the morning session was shortened, they plan to drop Friday afternoon, because on Friday the judge will be leaving on the boat for the island of Iloilo so as to begin his weekend on time, and there will be no hearings tomorrow: we decided in the light of the continuing delaying tactics that Brian will ask Hayden personally for a five-day continual hearing, a rota of stenographers, and a full-time prosecutor, and nothing more. Brian has already written ahead to Hayden to this effect. He has also made it plain that he will not enter into any deal to go home, so that there is no point in asking us to do so and causing himself embarrassment. We decided that from now on the lay leaders will meet the crowds, as we are overwhelmed with work.

Friday, 24 February
Hayden is in Manila.

I spoke on Radio Veritas: mentioned the five-day hearing and the need for a courtroom, and that the judge says he has no filing cabinet!

We all spoke on the BBC World Service and I took the opportunity to ask the BBC classical record request programme to play 'The Shadow of Your Smile' for my Auntie Doris. Charlie Bird did an interview with me in Irish for Radio na Gaeltachta (the Irish-language radio station). Also, a long call from the *Cork Examiner*.

Saturday, 25 February
Very bad night – mosquitos, subconscious worry about sniper on roof, and headache. Australian television men arrived at six a.m. and said that yesterday Marcos had granted the five-day hearing (so we got it at last!) and that Hayden is about to phone. The Aussies have patched in a tape to the phone (with our and Hayden's permission), and there is a cameraman at both ends, so that when Brian goes on the phone to Hayden they will have the whole thing recorded.

Six-thirty a.m. I am in the warden's office now with Brian. *Irish Press* just rang. I told them to ring back again as we were expecting a call from Hayden.

Six-thirty-five a.m. Hayden rang just after I put down the phone. Brian is now on. I reckon he will just say something about hearings five days a week. . .

Brian chatted easily with Hayden, who told Brian of his meeting with Marcos. Two points: our requests have been granted regarding the details of the speeding up of the trial, and the door is open for ongoing dialogue.

But we still have to fix up the security problem.

Sunday, 26 February
I am not sleeping that well since the night of the suspicious appearance of the men on the roof.

One of the guards with whom we are friendly felt that it was an inside job, the thing on the roof. We decided to take precautions. Apart from buying our own padlock and chain, so no group could burst in at night and put an end to the whole thing, we put chicken-wire over the grills, the gate and the bars of the window-slits so that no grenades could be rolled in. The colonel had warned the bishop recently that some army grenades were missing and that he (the colonel) could not account for them. A little reminder, so to speak.

We bought several flash-lights with long beams, and whistles; I got Garry, a living-out prisoner, to do night duty for a certain remuneration, and I distributed the whistles to the *bosio* of each cell.

Michael McCluskey talked at length to the prison officials about our safety. Minister Barry himself brought it up at a higher level, so that one day Brigadier General De Guzman arrived with an impressive entourage of armed men and discussed our safety with the warden. Before he left he gave instructions for stricter visiting hours to be posted on the outside gates. We were happy with the new visiting hours because we were hardly getting time to breathe.

TWENTY

Diokno Performs

Some pages from my diary:

Thursday, 1 March 1984
Case resumes today. We are all sporting new *barongs* with the logo NEGROS NINE embroidered on them. The warden has provided a new vehicle with six armed guards and a white armed police car behind. The judge now says no TV cameras in courtroom, but no mention of when the famous five-day hearings will begin.

They are presenting Juanito Boholano (Junior) a notorious murderer who claims to have been with us in the ambush. Today Boholano pointed out Itik as one of the ambushers. He identified him clearly in court.

In the evening we had Mass with Bishop McKeon of Bunbury. We hear Cardinal Sin has received a thousand letters, mainly copies of protest letters sent to various Filipino officials because it seems we have now been adopted by Amnesty International as prisoners of conscience. A lot of letters also from Ireland.

Senator Diokno arrived tonight on the seven p.m. jet from Manila. Diokno came to our cell late at night with his wife. He got down to work immediately and checked out Itik's story, and mine. He will be assisting Attorney Cruz, who appears for all of us, but specifically for me and Itik. Diokno's coming into the case is significant. He is the acknowledged leader of the Philippine Bar and he should be able to stand up well to the objections of *Fiscal* Diola for the prosecution and the stalling tactics of Judge Legaspi at the behest of the prosecution's motions. We shall see. Boholano Junior is giving evidence for the prosecution at the moment and Diokno will take

119

him on when our other counsel for the defence, Attorney Hagad, has finished with him.

Friday, 2 March
Boholano Junior is holding up well under cross-examination from Attorney Hagad.

Fighting in Cell 4. Edwin and Brik. I persuaded Edwin to change cells. So he took up his mat and was allowed to change. In the morning the members of both cells will discuss it. Edwin is only eighteen and has spent his youth in prison.

Saturday, 3 March
As usual no electricity on Saturday or Sunday This means that fans don't work.

We are visited by Toby, the son of a prominent politician. This fellow Toby is in for homicide. His father put him in prison himself before he could be convicted – smart move. No case has been brought against him, so basically he can come out whenever things die down. Meanwhile he has his own special house with all mod cons and more besides. Anyway, Toby came to visit us. He says we are being watched by certain guards who are connected with Major Galto (it was Major Galto who had been contacting the prisoner who was allowed to escape). He also said that a certain family is determined to get us one way or another. He said we should have someone watching all the time outside the cell gate at night. I discussed it with the others, and we decided to do something about it.

Assistant Minister of Justice Borromeo was in Bacolod last night. He took the opportunity to meet with our lawyer, Johnny Hagad. They used to be classmates in law school. Borromeo made a bizarre offer: he said that if we show the ministry our evidence out of court and the official records of the Philippine Airlines manifest, proving that I did not return to Negros from Manila on the fatal date, then they, the ministry, will arrange to drop the case! Strange, considering the court is supposed to be acting independently. After discussion, we agreed that if we show our evidence we will do so without suspending the hearings in court. Anyway, a dialogue has been initiated.

We have hired a living-out prisoner to stay awake from midnight until five a.m. watching our cell. Our original watcher, Garry, escaped; he has been caught again and is now in another prison.

Sunday, 4 March
Attorney Johnny Hagad is to go to Manila to meet Borromeo some

time. We met at night to write out for Attorney Hagad his brief for seeing the Deputy Minister of Justice:

1. dismiss all cases without double jeopardy (this is a legal term meaning the cases can never be brought up again);
2. personal guarantee of safety for the nine after cases are dismissed or in the process of being dismissed, and for the seven should the two foreign priests leave the country.

We had given our watcher cigarettes to help him to keep awake, but a guard named Buncalon came and asked him to leave, so in the end our fellow gave the guard the whole packet of cigarettes in order to be allowed to stay. This guard Buncalon is at the moment suspended because of the complaint we made about him for maltreating a prisoner.

I met guard Sanoy (the one who once beat up the little fellow during our Mass). I had had one of our lawyers send a legal warning to Sanoy. The little boy was terrified and could hardly speak. I finally got him to admit that instead of an apology Sanoy had threatened to kill him. I went straight to Sanoy and had WORDS with him; he appeared contrite, but I feel he is a vicious person.

Today I must follow up our Bacolod-based vocations. I phoned all the schools and candidates and the telephone operators were very co-operative. One of those operators is hoping eventually to go to Australia and is hoping for an introduction from Brian to the consul!

A group in Cell 7 is due to go to Muntinlupa, the state penitentiary, where there are nine thousand prisoners. This prison in Bacolod is basically more like a remand prison. If they go to Muntinlupa they will be there for years. They will be sent in a boat in chains. What kills them is never seeing their families again; they are all poor and no one from their families could ever afford the trip to Manila to see them. Muntinlupa is a hell-hole, and what with the gang warfare it's hard just to stay alive there.

We had a meeting of all the *bosios* to start a prisoners' committee. They elected an overall chairman, vice-chairman and secretary. Every cell will meet before Wednesday, and the larger problems of each cell will be brought to the committee. We stressed the idea of the dignity of the prisoners.

We had a visit from Ben Alayon. We call him the 'barefoot lawyer': through his own efforts, though with no law degrees – just high school – he has got 171 prisoners out of jail in two years. He needs just the fares to go around the prisons and courts. He has been elected barrio captain of the little area around the prison. A most unusual barrio captain! He was 'in' himself for two years, for embezzlement – apparently he was the 'fall guy'. He decided that if he got out he would work for other prisoners. He came in the other day to ask for help for the sick wife of a prisoner.

Tuesday, 6 March
Father Mickie Martin has been digging up the legal papers of the old murder cases against Boholano.

Wednesday, 7 March
Today is Ash Wednesday, so we decided to have a special penitential service for ourselves and the other prisoners. We sat down and planned it together. The six lay leaders had been used to planning such liturgical events so the session went along smoothly. There is no point in hitting every note on the scale simultaneously. Hence, we felt that an indiscriminate attack on 'sin' might lead our fellow-prisoners astray and might make them imagine that they are worse than everyone else, which is not true. Our survey of the cells shows that most are here for reasons that have little to do with sin, so we decided that the note we should hit would be over-acceptance of our fate – fatalism: the tendency to ascribe our fate to the 'will of God'; our lethargy; our waiting for a *Deus ex machina* to save us; our *not* doing the little we can to change our situation here in the jail itself. Omission, in this sense, is to be the theme.

Some women brought blessed palms from last year's Palm Sunday (in the Philippines we use the top fronds of the coconut palm). We burned these and mixed them with oil and so produced the holy ashes. In Ilongo we sang the old Latin refrain *Attende Domine* (Here my cry, O Lord) to its gregorian melody. As we sang, each prisoner came to the altar with a piece of black paper, burnt it in the candle flame and symbolically did away with the things in his life which he felt were impeding his growth to being a genuine human being. After that we gave out the ashes, to the words *Memento homo*: 'Remember, man, thou art but dust and unto dust thou shalt return.' We ourselves took part, as did some of the guards. We invited everyone who wished to private confession – not so easy to arrange in our cramped conditions, but we managed.

Then we held the Liturgy of the Eucharist. At the kiss of peace we emphasised the reconciliation aspect of Lent. I got the chance to give the *pax* to one of the guards whom I had had a row with because he had beaten up one of the prisoners.

I believe that the secret of the Roman liturgy is moderation and the determination not to let it become a substitute for life; but the siren of spiritual consolation is always beckoning the religiously

122

inclined, and that lady is frequently a deceiver. Be grateful for the glimpse of the 'Other' which you will often get, and avoid becoming a spiritual voyeur – such is the advice I often give myself.

There is an organisation called VIPS (Visitors in Prison Service). They are a very fine group, rather like the Vincent de Paul. They write letters for the prisoners who cannot write, and bring medicines. The organisation has spread throughout the Philippines. It is almost completely lay and they have an excellent charter. They are headed by a wonderful woman called Manggi, who has reared twelve children of her own and has great compassion and patience.

We rose early to go to court. Who should appear as we were going to the vehicle, but the same man who had threatened Brian before. He was stocious, as we say in Dublin – very drunk. He had two armed guards (Philippine Constabulary in civilian clothes) and a driver, and almost had a run-in with Brian, whom he called *tonto nga pari* – loosely translated as 'a priest who causes trouble'. Brendan O'Connell appeared just then and had his video-camera with him, so he got it on tape (to the embarrassment of the army fellows).

At the court, Attorney Hagad told about Boholano being involved in an abduction case; the prosecutor blocked everything and the judge didn't seem interested that a prime witness might have a criminal record. He upheld the objections of the prosecutor.

Senator Diokno spoke today. He started by taking on the prosecutor who questioned his right to appear for us. *Fiscal* Diola objected to Diokno's taking over the defence brief during the course of the trial. Diokno asked in a loud clear voice: 'Who is running the court: the judge or the *fiscal*?' There was great applause because that is the question in everyone's mind.

Diokno really took the floor. Striding back and forth across the courtroom, and speaking with great emphasis, he made it clear that he would not be cowed by prosecution quibbling and blocking tactics. He destroyed Diola's objection to his presence and asserted the rights of the defendants to use their resources as best they could. As far as he was concerned, the accused were entitled to the best defence they could get under the Constitution. He was there to see they would get it! The packed courtroom applauded again. It was a kind of psychological turning-point: the defence had gone on the attack. The sense of relief and satisfaction in the courtroom was palpable.

Then Diokno got to work on Boholano and made him admit that he really had no evidence against me or Itik. It was a brilliant performance. A strange contradictory sort of thing happened: both Itik and I felt such relief surging up that we even began to feel angry and we found ourselves intervening with remarks. At one stage Itik almost shouted '*Butigon*' (Liar)! at Boholano. I kept my arm on his shoulder to make him feel my empathy and that I was also angry.

After lunch Diokno again. As I anticipated, the prosecutor had re-grouped his forces and was blocking like hell. It almost unnerved Diokno, but he broke through in the end and got two significant contradictions from Boholano. . .

Saint Patrick's Day cards and letters continue to pour in. Every time we get back from court there are more, and even in court we are handed fifty letters at a time. I have replied to some, and Itik has also replied. Old friends have written, and I love that.

I finally finished my Negros Nine document; it is supposed to be a complete summary of the case up to now. We need to get ten thousand copies printed and hand them out to visitors as they come, and we will ask them to distribute and multiply them.

A letter with an Irish stamp and postmark arrived to a Negros *haciendero* threatening to kill him and burn down his farm should anything happen to me. The sender claims to be a member of the Irish National Liberation Army and to have Philippine connections. The letter has been printed in the daily papers. I assume it's a fraud or a 'nut', but I bet the colonel is delighted.

Friday, 9 March
Morning session in the court very good. Diokno really proved the witnesses to be lying. We were all in good form, but exhausted.

After the morning court session we had a meeting with the lawyers at four p.m. We discussed getting more details regarding the crimes of Boholano Senior and Junior: they seem to have done everything in the book.

At the end of the session the colonel, surrounded by his entourage and with a smirk on his face, called me over and said, 'I have a letter here which I think you would like to read.' I guessed what letter it was and said, 'No thank you, Colonel. I don't read other people's letters – nor do I listen to their phone calls.' (A bit pompous, I think now.)

Saturday, 10 March
This is the anniversary of the mayor's death. Morning started at four-thirty a.m. with Ricardo, a prisoner who helps in our cell, clashing pots around as he put on rice and eggs to boil. Does he have to make so much noise? We are all very tired. It is hot, and there are too many visitors.

A letter arrived from Father Tom Cusack in the United States. He says fifty US congressmen (including Tip O'Neill and Geraldine Ferraro) have signed a letter to Marcos to drop the case. The letter was sponsored by Congressman Mrazek. It seems that before sending the letter they contacted the US Embassy in Manila, who reassured them that the case is trumped up!

Over a thousand copies of Negros Nine documents are nearly ready, and before we went to bed I said to Brian, 'We must prepare for the worst; we must not let up on our information campaign; we must have more hand-outs in Ilongo and English for the ordinary people.'

Sunday, 11 March

Itik's turn to celebrate the Sunday Mass. He taped his sermon and then had it played over the local radio. He speaks very strongly!

Bishop Pat Hurley C.SS.R, Redemptorist from Samoa, visited us and brought the support of the West Samoan bishops. He invited us to come – told us that the cardinal there lives in a reed hut and walks from village to village in his bare feet, like the people.

I was over in the office making a phone call telling all and sundry about Boholano and his killings, when Dayot (a trustee prisoner) intervened and said he personally knew of Boholano's crimes in Himulalud and Sadun. Murder and robbery against a certain Tison and a Doctor Damo from Bayawan. He told me to contact Thomas Threeambulo of Bayawan for more information.

Community leaders from Kenya, Indonesia, India, Sri Lanka, Burma – very fine fellows. Swedish journalists.

Monday, 12 March

Seven a.m. Fierce rumble broke out, with Cells 8 and 10 fighting. (A rumble here is a fight between cells – a sort of internal riot.) Brutal fight just outside our cell gate, with no holds barred: scalpels, bricks, planks in use. Brian had just got up and he went to the gate and tried to quell the fighting by shouting. One of the wounded (Elmer) dashed into our cell for sanctuary. Brian attended to him. He had wounds front and back, and there was blood everywhere. Suddenly Brian sat down heavily and I thought his stomach had turned because of the sight of the blood, but when I looked at him his pallor seemed to be that of heart trouble. He also appeared to black out for a moment and couldn't move at all. His breath was short, but he had no bad feeling in his stomach. I suggested the hospital, but he disagreed. I insisted, however, and phoned direct to the Riverside Hospital and got them to send an ambulance with a doctor and nurse and two attendants, knowing that Brian is so heavy. Meanwhile, guards had arrived, and now a sort of daytime curfew has been imposed. Two of those in the rumble were carted off to the provincial hospital. The ambulance arrived and they immediately wheeled Brian out. (I got a photo of him and gave him a wink, saying that I wanted the last photo of him alive!)

After a brief consultation with the others I phoned Attorney Cruz and told him that the case would go on – no postponement. He said we need a waiver, whatever that is – maybe it is waiving our right to be in court when a case is being held against us!

Crowds of visitors. Charlie Bird back from Cebu and the whole Oringao crowd from Brian's parish arrived, including Pulo who witnessed Boholano killing five people! Pulo was tortured, bullets put between his fingers by the army to try to make him be a witness against us. He still has marks on his wrists.

Three hundred and fifty cards from Ireland for Saint Patrick's Day. We have put a lot of them up on the walls. We also got shamrock.

I have arranged for a waiver allowing for Brian to be absent from court; also a doctor's certificate which has to be notarised by a lawyer.

Charlie Bird says I look very bad, much worse than when he first came here. I am going to try to get to bed a little earlier: I rarely make it before one a.m. I phoned my mother, so she would not be worried about Charlie's one-thirty news today, which would say I look tired, etc.

Attorney Hagad stood up in court and said: 'Father Brian Gore, whose very name connotes blood, will not be in court today. There was a riot in the prison and at the sight of blood he took a bad turn. This is the same Father Gore who is accused in this court of multiple murder!'

Our waiver and doctor's certificate almost did not prevail because the judge said that if there was a new witness who wanted to identify Father Gore, how would he do it (talk about casuistry!). Council for the defence replied that the witness in question should go to the hospital and identify Father Gore there. So another attempt to postpone was foiled by a hair's breadth. Our counsel, Romeo Subaldo, got Boholano, who claims to be a member of the Christian community, to admit that he could not say the Our Father!

Then Des Quinn passed me a note saying that I was wanted in a little room off the dock, in fact the judge's office. I nodded to the judge as if I were going to the bathroom and passed underneath his bench and entered the little room. The court secretary was there and she said, 'Phone-call, Father.' It was a long-distance call from a radio station in Sydney. I was on the air live: they were all worried about Brian, and I told them the story in 'glowing' terms. I finished by saying, 'By the way, this call is probably making history: it is not often a fellow is interviewed live on radio direct from the dock!'

TWENTY-ONE

Borromeo Initiative – False Hope?

From March until 4 May we had to dance to the most extraordinary tune. The court case continued, with the prosecution presenting their witnesses Boholano, Mendoza and Captain Malvas. Boholano was a notorious criminal, but, when we presented in court the actual legal charges against him from the *municipio* of Kabankalan, the prosecutor claimed that the spelling of his name was wrong. Now, people living in the mountains do not have fixed spellings for their names, and the prosecution themselves had used different spellings for Boholano's name. However, the judge upheld the prosecution and asked no more questions. On that argument the cases should have been dropped against all of us, because almost never did the prosecution get the names of the nine of us spelled correctly. In exasperation, when the cross-examination was finished, Attorney Cruz concluded quietly, but with great clarity and an edge to his voice: 'That'll be all for the defence, bring on the next lying witness.'

The next witness was Mendoza, the army investigator of the case. In the government story our ambush party drove from Brian's parish of Oringao, through the large town of Kabankalan, up the mountain again to my parish of Tabugon, where we called for the cook, and back to the ambush site, taking the long way which passed many military or police outposts and using the best-known vehicle in town – Brian's blue Fiera jeep.

Painfully, Diokno tried to get Mendoza to admit that such a plan was downright foolish when, if we had gone on foot, we would have reached the ambush site in a few miles instead of fifty which the alleged plot said we did. Even then it was clear from the prosecution description of our 'plan' that whoever wrote the so-called plan did not know the roads at all because even using the jeep we could have done it in twenty miles instead of fifty. However, since the plot called for my ex-cook to be a witness, it was necessary to collect him at my *convento*, hence the long journey. Although Mendoza was supposed to be the investigator, he announced 'I don't know' to every question from Diokno regarding the distances involved, so that he would not have to admit the patent weakness in the plot. The judge made no attempt to quiz him as he, the judge, so often did later when *our* witnesses were on the stand. However, endless answers of 'I don't know' or 'I don't remember' made Mendoza lose credibility before those attending the hearings and, it was to be hoped, before any Supreme Court review of the case, should it come to that.

Finally, finishing with Mendoza on the stand, Attorney Cruz shocked the court by saying, 'Captain Mendoza, please tell the court where *you* were at five-thirty on the afternoon of 10 March 1982 – the hour at which the mayor was killed.'

Mendoza: 'I was at the Sonedco outpost.'

Cruz: 'Yes: less than two miles from the site of the ambush. Thank you. That will be all, Your Honour.'

And Cruz sat down, leaving everybody stunned at the implication which up to this moment had not crossed our minds. The prosecution moved to have the last words of the defence struck from the record, and the judge obliged.

Next came Captain Malvas, who was to be the last witness for the prosecution. The strange thing is that he was the station commander of Kabankalan Integrated Police before, during and after the killing of Mayor Sola, but, before we were accused he was, conveniently, changed. If anyone ought to have known about the case, it was he. But he was pathetic on the stand – and he did not lie. He admitted that all documents, photos, sketches etc., pertaining to the case had been lost, and in no way could he explain the loss. Diokno told the court that the documents were clearly 'lost' because they contained evidence which showed we did not kill the mayor.

Diokno walked up and down the small space allowed him, chain-smoking and hardly looking at Malvas, as one question after another tumbled out.

Diokno: 'Where are the empty shells you picked up at the site?'

They were produced.

Diokno: 'Did you have them finger-printed?'

Malvas: 'No.'

Diokno: 'Did you have them sent for ballistic tests?'

Malvas: 'Yes.'

Diokno: 'Where are the tests?'

Malvas: 'We got none, sir.'

Diokno: 'Did you mark the shells before you sent them?'

Malvas: 'No.'

Diokno: 'So you cannot be sure that these shells here are the same shells you sent away?'

Malvas: 'No.'

By the time Diokno had finished the only material evidence of the prosecution – the empty shells – was in tatters. Most people felt sorry for Captain Malvas, because he was in an impossible position – presumably if he had been the sort of person who would have co-operated in the case he would not have been removed from Kabankalan police station and replaced by a more pliant man.

All the time the case was going on, messages were emanating from the Ministry of Justice. We called them the 'Borromeo Initiative' and it amounted to this: Borromeo, Deputy Minister for Justice, made it clear that if we showed the ministry *our* defence evidence ahead of time, and if we produced the Philippine Airline manifest (that is, the list of all the passengers who flew on Philippine Airlines between Manila and Bacolod between the fatal dates that I claimed to have been in Manila) and if that document corroborated my claim, then during the break between the end of the prosecution's presentation of witnesses and the beginning of the defence presentation, they, the government, would be prepared to drop the case. *We would have to trust them, of course, by showing them our cards, or some of our cards, in advance.*

We met again and again – alone, with lawyers, and with our superiors. If the offer was sincere, it held possibilities, but we ruled out showing evidence of any witness who could be easily harassed. If the airlines manifest and the requested affidavits were acceptable, our plan was to go ahead with the case and at the break to present a motion for dismissal. The prosecution could then, on a nod from the minister of justice, co-sign the motion for dismissal with us and the case could be dropped without going into the hundred and thirty witnesses for the defence, with all the delays and dangers that that meant.

During all this time reporters thronged the cell and visitors came in droves. Also came letters and cards; on one day we received two thousand Saint Patrick's Day cards, and in all we must have received about ten thousand. The post office brought them over in boxes. They got very confused and presumed that every Saint Patrick's Day card that arrived in Negros was intended for us in the prison. Hence we received not only our own cards but everybody else's too. I was sent so much shamrock I tried to see if it would grow. Brian delighted in showing the shamrock to the visitors as an example of Irish chauvinism. However, *we* could hardly survive in the cell, so the shamrock did not stand a chance and it wilted very quickly.

On Saint Patrick's Day we had a special Mass, which I think Charlie Bird taped for home. I gave no homily, I just did not have it in me. However, I was still deeply touched by all the cards, and I am sure the Bacolod post office will remember the occasion for a long time.

I used to stay up late to answer the letters which were now flooding in from all over. There were a great many from Scotland and England, as well as Ireland and Australia. Because of the Amnesty International connection there were letters of protest coming from people like Protestant pastors in Sweden and Denmark and from South America, and copies of those letters of protest sent to various officials also reached us. What with the cuttings and the cards and the letters and the court documents (there were now thousands of pages of stenographic notes), there was a certain amount of paper chaos in the cell.

Filipinos are notoriously tidy and careful, and keep all their things together neatly, which is what saved us from drowning in a sea of paper. Peter used to slit open the letters and unfold them; then i would read them and answer them and he would put them away carefully.

Finally, one night at about one a.m. as the pile of unanswered letters grew higher, I told myself that the people who wrote would surely not want me to get a breakdown trying to answer them, so we made the decision to ask the Presentation sisters to answer them for us. We had two thousand cards printed with a picture of the nine of us behind bars and our signatures on it, and Sister Alice and Sister Bridget and their community took on the major part of acknowledging the letters, passing back to me anything of a personal nature.

Meanwhile Brian and the others were doing their own answering. However, Ireland had outdone itself with letters. In fact, one class out of one school alone, that of Sister Bríd in Killester, organised five hundred letters to each of many different officials and passed the campaign on to other schools. Sheafs of school letters were pouring in; in all (cards included) there must have been fifteen thousand received in the cell, though I stopped counting after ten thousand. Some were very touching, many were deliberately written to cheer us up, and there is no devotion in Ireland or Australia in which we were not enrolled. Apart from this there were also the letters sent directly to the various officials.

Local newspapers would come over a couple of times a week to look through the letters and do a regular column on the special ones. Brian, Itik and I particularly enjoyed some from a group of elementary school-children which were meant for President Marcos, but maybe it is better that they found their way to us as they might have been misunderstood:

the little boys were only ten years old, but in no uncertain language and undaunted by spelling problems they told President Marcos what he ought to do and what they would do to him!

Anyway, as soon as the last prosecution witness, Captain Malvas, appeared we began to hammer out the motion for dismissal which we would then present to the court for co-signing by the prosecution as soon as Malvas had finished.

TWENTY-TWO

The Long March

When news of the accusation first came in 1982, our two parishes of Oringao and Tabugon met. Father Dangan was still not implicated, but our lay leaders met on their own and decided that if we were imprisoned they would march all the way to Bacolod from the mountains to protest. Neither Brian nor I was at that meeting. It was their own idea.

The idea of mass walks as a form of protest had been gradually developed in both our parishes as part of the non-violent tactics for dealing with various cases of injustice. We had walked all the way to confront Angelito Rio, and we had walked over the mountains to protest at military atrocities in Sipalay. Brian had used this type of mass action on many occasions, for example, when a group of five hundred members of his small Christian communities helped some peasants to plant their land as an act of defiance against those who were trying to force them off the land illegally and unjustly. The members of the small Christian communities did this in spite of the threatening presence of paramilitary groups belonging to the army. We had discovered the power of walking, but this planned walk sounded a little ambitious: from the mountains to Bacolod, about eighty miles, in the heat.

As soon as we were let out on house arrest the plan seemed to subside, but our sudden return to prison brought it up again and our two parishes shared it with the Christian Community Pastoral Group (a group of twelve parishes all trying to implement the diocesan small Christian community programme). They met regularly, and the other parishes decided to take it up. But the problem was the date. We wanted it on 6 May, the anniversary of our arrest, but that would be too close to a huge boycott march planned by other groups for the date of a forthcoming election; so there was nothing for it but to push our march forward to 9 April, as two long marches so close together would not be good.

The Christian communities decided to call our march Exodus, which seemed to be apt: the theme of God's people on the march to the promised land, echoing the words of Moses, 'Let my people go.' The march was called not just for us but against the general government policy of attacking the Church. The decision to change the date and the decision not to include any specific political call in relation to the elections took many meetings and there was much misunderstanding. We tried to keep abreast of the preparations, but this was not so easy since we were 'inside' and the organisers were 'outside'.

Eventually the plan was this: the people were to congregate at Kabankalan at the southern end of Negros and at Sagay in the north, each about sixty miles from Bacolod. They could be trucked to these spots, but they would walk the last sixty miles. Since Itik's parish was nearer Bacolod, his people would join the Kabankalan march as it passed. The march was to finish with a demonstration in the *plaza* at Bacolod with speeches against government oppression of the Church.

None of us, of course, could attend the march and only heard it over the radio, so I have decided to stitch in here the account of Father Bob Burke who took part in it. Father Burke, a Chicago Columban, comes from a parish way down in the south of Negros and his group had first to travel sixty miles to Kabankalan before they began the real march. Here is his account:

> This is about the Long March, or Exodus '84, to allow it a scriptural description, three days of torrid sun and long kilometres from Kabankalan to Bacolod, a distance of about ninety-five kilometres, or approximately sixty miles. I was there. A long line of marchers (numbering at the start more than 1500) carrying streamers and placards moved over a hot asphalt road like a colony of ants, twisting into curves, seemingly endless.
>
> Leading the march were the people of Oringao, their parish priest a prisoner in the Bacolod Provincial Jail; behind them, the people from Tabugon, their shepherd a prisoner too. The two groups set a furious pace the first long day, as much as to say: We are coming, we are on the way! Stringing along behind them were groups from different parishes, carrying identifying banners to announce the Christian community and the parish of which they were members. I walked with the Bacuyangan group, thirty-five who had travelled one hundred kilometres north to Kabankalan to join the march.

The Marchers

A little about my group. The woman walking behind me wearing the conical Philippino straw hat was a mother of eight, with little ones at home. Why was she here? The fellow just ahead of me, denim pants, a faded T-shirt, a crushed straw hat, his feet calloused and toes spread wide from long bare-footed walks in the mountain. What was his reason? The several teachers, still young, carrying banners, shouting with the rest. Why? The seventy-one-year-old catechist, dressed in black, carrying her own bag with a few boiled eggs and a change of clothes. Had she nothing better to do?

My group was a microcosm of the Long March that stretched beyond sight before us and behind us. Mostly they were poor farmers, fishermen, laborers who would describe their lives: '*Isang kahig – isang tukal*' (One scratch – one peck, i.e., living just from day to day).

Down the line from me, Father Demit Gatia, Scripture scholar, Rome-educated, diocesan priest, and beloved, and further down the line Father Nanding Reyes, dedicated assistant of the Kabankalan parish. Ahead of me, walking with brisk strides, Father Eamonn Gill, story-teller of exceptional ability, moved up the line in search of an ear for his many stories.

As the heat of the day intensified, drop-outs sat by the side of the road and awaited medical aid from the Ford Fiera marked with a large red cross that scurried up and down the line of marchers like a water-bug in a lily pond, driven often by Father Terry Bennett. A second Fiera with a mounted camera operated by fifty-one-year-old Father Brendan O'Connell (a capable photographer) patrolled the march, and the camera recorded for television this assault on Bacolod. Why – why so many?

The marchers moved north like a long freight train, and its whistle at every crossing, every town, was the shrill voice magnified by a portable sound system that shouted: '*Singgit sang banwa!*' (The cry of the people!)

An avalanche of voices responded: '*Kahilwayan!*' (Freedom!)

The microphone: 'The cry of the Negros Nine!'

The people: 'Freedom!'

The microphone: 'The Negros Nine!'

The people: 'Let them go free! Let them go free!'

The Long March enters another town on its route. Deep-throated bells of century-old Spanish churches, like solemn old men, welcome the marchers and respond to the message they carry to Bacolod: an emphatic Yes! Yes! Yes! Crowds line the side of the road, pressing cups of water, fruits, candies, bread, into the hands of the perspiring

133

marchers. The day lengthens, the pace slows. Shirts are bleached and salt-crusted. There is silence now except for the slop, swish of sandalled feet on hot pavement.

Then the day's destination is reached, and the marchers sprawl on the grass-covered *plaza* of the town's church. The advance unit of cooks, supervised by Consing Perez, prepare supper for this huge crowd. For them it has been a guessing game: how many will have joined the march, and will there be enough for all?

After supper, darkness and quiet settle on the group, most of whom sleep immediately. Father Dodo Dejilla, energetic and capable organizer of the Long March, huddles with his lieutenants to evaluate and plan. As for me, I lean against a tree in the darkness, and my head is like a cage of mice – thoughts, questions scurrying about, bumping into one another. One day's march over, two to go. . .

The Final Day
The final day, the final march. The southern group, now swollen to about three thousand, reached Bacolod on the morning of the fourth day.

A sudden tropical storm drenches marchers, sags broad-brimmed straw hats, withers cardboard signs, as the group marches through down-town Bacolod. There is a cheer as the southern group meets the group from the north of Bacolod who have marched approximately the same distance, a thousand or more in number. The two groups like giant waves meet, swirl, unite and move on towards the provincial jail. Five thousand chant: '*Upud sa amon, Negros Nine, hilwayon, hilwayon!*' (Come with us, Negros Nine! Let them go free!)

It is a second Jericho assault as their voices bounce off fifteen-foot-high white-washed prison walls, and salt tears mingle with puddles of fresh rain water as marchers pass the jail gate where the Negros Nine watch, pressed against the bars.

It had begun to rain heavily, and we tried to unload the visitors so that we could get a few minutes to eat. We were in the middle of the meal when Brendan O'Connell appeared and told us that the marchers were coming and in spite of attempts to divert them would pass the gate. We went out to the gate and stood in the streaming rain, wistfully watching the groups passing by. Shouts, chants and some tears from people like Crispin who had walked all the way (he had helped me in my work from the very first day I arrived twenty years before). They were drenched to the skin, and some threw food over the gate – melons,

Top - A section of the Long March, 10-13 April 1984, when thousands converged on Bacolod to protest against the injustice of the trial. *(Fr Brendan O'Connell)*
Above - A section of the crowd at Bacolod during the rally held after the Long March. The clenched fist is raised during the singing of '*Bayan Ko*' (My Country). *(Fr Brendan O'Connell)*

and suchlike – to us. It was deeply moving to see our old friends, our own parishioners. The nine of us pressed our faces to the bars; the march was being rolled along fast by the marshals, but many rushed over to shake our hands and kiss us.

When we got back to our cell we tried to finish our meal, but the affair in the city *plaza* was beginning, so I lay down on my bed and let the messages from the *plaza* speakers, coming from all the transistor radios around the quadrangle, flow over me. Father Bob Burke's account continued:

> The march continues into the public *plaza* in front of the cathedral, where a short program has been arranged. At a signal from the master of ceremonies, the huge crowd becomes silent, and seven thousand voices mingle, the young, the old, the weary, the marchers, as they sing: '*Bayan kong Pilipinas*' (My country the Philippines).

Later, Donie Hogan arrived and described the extraordinary scenes as the marchers passed through the various places, such as Aguisan, where Father McShane waited with his people, all with gifts of food and water – tears flowed down their faces as they threw their arms around the marchers. We were beginning to feel that the march must have had a great effect on the people in the places it had passed through. My diary for that day also contained the following reflections:

> Four p.m. news came that Senator Diokno now has a full copy of the Philippine Airlines manifest. It shows me leaving for Manila on 8 February and returning on 22 March, and no trips in between. However, Borromeo is now asking for *more* affidavits – he wants some to cover the lay leaders. We are apprehensive that revealing the names of these forthcoming witnesses might put them in danger. We are preparing a motion for dismissal, but the hope of being out for Easter seems to be receding. If we are going to be here for Easter we'll have to start preparing our Holy Week ceremonies now.
>
> News also came from a high-placed Australian official that a hundred-million-dollar loan from Australia to the Philippine government has been halved. Only fifty million is being given now, and the official let us know that the other fifty million would come when Brian is out, although I presume this was not spelled out as such. It seems that there is such strong support for Brian throughout Australia, due to the media coverage, that people would protest if the whole amount were given.

Saturday, 14 April
Edwin came out of his cell all cut in the stomach and wrists. He did

Edwin, who spent most of his youth in prison, dramatically demonstrates his anguish by 'crucifying' himself. *(Fr Niall O'Brien)*

it himself with a blade. Why? It is not uncommon here. A need for attention? Afterwards he had himself tied up on the gate of his cell as if crucified. This gave a great opportunity for many to mock, led by Henry, of course. I had mixed feelings about the whole thing: it seemed to be strongly derisive of the crucifixion, especially the way they were mock-acting; however, having failed to stop it (I made some attempt), I realised I would be putting evil where none existed. If Edwin was looking for notice I could solve that. I got out my camera and took photos of Edwin, who acted up dramatically. I asked all to clap, and eventually , after some play-acting he came down.

As I look at the photographs now, I begin to realise that there was more to this event than I was aware of then. Edwin had been in jail for years, even though he was only eighteen or twenty. He had no lawyer. He had grown up in the streets, and in fact what got him into prison was an act of self-defence. He had let himself go. He used to beg, and we tried to make him understand that it was against the dignity of prisoners. However, I now feel that by cutting himself and ritually crucifying himself Edwin was really crying out to the world, saying, 'I am crucified,' thus acting out his own degradation in the only symbol he knew. I recall the words in the letter to the Hebrews: 'You crucify again the Son of God and make a mockery of him.'

And what are young children doing in a place like this, anyway?

TWENTY-THREE

Organising the Prison

Many things had changed in the jail since we had arrived. Each of us took on a different aspect of work: Brian looked after the physical side of things; Itik was in the crafts; and I was doing a lot of the paper-work. Brian had a toilet bowl put in our cell and a curtain put around it. Nena, Rosita and Mommy Paz were always ready to bring the things we needed. Then Brian got a hole dug underneath the wall to the outside and had a septic tank built outside. The warden arrived during the operation and gave us some advice. We papered the walls with the newspapers I was receiving, and Brian put in lights. He then gave fluorescent lights to each of the other cells and put a tap on the water supply so that the water would not be wasted. The Redemptorists gave us bookshelves and a little table for me to type on. Baby and Dodo Gonzalez, faithful friends, contacted the fire brigade, who came in and hosed out all the cells. Everyone had to put his belongings out into the quadrangle and when all that stuff was there it looked so pathetic – ramshackle little stands covered in tattered plastic. It reminded me of a concentration camp. Anyway, the firemen did their job well and hosed down everything, and then we gave Lysol disinfectant to each cell to wash out the place. We had told people about Lysol a few days beforehand and also let it be known how dangerous it was for ducks – the owner of the ducks quickly withdrew them and that meant a much cleaner quadrangle!

The VIPS, the Visitors in the Prison Service, a very good group, gave cement and we filled in some of the holes and covered other parts of the open sewer with wood. They also got us oil drums which were cut in two with an acetylene flame and made into four rubbish bins, one for each corner of the quadrangle. Each cell in turn emptied them on to the big dump outside, near the long house. Whatever money came in we gave to Brian, who used it for the various projects. He put up a basket-ball ring and a volley-ball net; when Mayor Bagatsing from Manila came to visit we asked him for a basket ball and a volley ball, which were duly delivered, and a contest was started between the cells.

With the improved lights the prisoners were able to work better at their handicrafts. Itik ordered lots of plywood and sugar-cane reeds and distributed them, with the help of the lay leaders. That meant that many of the prisoners were busier and there was money to buy food, which was, of course, the number one need. In fact, the range of products produced got larger and larger. Originally they had been doing just the Last Supper and an icon of Our Lady, but now they took on all sorts of designs, many with the words 'Free the Negros Nine' or 'Free all political prisoners' or various other slogans related to our case. We got them to do special ones for well-known visitors with the pope's words when he was in Bacolod: 'The Church will not hesitate to take the side of the poor and to answer their cry when they are not heard, not only when they demand charity but when they ask for justice.' Every day someone had a new idea for a design and the visitors began to buy them and order their own directly from the prisoners. The themes of justice and freedom began to dominate. However, my favourite image was of a hand grasping barbed wire, allowing the dove of peace to alight: there comes a stage when someone must absorb the violence and not pass it on.

The area of medicines fell to me because of my experience in our barefoot doctor programme in Tabugon. Mommy Paz and a Spanish nun, Sister Pilar, who was also a nurse, brought us in a large supply of medicines. Lydio's sister is a nurse in the local hospital. She visited him very often and would help to clean up wounds when she came. We used salicylic acid for ringworm and skin infections, and various anti-TB medicines, antibiotics and vitamins. At night-time I did the rounds of the cells until we became too busy altogether.

Since Mommy Paz was the head nurse in the hospital we were able to refer the serious patients to her. Except for one memorable occasion, I never saw the nurse who was supposed to be appointed to the prison. Prisoners going to the hospital were normally chained by one foot to the bed.

In the very next cell, Cell 8, a prisoner had asthma at night. It was a terrible thing to see him struggling, trying to get his breath. Since Brian also had asthma we usually had medicine for this. Another prisoner had epilepsy. Because he had had a fit in court the judge would not hear his case unless he had a doctor's certificate saying he would not have a seizure. We got some medicine, and Brian got the doctor's certificate, and he was released. . . Which brings me to the story of Ben Alayan.

As I said before, Ben had made a vow saying that he would help the prisoners. We made out a questionnaire for them on what illnesses they had and on the status of their legal cases. It was just unbelievable: of the two hundred prisoners in the top-security section almost none had been convicted, though many had been in prison for years and years. Nearly all the cases had come to a halt for one reason or another. Almost none had a lawyer and the cases were endlessly postponed. In some cases the judge had died and not been replaced, and in others the papers were lost. One prisoner had even been nicknamed 'Sorry Wrong Number'. His name was José Baloi, nearly seventy years of age, who had been finishing a sentence for homicide in the state penitentiary in Muntinlupa, Manila. When he was about to be released another recent case for murder was brought against him back in the island of Negros. He protested his innocence and pointed out that he had been five hundred miles away and under state custody. To no avail! He was shipped back to Negros to answer the second case. Ben Alayan went to the accusers and confronted them with the impossibility that this man could be guilty. The accuser, when he heard that José Baloi was nearly seventy years old, said, 'The José Baloi who killed my cousin is in his twenties.' It was a case of what the other prisoners called 'Sorry Wrong Number'. And then there was no one to get the old man out. We were working on his case, but it was explained to us that if we succeeded in getting it dropped, he would still have to be shipped back to Manila. He could be released only from there and it would be a long time before there was another shipment of prisoners to Manila.

Frequently a case would go on for a year or two without even one hearing. Sometimes the prison forgot to send the prisoner to court on the appointed day, even though the poor prisoner would be waiting to go from early morning, all ready in rented clothes. Then the judge would find the *prisoner* guilty of contempt!

Another man had been in for almost ten years. He had killed a man in a genuine act of self-defence when a gang attacked him. The judge, a cousin of the president, had adjourned the case to make her decision. Almost five years later she had yet to make it.

People usually got five or ten minutes' hearing every two months if they were lucky. State lawyers were divided into two classes by the prisoners: 'Attorney Carabao' or 'Attorney Guilty' – the former wanted to know whether their family owned a carabao (which could be sold) and the latter just told them to plead guilty because they would get out more quickly that way.

I calculated that there were five classes of murder prisoners in our section: self-defence, revenge, falsely accused, armed robbery, and paid killer. Needless to say the latter two were the harder types. The first two were frequently victims of circumstances and came from a part of the mountains where there was no genuine police force, nor any law and order, so that it was up to each person to defend himself, so to speak.

However, there were also those who were in for theft or robbery. One fellow was nicknamed 'Robbery With Music'. He was aged only fourteen, but he stole a tape-recorder from a teacher in a mountain school. The story went that he did not know how to turn off the tape-recorder so that while he was running away it went on playing, hence the nickname.

Gary, in the next cell, had stolen an expensive camera from a French tourist. The tourist got his camera back, but two years later Gary was still in prison. He asked me to write tô the Frenchman, whose address he had. I am sure the same man was taken aback to receive a letter in French from Gary's co-prisoner. I explained that Gary had a family and had paid enough for his misdemeanour. Could the man have the case withdrawn? I received no reply.

The most notorious case of all was Roney, whose picture went all over the world. As I have already mentioned, he was put in for firing a dart at an assailant of his father. We lost no opportunity to get him on television, and doubtless there were many outraged calls to the Philippine ambassador in Canberra. Roney was eventually released 'into the custody of his mother'.

Try and imagine what it is like when nearly every prisoner has a case which needs to be followed up. Finally we decided to start the barefoot lawyer programme. Most of this work was done by Brian and Itik. We collected the completed questionnaires and engaged a man full-time to help Ben Alayan. He came to the jail each day, and on Sunday at the homily we encouraged prisoners to go to Ben so that their cases could be followed up. It was remarkable how many cases could be caused to be dismissed by an intelligent layman who knew a little about the law. Failing dismissal, such a person could at least get the cases moving along faster.

Of course we were not always right. Sometimes we took the side of a prisoner, only to find ourselves embarrassed. For instance, Felix was in for stealing scrap-iron, and Ben said we would undoubtedly be able to get Felix out because he had already been there three years. However, when the verdict came back Felix had been given six to ten years. We were shocked: we had pressed the case along precisely because we thought it would be dropped. Brian and I were angry, and I said, 'You know, Brian, property has all the rights: this little fellow gets involved in stealing some rusty scrap-iron worth a couple of hundred pesos and now he's in for six to ten years while people who stole a hundred thousand pesos are out walking about.' Brian agreed heartily. I saw Felix next day, and needless to say he was downhearted. 'Tell me, Felix,' I said, 'how much was the scrap-iron worth?' 'Oh, about two hundred and fifty thousand pesos, Padre,' he said!

The barefoot lawyer programme meant that we could direct the ever-increasing number of cases to Ben and his assistant and leave ourselves time to prepare for other matters, such as our own court case and the Easter ceremonies, which were now just around the corner.

One of the saddest days for us was the day of the shipment. We knew this day was coming. The first hint I got was when I asked a fellow-prisoner who was gazing strangely out through the bars what he was thinking of, and he said, 'My mother: I'll be leaving on the shipment in two days' time; I come from the mountains in Victorias, and she is too poor to visit me to say goodbye.'

On the morning of the shipment day we celebrated Mass for them, and then we went off to the court. For days they had been collecting their things together. The shipment was always a moment of fear, because it was then that the guards could get their revenge on any prisoner whom they had not been able to get at in a cell; it was easy now, because the prisoners were chained.

When we got back from court at midday, we were appalled to see thirty-two of our fellow-prisoners chained by the legs in pairs. They were the shipment and were due to sail on the cargo boat *Santa Maria* for the national penitentiary of Muntinlupa in Manila, on the island of Luzon.

Saint Vincent's Orphanage came to visit us, and when they saw the prisoners in chains ready to be shipped they sang and danced for them. One fellow wept openly, although they tried to stop him. I feel deep sadness at the whole thing; they are like cattle going off.

Manggi, the head of the VIPS, arrived with her group. They had been faithful to the end. She is a great woman, and she visits them in Manila too.

I gave advice: keep away from gangs; save money, you'll soon be out; get to know the chaplain; be a leader and a light to your fellow-prisoners.

I was very disturbed, and even more so by their trying to stop the fellow who was crying. I felt it was time for tears.

Our military escort came to collect us. Brian gave them his blessing, and we were driven away to the court.

We we returned they were gone.

TWENTY-FOUR

Resurrection Behind Bars

Great comings and goings were taking place over the 'Borromeo Initiative' – the indications we had been given that the case would be dropped. My diary is packed with details, rumours and contradicted statements about the Philippine Airlines manifest, our affidavits and the Hagad-Diokno motion for dismissal. The media were pressing hard to be first with the good news, but it gradually became clear that nothing would happen before Easter. I telephoned home to put them at ease, and we resigned ourselves to being 'in' for Easter and began to plan the ceremonies.

Domingo de Ramos (Palm Sunday) went off well, with a procession of palms cut from the already forlorn coconut trees in the outer prison yard.

We sat down and planned the rest of Holy Week:

1. Holy Thursday would be a day emphasising love;
2. Good Friday would be a day emphasising repentance for not loving;
3. Easter Sunday – 'He is alive, with us now, struggling to build the kingdom of love and reconciliation.'

Itik was to take Holy Thursday. Someone suggested that after Itik had washed the feet of the 'apostles', each cell would hold its own ceremony. One of the prisoners would read from the Saint John's Gospel:

Jesus got up from the table, removed his outer garment, and taking a towel, wrapped it around his waist. He then poured water into a basin and began to wash the disciples' feet and to wipe them with the towel he was wearing. . . When he had washed their feet and put on his clothes again he went back to the table.

'Do you understand,' he said, 'what I have done to you? You call me Master and Lord, and rightly so! So I am. If I, the Lord and Master washed your feet, you should wash each other's feet. I have given you the example so that you may copy what I have done to you. . .'

Then each *bosio* would wash the feet of his own cell-mates. It was objected that the fellows would ridicule the *bosio* and laugh at the idea, but then someone said, 'Okay, let it be that way, because in fact in life if you do try to serve you will be laughed at and ridiculed sometimes, so that it is a good test – the symbol becomes the reality.' So we agreed, but left it to each cell to decide what they wanted to do.

When I toured around and quietly looked in at the cell gates I was deeply touched by what I saw. With rapt attention they listened to the words of Saint John, and with reverence they carried out the washing ceremony, as they sang the song 'Whatever you do to the least of my brethren. . .' They had gone to great trouble to prepare their group meal (Last Supper) and it lay there waiting for them. Our doubts had been unfounded. I wonder if we really ask enough from people!

Sunday, 5 April
I picked up the 'flu. Last night I awoke to discover I had fallen asleep without a blanket. I had a raw throat getting rawer. I have tried to remain lying down, but it is impossible with the conditions. I am so disappointed, because I was supposed to be in charge of the Good Friday ceremonies.

Decided not to go to hospital. All the private rooms in the provincial hospital are full and I would have to sleep in the corridor, Brian says. As for the private hospital, I suppose I feel a reluctance to appear to be wanting to escape from here to that hospital. It is difficult being sick here. Lights keep burning all the time, transistors on at full blast, and the beds are hard. Even as I write, there is a meeting going on in the cell over a rape case that is being solved by the barefoot lawyers. I am an object of curiosity in the bed, unshaven and unwashed; I feel uncomfortable and suffer from the lack of privacy. I would love to be away somewhere in a private room!

I got a massage and took some aspirin and muscle relaxant and one Dalmine, and slept well. Perspired, awoke, felt lighter, and the rawness of my throat was gone.

Newspapers arrive: big announcement that the First Lady is in Rome with large clerical entourage. We feel bad about it. I phoned our Rome house immediately where Bill Halliden, my old history teacher and chant teacher, is now Procurator General, and asked him what we could do because we felt that the whole trip, apart from being a blatant pre-election stunt in an eighty-five percent Catholic country, is also meant to give the impression that all is rosy in the garden of Church-State relations. Bill got to work immediately and had the pot boiling before the week was out.

One of the sisters later told me how their mother general had been inveigled into the trip. She got a call in the morning from the nunciature to say there were two places on a plane going to Rome – no mention of which trip. The mother general had a job to do in Rome, anyway, and she thought this would be a great saving. She got her things together and went to the airport, with a companion.

To her amazement there was no crowd waiting. She looked around and was ushered into a different reception area and onto a jet. As soon as she got on the plane she saw fresh flowers all the way down the aisle.

She had hardly taken her seat when the President of the Philippines arrived, followed by the First Lady. He immediately called for cameras. Mother General fled to a back seat as it dawned on her what she had walked into.

However, Father Hallidan's initiatives in Rome meant that our case was brought to the fore precisely during the visit which was meant to cover up our case (among other things).

On Easter Sunday our very beautiful ceremonies started at four in the morning and finished at dawn. We started in the dark with readings from Exodus:

Accordingly, task masters were set over the Israelites to oppress them with forced labour. They had to build for Pharaoh the supply cities of Pithom and Raamses. Yet the more they were oppressed the more they multiplied and spread. The Egyptians, then, dreaded the Israelites and reduced them to cruel slavery, making life bitter for them with hard work in mortar and brick and all kinds of field work – the whole cruel fate of slaves. . . But Moses said to Pharaoh, 'Let my people go.'

(Extracts from Exodus 1 and 5)

Next we had the New Fire to indicate the Resurrection and we lit a huge candle from it and went in procession around the quadrangle singing 'Light of Christ'. All lit their candles from the candle, and I sang the 'Exultet' – the song of praise of the candle and of the risen Christ. It is so elemental that it is always moving. Then the 'Gloria in Excelsis Deo' with bells and lights, then the blessing of Easter water and the baptism of some ten of our fellow-prisoners who had asked to be baptised. We had given them a seminar beforehand, but now we asked them to declare publicly their readiness to accept the consequences of becoming a disciple of Christ. 'Do you believe we are all brothers and sisters in this world? Are you willing to stand for the rights of the poor? Do you renounce oppression? Will you follow Christ?' Baptism is a commitment to build the Kingdom. All the congregation joined in renewing their commitment, and we sprinkled them with the Easter water.

Each cell brought a symbol of life, and I could not help smiling at some of the exhibits. Cell 3 brought a stone, and announced: 'We want to be soft – not like this stone!' I suppose you could call it an anti-symbol. Each showed the symbol to the congregation and explained its meaning. By the time the consecration came, dawn was breaking. After Mass there were games, food and fiesta: it was like Christmas, with a great air of joy.

We hoped that now the Easter holiday was over the negotiations regarding the Borromeo Initiative would maybe be speeded up. Like All Souls Day, Easter closes everything in the Philippines. Now our hopes rose again and lines started buzzing. The problem was that there was soon to be an election, and we wondered whether they would want to get the case over before the election (we tended to this view) or whether they would wait for a 'landslide' victory which would strengthen them.

TWENTY-FIVE

The Guards

I have never taken you outside the quadrangle yet, and maybe we have time to do that now. So far, we have only been inside, where two hundred or so high-security prisoners live in ten cells, but outside this, yet still inside the walls of the prison, is a sort of village, several acres in size.

The warden's office and house are the most prominent structures, and next is the long house – a very long *nipa*-roofed building, a hundred yards long, in which most of the other three hundred prisoners live, frequently with their families. This building is in such a state of disrepair that when there is rain it pours in, in spite of the make-shift plastic patches over the holes. Beside the long house is the prison dump – open to the eye and the nose. And beside that again is an iron lavatory, almost equally exposed. A walk through the overcrowded long house to the dump and septic tank shocks most visitors profoundly. Near the dump are small corrals where fighting cocks are kept and looked after by the prisoners on behalf of the guards who own them. The guards themselves live in houses dotted around the compound.

The system of running the prison has developed over the years. Prisoners are divided into top-security and trustees. The trustees are those who are allowed the privilege of living outside the cells, provided one of the many guards takes responsibility for them; in other words, he trusts them. They help in various ways in the running of the prison and frequently in the house of the guard, doing the cooking and cleaning, and minding his children. Some are sent to clean the courtroom, and we meet them there during our case. Others have to do work in various public buildings around the city. It was one of these trustees who witnessed the colonel's report to the governor on our escape from the constabulary headquarters. Sometimes they are detailed to go on a regular trip up the hills to look for firewood for the kitchen, and on these occasions the truck is always accompanied by armed guards.

The kitchen is basically two or three enormous iron cauldrons set in brick, with a hole underneath to allow a fire to be lit there. The cauldrons, called *kawa*, seem to have been here since Spanish times. Certain prisoners are detailed to cook, and to deliver the food in aluminium vats to the cells, and wash the vats afterwards. One tap serves the kitchen and all the inmates of the long house. If we count the three hundred prisoners, the families of those who have joined them, the guards and their families, there must be a population of six hundred to a thousand. Hence, many stores have been set up by the guards' wives. Then there are also little stands or spots where prisoners themselves put out vegetables for sale to fellow-prisoners. It is a veritable village, throbbing with life.

What are the families doing here? Well, basically they are here because of the innate humanity of those running a very inhuman system. If a man is in prison, his wife will sometimes bring him food or clothes, or she will come simply because she had no one to protect her and the children. She will just arrive, and if he has managed to become a trustee they can live together in some little spot with the children. Who feeds whom is very hard to know, but she will probably do the washing for the guards' families or look after a guard's children, or get involved in buying and selling. Usually wives just visit for a while, keeping up the contact with their husbands; they are lonely for each other, and I suppose the guards do not have the heart to strictly enforce whatever rules exist. In any case, these prisoners have become the trusted servants of the guards and so a human relationship has been built up between them. In fact, trustees are expected to defend their guard in a rumble, and guards are expected to defend their trustee against other prisoners. I suppose you could say it is a feudal relationship, the trustee becoming the guard's unpaid serf.

Wives and relations bring food, clothing and medicine, and as a sorely under-budgeted institution the prison needs these things – to cut off the visitors would mean cutting off support for the prison. Also, marital rights are taken for granted, all the more so because the prison is, to a great extent, a remand prison where people await sentence. I have almost never met anyone here who has actually been sentenced; they are usually in so long that they pass the legal maximum sentence, and then, if they are lucky, they manage to plead guilty and be released.

In theory, there are government lawyers attending to the prisoners. However, we see very little sign of them, and I do not think the provincial government has ever realised that half the prisoners could be dismissed in a week given proper legal attention, thus saving the province huge sums of money (because the expense per prisoner of running the prison is extremely high). I would say there are about eighty guards attached to Bacolod Provincial Jail. They are sorely under-paid, and they do not seem to have undergone any training worth talking about. They are basically decent fellows, many sent in because they are athletes, and they double as the province's athletic team, of which Negros is proud.

It is very hard for guards, no matter how good, not to be corrupted by the system. They were good fellows coming from the farm, but as guards they have to stick together. If one guard maltreats a prisoner, there is no chance that he will be corrected or censored by his fellow-guards. And we have found that nothing comes of the many protests against cruelty and maltreatment we have made – because it is the guards who investigate the guards! We wanted to have an outside group set up who would be independent and do the investigations, a group of lawyers who owed nothing to the prison. The VIPS are a noble self-sacrificing group, but their continued entrance to the prison depends on the goodwill of the guards. If they criticised the guards, that would put an end to their entry, so it is the old problem of who guards the guards: *'Quis custodiet ipsos custodes?'*

Needless to say, we have had many run-ins with the guards. On one occasion I was embarrassed by my own rashness. I saw what appeared to be an old man being beaten up by a young man. I could not contain myself and roundly gave out to the young fellow. I asked him his name, but he would not give it. I asked the victim, but he would not give it either, and neither would the by-standers. It began to dawn on me that I had been giving out to a guard. I was a bit angry, so I gave out to him further for not wearing his uniform. We parted, and I felt bad about the whole thing. Having investigated the matter, I found it was a very complicated affair and that the guard was not totally unjustified, as the old man had hit a child who was the son of this guard's trustee. I decided it was a case for an apology, so I went to him next day. He was in full uniform this time. I said I was sorry for giving out to him in public as I knew that took from his dignity, but that I would not have done it if I had recognised him. I also told him I realised the complexity of the actual event.

I distinctly remember a guard, sent by the warden to lock our gate, who looked at us first, literally asking permission to turn the key. He found it so hard to do, which is understandable when you remember that these guards are, when all is said and done, our parishioners.

We have also made friends with some of the guards, especially those who have not been corrupted by the system. Itik has become god-father to a child of one of them. If they need medicine the guards come to us, and we give it, as they do not have any medical care either. They also have family problems which we are willing to help with. I suppose it is only those guards inclined towards bullying that we lock horns with. We have had one suspended, made complaints about another, and had a lawyer's letter sent to another.

The guards have their work cut out for them too, because if one of their trustees escapes they lose their job if they do not catch him. They receive a note from the warden's office saying 'Within forty-eight hours please give a reason why you should not be immediately dismissed.' They are then expected to travel over mountain and valley and on to other islands until they catch the trustee. This happened to one guard recently: he had let his trustee home secretly as the latter had pleaded a family problem – this was illegal, but the guard covered for him; but the trustee never came back. One could understand that if such a fellow were caught, he would be liable to receive a hiding. Indeed, there are many escapes, but the system seems to work because the guards usually catch the escapees quite easily, mainly because the first thing an escapee does is go straight home for a decent meal. He will hardly have finished the meal when the knock comes on the door, and for him it is straight back to the *bartolina*, frequently with a beating. One fellow, who had been helping in our cell, escaped one night. However, he got lost in Bacolod city, being a mountain type. He just came back to the prison and they let him in with no questions asked.

It is strange: when you categorise people, it is easier to dehumanise them. You say 'the guards' or 'the prisoners', and somehow it seems that regarding them simply as a member of a group is a way of hiding from yourself the true person behind the face. That's how ideology works.

On one occasion while we were in court we noticed the Bombo Radio people reporting our case. We were listening to the radio at lunchtime and noticed that the report was inaccurate. I went straight to the telephone, called up Bombo Radio and complained. They apologised and agreed to retract what they had said. They then asked me if I would like to give a talk to the people in Negros, and I said Yes. The one condition was that I should not speak about politics, and I answered, 'Don't worry; I never enter into politics.' I said I would speak on vocations to the missionary priesthood. Anyway, I gave my little talk on becoming a missionary, and it seems that in a far-off part of the prison (which has all sorts of outlying parts) there was a guard at his lunch listening to his transistor radio. This guard had always had it in mind to become a priest, and he had in fact done a lot of extra study by himself at night-time, even though he worked as a guard during the day. He suddenly discovered who was talking on the radio. My final words were: 'If you are interested, you can apply at Cell 7, Bacolod Provincial Jail.' He thought to himself, 'Well, that's very close; I might as well try,' so that evening he turned up, his armalite hanging from his shoulder, to apply for the seminary. I tell the story just to show that it takes all types to make up a prison guard. However, since the guards, receiving no specific training and undergoing no psychological screening to eliminate the inevitable sadist, were nevertheless given absolute power over fellow human beings, that power inevitably corrupted most of them.

I once remarked to a Bacolod matron that the prison compound was like a Japanese concentration camp, and she said, 'Oh, no! The Japanese camps were better than this.' However, I think we were both wrong. The amount of decent humanity at play inside these walls is amazing. What society has taken away with one hand, human nature has returned with the other.

TWENTY-SIX

Motion for Dismissal

Thursday, 3 May

Frantic activity by the media. Everyone expects the case to be dropped. Charlie Bird is on his way back to the Philippines. All the papers required by Borromeo are ready, and the motion for dismissal prepared by Diokno and our lawyers is finished; it is a powerful document, very well put together.

Friday, 4 May

What a day! Everyone keyed up! All in court by nine a.m.

Our counsel moved for dismissal.

Then the prosecutor stood up and said that Mr Puno, the minister, had informed him *yesterday* that he should oppose the motion for dismissal; in other words, he would *not* co-sign it.

We were stunned. Borromeo is supposed to be saying one thing and Puno says the opposite – and to think we have already shown them the affidavits of our forthcoming witnesses! Then the prosecutor says that Puno has said we can have a five-day hearing. (Big deal!) Was this all a ruse to see our evidence in advance?

Discussion ensued on how many days would be given to the prosecution to reply to our motion. Prosecutor asked for five, and eventually got seven! The judge will then have five days to decide whether to grant the motion for dismissal or not – so the election will be over!

It seems we will not withdraw our motion. We fixed a date for the next court hearing for 22 May (not that it has ever mattered what day has been fixed, they have always been changed).

Channel 7 from Sydney did a review of the case. Brian and I both spoke strongly to the *Evening Press*.

I am angry and disappointed, and I feel we ought to see now that we made a mistake in trusting Borromeo. Everyone expected the case to be dropped, and now there's another wait for the judge's decision, with more false hopes!

I am exhausted now. I hope my bronchitis clears up.

Brian feels that if they are not willing to get out of it at this stage they will find us guilty. (After all, it's been handed to them on a plate.)

TWENTY-SEVEN

Cárcel Pública de Negros

When Magellan's ship sailed around the world in the 1520s he 'discovered' the Philippines, or I should say that in an attempt to discover a new route to India he came upon the Philippines, and, by accident as it were, sailed around the world. The first of the Philippine islands he visited were the Visayan islands, that central bunch situated between Luzon in the north and Mindanao in the south. Many of the Visayans were tattooed, so that for a while the Spaniards called them *Los Pintados*, 'the tattooed ones'.

Like many another pre-Spanish trait, the art of tattooing did not disappear completely with the coming of Spanish cultural domination. It just went underground. And, strangely enough, the place where it best survived was in the prisons. Maybe that is not so strange, because I presume that in the early days prisoners tended to be predominantly political and of the sort who most resisted the new cultural invasion. Anyway, the art of tattooing is flourishing in Philippine prisons, and thus in Bacolod Provincial Jail.

The master tattooer in the jail was Diutay Millian, who was thirty-two years old and told me that since the age of thirteen he had been more years in than out of prison. He himself displayed multiple tattoos by way of advertisement for his trade, on both his legs up to the thighs – almost like long black stockings – and on his arms. He had none on the chest, however, as others did, so he could wear long pants and a long-sleeved shirt open at the neck and no one would know he was tattooed, he said.

On the back of his thigh on the right leg he had a picture of a beautiful girl and the name of his girl friend written under it. Further down the same leg he had a snake wrapping itself around the shin. Other people had snakes wrapped right around their bodies. On the front above the knee he had a consortium of writhing devils. On the other leg he had a well-done picture of Our Lady of Perpetual Help, and further down, a grim dragon. His earliest tattoos were done when he was just thirteen, and were on the upper arm. Other items in demand were witches and spirits from Filipino demonology, and it seems to me appropriate that they have survived as they were part of the heritage the Spaniards sought to eliminate.

I asked Diutay how he did the tattoos, and he told me he had Indian ink and a special instrument consisting of sixteen needles sandwiched between two bits of bamboo, so that one dab of this instrument simultaneously delivered sixteen pricks in a row. A rag binding the two bits of bamboo together was soaked in ink and the ink dripped down onto the needles, so that as they pricked they delivered the ink into little wounds – frequently not deep enough to draw blood, but always deep enough to be very painful which lent the whole thing a touch of *machismo*.

While I was in the prison, Diutay finished a job on another prisoner who happened to be a polio victim. The tattoo was done on the 'thin' leg, and the result seemed to me grotesque. Frequently the operation caused a swelling in the lymph nodes at the joining of the arm or leg, which would seem to indicate that some poisoning took place. However, they would get over it.

Various words and slogans were often tattooed on prisoners – the name of a friend or protector, their own nickname, such as 'Lover Boy' or 'Diutay' (small fellow), and many had a gang logo, such as *Pangkat Paghida-et,* which in prison argot means 'Peace-seeking group'. In fact, on one occasion when I was explaining baptism to the prisoners, I used this as a simile and said that, just as being tattooed with *Pangkat Paghida-et* was supposed to mean that you were for peace, so one aspect of baptism was a public demonstration that you intended to defend the rights of the poor and was a sign of your allegiance to the Kingdom of God. It seemed to fit in well enough with that elusive theological concept of the 'character of baptism' which was prominent in the catechism when I was a boy.

Whatever vestigial connection the tattoo may have with early Visayan practices, or whatever possibilities it lends a would-be catechist for illustration, the tattoo has a darker side to it. It is a symbol of fatalism, of the hopelessness of being in jail for ever; and indeed the longer the sentence the more likely the prisoner is to have more of his body covered in tattoo. I was told that those in Death Row in Muntinlupa (the national penitentiary) cover their faces with tattoos, even giving themselves horns. Sadly, they have internalised the image the public has of them.

Some prisoners realise the negative value and strive to remove the tattoo, but too late, because all the methods, as far as I know, are painful (such as re-tattooing in milk) and they mess up the tattoo instead of removing it. The prisoners who leave the jail alive carry with them for ever a primitive reminder of their dark years in jail and a warning to the public that they are ex-convicts.

Diutay offered to tattoo me, but since I still cherished the hope of swimming in the 'Forty-Foot' in Dublin Bay again some day, I decided to decline.

One day I was delighted to discover an old plaque on the wall of the prison. An annex had been added for the dozen or so women prisoners just at this part of the wall, distracting the eye from the plaque and casting a shadow over it, so that it could only be read at certain times of the day. It read grandly:

CÁRCEL PÚBLICA
DE LA REGIÓN OCCIDENTAL
DE NEGROS
AÑO DE 1890
Ad Majoram Dei Gloriam

So the prison had been built for the greater glory of God. Did I detect the hand of the Jesuits there? Well, a little bit of research revealed that the prison had indeed been built by a priest, but not a Jesuit. He was Father Mauricio Ferraro and he was an Augustinian Recollect. It seems that around 1870, Father Ferraro was building Bacolod Parish Church (now the cathedral) and he asked the military governor of the day for the loan of prisoners to do the job. (In those days Church and State were very close.)

The military governor realised that Father Ferraro was a good builder, so he decided to loan the prisoners, provided the priest would design and oversee the construction of a stone prison for Bacolod. Father Ferraro agreed, and finished the construction of the prison twenty years later. Maybe that was why he put the words 'To the Greater Glory of God', because the prison was a payment for the church, but I suspect that there was a deeper reason. I suspect that he felt that prisons were a part of the 'gift' of civilisation; and this is not as outlandish as it may sound, because prisons do at least imply the principle of adjustable sentences to suit the alleged crimes, whereas a régime which takes no prisoners is left with the uncomfortable alternatives of maiming or capital punishment.

Lest I be guilty of being wise after the event, let me say that the Spanish laws regarding the use of citizen labour on public buildings were not as cruel as they look. In fact when they were introduced they were quite enlightened, because at bottom they were a substitute for slavery. Several centuries earlier Spain had been ahead of its time in abolishing slavery and hence slave labour. For public works they had the following system: instead of paying your poll tax you did X number of days' labour on public works – roads, bridges, ship-yards, defence works and (wait for it!) churches.

Of course the whole system was open to endless abuse, as some could afford to pay and some could never do so – therefore the latter had to do all the work. And many of those who could pay were probably able to avoid paying anyway. By 1888 when Father Ferraro was beginning to build the prison, the poll tax system had petered out, hence the friar's special request to use prisoners.

As I sat writing my diary, I would look up at those solid walls and imagine the good times the prisoners had as they built them, with Father Ferraro walking around in his long white cassock and black leather belt, casting a cold ecclesiastical eye on the work and uttering the odd unecclesiastical phrase at work badly done.

What is interesting about Father Ferraro and his confrères is that they also built a lot of roads and bridges and introduced various types of new crops, and found no contradiction between that and their vocation. Whatever the theology books were saying then (and I suspect that Vatican One had not yet filtered out to the Philippines) their pastoral practice tended to regard human beings as a whole and not to be split too severely into bodies and souls.

However, Father Ferraro and his companions did regard the Spanish government highly and felt that what was good for Spain was good for the Philippines. And the Spanish government at this time regarded the missionaries as 'handmaids' in the work of colonisation – so much so that when Spain closed seminaries on the peninsula a short time before, they thought it better to leave the missionary colleges open.

Anyway, to cut a long story short, there came a time when the local élite decided to throw off the Spanish control. That was in 1898. The Spanish friars had been so entangled with the government that they were seen as part of the one institution, so they were all rounded up (with a few notable exceptions) and placed – guess where? – in the *Cárcel Pública de la Region Occidental de Negros!*

So we were not the first priests to inhabit those cells. However, one of the 'notable exceptions' mentioned above was Father Ferraro himself, who was allowed house arrest because of all the public works he had done. Thus he avoided the humiliation of being incarcerated in his own *Cárcel.* He did not escape expulsion, however, and few months later he and his companions were deported on a ship called the *Monserrat.*

Strange – house arrest, imprisonment, deportation – the same realities occurring a hundred years later, but now the circumstances were reversed. Father Ferraro and his companions were seen as very close to the Spanish élite, pillars of the colonial government, and therefore sharing in the darker side of their rule. But many priests today are seen as being too close to the restless masses, critics of military abuses and, by implication, of the neo-colonial government.

A statue of Father Mauricio Ferraro stands outside the cathedral. He looks overly pious – rather as if he had just descended from heaven – but I suspect that, successful building foreman that he was, he looked a lot more earthy and, though he built this prison *Ad Majorem Dei Gloriam*, he would probably be amused at the way in which his wish was currently being fulfilled.

TWENTY-EIGHT

Trouble Brewing

Tuesday, 8 May

Restrictions began today. This is in preparation for the national elections on the 14th. There is a huge boycott lobby; they probably don't want the prisoners 'infected'. (Five hundred votes are not to be sniffed at.) Visitors are no longer allowed into the cells.

We made a petition to the Negros government to improve conditions, particularly the food. It was signed by every cell and then we gave it to the *Daily Star* newspaper. . .

Siting has the 'flu. I feel exhausted, as the heat is really strong. And today there was a lot of tension. Itik had 'words' with Conrado. I joked Itik about it later and it seems it was due to the fact that his blood-pressure was up. I said: 'I like it, Itik, when you get a bit mad; it's the Irish coming out in you. It's terrible if I'm the only one getting angry.'

Today I almost had a fight. I heard shots and went out to see what had happened. I was at the visitors' gate, looking out towards the outer yard, when I was grabbed roughly by a guard named Tagalog. I resented being manhandled and told him so – 'Take your hands off me!' We had 'words' and he ended up by shouting '*Iho de puta!*' (Son of a bitch!). I was a bit shaken at my own anger and thought up lots of justifying things for myself, but afterwards I felt I should apologise and at least remove any hate or anger from both of us. After all, he was only doing his duty. Gradually we are having more and more fights with the guards.

In a way it was a break not to have visitors in our cell. Little children keep coming in from the outer yard for bread; one child's mother has just died. We are all against hand-outs, since it destroys people's dignity, but it is impossible to refuse children. . . and there is such a thing as crisis intervention.

Wednesday, 9 May

Colonel Billones came to see me. It seems someone had made a report to him about my little fracas with the guard Tagalog – possibly an enemy of Tagalog. I told the colonel that Tagalog was not at fault today. During prayer I examined the case in my mind and felt that was the correct judgement. Tagalog was doing his best to keep people away from the firing. The fact that he grabbed me was not intended in a malicious way. Later I met him and he said something like, 'We're both forgiving each other?' I was happy at the outcome.

RTE 'Day by Day' phoned and asked if I had heard the news. 'What news?' I asked. They said, 'The news that if you are condemned you will be deported.' This was supposed to come from Minister of Justice Ricardo Puno. However, I heard a tape later of Minister Puno's statement. He did not say we would be deported, but that the death penalty would be commuted *if* the Minister of Justice saw fit; he did not say commuted to deportation. Deportation would come if there was a pardon, but we will not accept a pardon. (Anyway, Reyes, the Commissioner for Deportation, told Bishop Fortich that if Brian was deported it would only be after he had served his jail sentence.) So we are heading for life-long jail sentences. I think the Irish practice of deporting foreign criminals has influenced the opinion in Ireland on this. In actual fact, the last person to be executed here in the Philippines was a foreigner; he was executed by musketry for allegedly being involved in drugs.

Itik celebrated Mass, and during the Mass he asked pardon of Conrado. He had explained earlier he gets high blood-pressure, which makes him fly off the handle.

I telephoned my parents to put them at ease. I worry about them and their long wait, but they are in good health and able to take these things.

Thursday, 10 May
Now that it looks as if we are going to be here for a long time, Nick has put me full-time in charge of vocations. (I was about to hand over the job to Donie Hogan.)

Call from Bishop Desmond Tutu of South Africa: very supportive. Minister Peter Barry telephoned and chatted with me. He asked me what he could do and I said that as soon as the election was over he could put the heat on, especially from 22 May which is supposed to be the date on which the trial will resume. He said he would.

When Charlie Bird interviewed me about Reagan, I said that as a guest he should be treated with courtesy, but also with honesty, and it would be dishonest not to tell him how we feel about the Philippines – and, for that matter, El Salvador and Nicaragua.

Saturday, 12 May

Father Michael Martin is well advanced now in producing a book of the documents of the case, and it will be out soon. A *Sunday Times* of Australia reporter phoned Brian and asked for his comments, because they heard on the radio in Perth that we will be released next week! Brian, in straight Australian fashion, told her that we were fed up with hearing this sort of thing.

Sunday, 13 May

The cells will not be opened for Mass today. (Tension building up before the election tomorrow.) Itik spoke to the warden and told him we were guaranteed religious freedom by the Constitution, and the warden said that it was orders 'from above'.

A sister came to the gate. She passed in the news that the two foreign priests would be found innocent and the seven would be executed. I asked her where she had got this, and she said from X, and I asked where *she* got it and she said, 'From the Columbans.' I said that this information was surely false and I asked her to check it out again with X and come back and give me the result of her inquiry; I pointed out that otherwise it would be disturbing for our group. Since she never verified it, I didn't pass it on to the group.

Just now the guard Prescante came and said he would have to lock us in. Brian told him that since there was no electricity we could suffocate with no fans – and Brian, of course, has asthma – so Prescante agreed and went back to tell the warden. The electricity has just gone on, so the warden must have received the message. We have just been locked in by a trustee, with Prescante watching. I wonder is this a preparation for elections, or a preparation for deportation?

However, the night was only beginning, and the next few hours would be the most frightening of the whole two years.

TWENTY-NINE

The Night of the Riot

Monday, 14 May

What a night! I really felt fear, and I am still trembling a lot as I write. It all started because of Itik's birthday. We sang 'Happy Birthday' and since our gate had been left open I put my head out and encouraged the other cells to join in the singing. Then a couple of cells (8 and 9) rattled their gates.

The guards were annoyed, and two of them came and demanded to take Nene Martinez, head of Cell 9, and Moldez, head of Cell 8, away. Nene and Moldez would not come out of their cells because they knew they would be beaten up. Finally, Cell 8 (right next to us) opened and Moldez was delivered to the guards. The guards kept insisting on taking Nene as well. The guards were armed, but the cell or Nene himself would not capitulate and the guards were afraid to go in. At least two of them held a carbine. Through the window slit I took flash photos of the guards, not sure whether they would come out, but sure that the guards would know that there was a record of who they were. In fact one of these very guards had been involved in beating a prisoner to death on that very spot three years before and all the prisoners knew it. Anyway, the guards shouted at us: 'This has nothing to do with you.' We answered that it had, and that we knew of the previous killing of the prisoner.

The next thing that happened was that one of the guards loaded his gun with a loud crack, threateningly, as if getting ready to fire. That was the panic signal for all the cells to smash their lights, and we heard the crash of bulbs bursting. The prisoners started to shout and rattle their gates. In prison terms this is an act of defiance; at least the guards regard it as such. It is a frightening sound and can be heard far away.

Then one of the guards fired his gun. Everyone scrambled for cover and an eerie silence fell over the prison.

We decided to leave our light on, as it was the only light illuminating the quadrangle because for some reason the flood-light was off. We were afraid that the guards would shoot into the cells under cover of darkness. If our light was on they could be seen.

Lydio says he heard a guard saying that Colonel Billones was waiting for the prisoners they were taking out. What are they up to? We intend to have a few words with Billones tomorrow. All day there has been tension because everyone has been locked in most of the day. The prison authorities have created this trouble. . .

Now as I was actually writing the above in the silence which followed the taking away of Moldez, and Brian and the others were reviewing what had happened, we all suddenly became aware of a great number of flash-lights in the quadrangle. Brian caught the gleam of many riot shields and helmets and we suddenly saw that crowds of soldiers with machine guns had moved silently into the quadrangle and a huge search-light had been wheeled in. We could also see firemen with hoses. The soldiers had tear-gas, and white handkerchiefs tied around their foreheads – a sign that shooting could be imminent and anyone with a white band was not to be shot. Without a sound they took up positions. . .

(Meanwhile, outside, unbeknownst to us, several hundred troops blocked the streets nearby. Father Martin Ryan, a Redemptorist priest from Tipperary, was passing by and saw them and realised something serious was going on inside. He desperately tried to get in at the prison gates, but was barred.)

A Philippines Constabulary man, Campolargo by name, approached Cell 9 and shouted out to his fellow-soldiers: 'Herbelario is in here. He's the one who knifed the soldier in Himamaylan.' Campolargo kept repeating this, as if to work his peers up, and he also demanded that Nene be handed over. (This was not the Nene who was the head of the cell, but another person by the name of Nene Herbelario whom he was now planning to take revenge on.) This was a radical change from the earlier request which was to hand over Nene Martinez because he was head of the cell and responsible for the rattling of the gate.

After a while Brian noticed the Bacolod Chief of Police, Colonel Diolingo. Brian called out to him, and he came up to our gate. We pleaded with him not to go near the prisoners until the morning. We told him of the legitimate fears of the prisoners because of the killing of Bebot Reyes, a prisoner, by the guards; the prisoners were afraid that something like that would happen again, and that was why they had smashed their lights and barred their doors. In fact they had electrified their gates by the simple expedient of attaching the electric light wires directly to the iron rungs of the gates; the soldiers knew this, and so it would have been a bloody assault because the soldiers would have used their guns as they were, naturally, afraid to approach personally.

First of all, Colonel Diolingo had our gate opened. We priests were allowed out to 'quieten' the cells. We got a promise from the colonel that he would not open the cells tonight, and we went around all the gates, calming the fellows down and telling them to relax and take down the barricades: no gate would be touched. They should put on the lights that weren't smashed, and it would all be discussed in the morning.

However, Nene Martinez, *bosio* of Cell 9, said he would not take down the barricades until Moldez was returned. I was taken aback because I had completely forgotten about Moldez in the tension, but I was deeply moved that *he* had not forgotten Moldez.

We approached the colonel and asked him. He ordered the warden who was standing in the shadows to return Moldez. Moldez was fetched, and the warden carefully asked him in front of everyone if he had been touched. Moldez said No.

The colonel now withdrew his troops with a final warning that if there was any more trouble he would use tear-gas, and there would be an investigation in the morning. (There never was. Not that it mattered: how could you have the security forces investigate the security forces? Nothing has ever come of that.)

Eventually, when all had left, we took Moldez into our cell rather than have Cell 8 opened, because of the fear that would cause.

We tried to analyse the causes of the whole thing.

1. Build-up of tension the whole day: no visitors, no sunning, no Mass.

2. Singing of 'Happy Birthday', the angry guards, the rattling of the gates.

3. But it seems from a letter that was slipped in to us that the real reason is that thirty-five thousand people are marching from the north and the south to protest against the election tomorrow and to proclaim a boycott. There are some who feel that the prison authorities are afraid that these people are going to come to the jail and 'rescue' us.

Our problem now is how to get the news out. We are totally incommunicado. We have made sure to lock our cell from the inside as well tonight.

Tuesday, 15 May: Election Day
Great tension. Itik is sick. His blood-pressure is up so high that he looks bad even though we are able to give him Aldomet which is for high blood-pressure. (We have some in the store of medicines I have for the prisoners.) We have tried again and again to get attention, but can't. Conrado is an official poll-watcher for the election. (The bishop is chairman of the poll-watchers and has had Conrado and Itik appointed to watch the poll in the prison.)

We got a note to the warden demanding that Conrado be allowed to fulfill his neutral poll-watch rôle, or otherwise the election in the jail would be invalid. This worried the warden, so he let Conrado out and over to his office to watch the poll. Itik was too sick even to stand.

We told Conrado to do his best to get a message out while he was poll-watching. Meanwhile I sent several letters to the warden.

Finally a nurse, Mrs Lasco, came. She is the nurse who is supposed to be appointed to the prison, but we have never seen her before. She took Itik's blood-pressure and said it was normal. I could see plainly that it wasn't. I asked her assistant to take it, and she came up with 150 over 90. I still felt by the purple look on Itik's face that it was more serious. (Little did we know at the time that Itik had the added complication of diabetes.) We sent yet another letter to the warden:

Cell 7, Bacolod Provincial Jail
15th May 1984

Dear Warden,
This is our fourth request to take Father Vicente Dangan to hospital. He has high blood-pressure, and it was increased last night by the arrival of riot squads, etc. In our presence the nurse took his blood-pressure, which is 150 over 90 in spite of the fact that he is taking Aldomet and other remedies. Father Dangan is supposed to be a poll-watcher and would much prefer to stay here, but just now his head is paining and he needs immediate medical attention.

Yours respectfully,

Father Niall O'Brien

Copies furnished to Bishop Fortich and Colonel Diolingo.

We asked Conrado when he was doing his poll-watching at the warden's office to try and get a note through the outside gate to the bishop. . .

No sign of anything yet, but Sister Gwendoline's basket of vegetables came in, and in the empty basket we hid a note for Bishop Fortich, asking him to come at once as Itik is sick and we cannot see a doctor. . .

I feel very angry. We sit here feeling so impotent. Itik is really sick, and looks very bad. We (I) am being too angry. What is the spiritual meaning of this powerlessness? To have runts of guards and prison-on-lookers coming to your cell as if you were a non-person. No privacy. No power to say that this is my home. My room. Please wait outside until I invite you in. But this is the condition of the other prisoners: the majority are totally powerless. Everyone in the town has more power than they.

All this must be a real grace to experience, because it is hurting my pride! I feel so humiliated. We know the warden has received instructions 'from above'.

We were not permitted Mass yesterday for the prisoners. That seems impossible in a Catholic country; no wonder we feel powerless. And, of course, as priests we are used to receiving respect and help from all quarters, even from non-believers, and that makes it even harder.

I thank you, Lord, for allowing me to feel a very little of what most people in the world feel – powerlessness, before authority and disease. Now I begin to understand those words, 'Christ emptied himself, taking on the condition of a slave'!

I had nearly finished my Lauds when two doctors arrived from the provincial hospital, Doctor Augustus Tan and Doctor Henrichi Parr. They were pleasant, but one felt that, like the nurse, they were specially chosen. They took Itik's blood-pressure, which is now 150 over 100, and therefore still going up, in spite of the medicines. He looks very bad and cannot move; it's not like Itik to lie down. (We were obviously right about Nurse Lasco, who was very definitely an administration nurse. Doctors and nurses should be from *outside*.) Anyway, they said they would recommend hospital, but until now there is no sign of this taking place. The warden has clearly been warned not to allow Itik out. . .

We have been waiting and waiting, but there has been no move to the hospital all day. All the time the radio has been giving reports on the election in an excited voice.

Cell 8 has a window through which they can catch a glimpse of the road. All day long they have been watching for signs of the boycott marchers and they pass their news to us through a hole in the wall. It has just been announced on the radio that the marchers stretch more than a mile from the *plaza* to the Sugarland Hotel. No wonder the authorities are worried!

THIRTY

The Langoni Massacre

We waited all day for news from the doctors, but nothing came of their promise to arrange that Itik be moved to hospital. Then at night Bishop Fortich finally arrived with Toto Suplido, his secretary. He had eventually received one of our many notes. The bishop was alarmed at Itik's appearance. He asked to see the warden and told him that he himself would take Itik to hospital immediately. The warden said that the doctors had gone off saying they would return, but had not done so.

The bishop kept on insisting, and eventually the warden rang someone (who had, apparently, given the order). After a while he came back and said that Itik could go to the hospital, but that he would have to have three guards and stay in the provincial hospital.

The bishop returned to our cell to collect Itik and we told him the whole story of what had happened the previous night, with a riot among the guards being stopped by the prisoners! Toto had tried to get in twice during the day and failed.

Tuesday, 15 May: Evening

We felt so much anger today that I thought we should have a Mass. At the Mass we discussed our fear. Geronimo said there was a difference between *kulba* and *hadluk*. *Kulba*, he said means the natural physical trembling which you have before something which frightens you, but *hadluk* is the fear which paralyses you and stops you from doing anything, a fear which is in your spirit rather than physical fear. What Geronimo was saying was that the natural action of being afraid – the actual feeling of fear – was acceptable and even a thing you ought to have. But if the fear reaches the stage where it paralyses you and stops you doing something, that we call *hadluk*. *Hadluk* would be a minus. *Kulba*, he said, was a plus. He seems to be saying we had *kulba*. (Was he saying this to console me? Had I exhibited more *kulba* than the others?) Geronimo also said that the other prisoners were prepared to die for each other. They were ready to oppose the riot squad rather than let either of the Nenes be taken out.

Late in the evening our cell was opened, so when I got the chance I went to each cell and asked Nene, Dodo and Sonny for details of the killing of Bebot Reyes, the prisoner who was killed outside Cell 9 by the guards. We got quite a lot of details and we told them that we would put these together and tell the guard Campolargo and the guard Tayum that if they touch the other prisoners our lawyers would reveal these documents.

I am not happy with my own angry feelings and am glad I did not speak to Colonel Billones. I felt so insulted by the fact that they wouldn't let Itik into hospital.

News has just come that Itik is in the Riverside Hospital, Room 449, with three guards! He is quite serious. It turns out he had developed diabetes, which has complicated things.

Wednesday, 16 May: Morning

Father Pat Sugrue arrived with the horrific story of killings in Inayawan yesterday. Eleven young Langoni men were tied to a pole

164

and walked through Inayawan, where everyone saw them. The eleven had been picked up by the military as they alighted from a Ceres bus in the village of Tambo, about two and a half miles south of Inayawan. Later, shots were heard. Nine bodies were seen laid out at the side of the Inayawan outpost. They were identified as nine of the eleven who were paraded through Inayawan. It was no ambush, but in this morning's paper it came out as an ambush: the colonel announced this – with all the fine details of the non-existent ambush. Father Brendan O'Connell sent up the real story.

Afternoon
More news on the Tambo massacre. When the parents and widows arrived at Langoni with the bodies they were met by the children and relatives. It seems that the whole population was there and the wailing reached out into the foothills of Inayawan. The strangest thing is that the ambush is recorded in the newspapers as having come from the sea, and now Brendan has discovered that on the morning before the massacre the local army captain was trying to hire a boat precisely at the spot where the newspapers later reported a boat ambush from the sea. It looks very much as though someone wrote the script of the ambush news release *before* the massacre. They were foiled because Brendan got the story out to the world press so fast. Luckily Tony Brazil was here and he brought it straight to Ireland, and there have been protests from Ireland already. At least one of the original eleven escaped and we have got some of the details from him: it turns out that the boys had just voted and were on their way to a basket-ball match.

My thoughts go back again and again to trying to help our guards to become more human. . .

Today I saw Nene Martinez sitting down, despondent. After a while I went over to him and asked, 'What are you thinking about? The words of Teresita Tayum?' (She was said to have said that Nene and his friends would 'get it' once the priests had left.)

'No.'

'What, then?'

'I'm thinking about the guards.' And from the way he said it, I knew he was thinking of the near miss last night. He was anxious and angry.

I said: 'Like you, Nene, I am angry. I feel deep anger at what happened last night. I feel angry at the guards. I was deeply touched last night when you refused to take the barricade down until Moldez was returned. I didn't think of that, but you did, and you were putting your life on the line for him. You know, Nene, that's what being a follower of Christ is all about. That's what we were trying to teach in our small Christian communities and I suppose that's why we're here. We taught that we are all brothers. But so too are the guards our brothers, even if they don't know it. That's the Good News and we must bring it to them. It doesn't really matter how long we are in here, as long as we never forget that. If we ever forget that, then they have won and my twenty years in the Philippines would have been for nothing.'

Nene gave a strange smile, and I knew by that smile that he understood me.

Gates are being rattled as I write, and they are coming around to count us. As usual I am the only one still up in our cell at this hour.

The shared fear of the last days has brought about a new solidarity in the prison. We feel as close as brothers to our fellow-prisoners, and they feel that way towards us. For the first time I have begun to talk to them about our Christian communities.

THIRTY-ONE

Strange Verdict

Friday, 18 May

The warden gave me permission to phone, so I called Itik and advised him not to hurry out of hospital: high blood-pressure and diabetes is a dangerous combination.

My mother is getting deeper into the Reagan campaign. Reagan holds the real power here, what with the huge US trade, the enormous bases, and a twenty-five billion dollar IMF/World Bank debt. However, in case my mother felt under pressure, I decided to phone Janine (my sister-in-law) and suggest a demonstration by my nieces and nephews to take the pressure off my mother should she wish to decline. She is working well with the Negros Nine Committee, while my father keeps links with Foreign Affairs.

While I was asking permission to phone, the warden was complaining about the price of quality padlocks for our gates. I smiled, thinking how one's life could be filled with the knowledge of padlocks, handcuffs and footcuffs.

166

Saturday, 19 May

Many visitors, including Marian Cadogan from Trócaire. (She was here in November 1982 on the very day when the news first broke.) She brought gifts and letters from home. Trócaire is going to take a strong stand on the Reagan visit.

Baby Gordoncillo sent over the galley proofs of the book of court documents, which will be called *The Negros Nine*. We are to help correct or improve it. . .

It is very touching when parents come to visit their children. They are so poor, and they have to come such a long way. They bring the most pathetic little gifts; a few vegetables is often all they have. I always try to console the parents. Sheer poverty may prevent them from visiting their boys more than once a year.

However, I am not a patch on Brian or Itik for talking with the prisoners. They talk for hours, getting the background. I want to escape off and be reading or writing or something.

Sunday, 20 May

Mr Ricardo Puno, Minister for Justice, lost his seat in the election. That will give them a chance to drop the case if they want to. The government seems to have done badly, even though *they* tally the votes, and in spite of the large boycott. The First Lady's candidates in Metro-Manila nearly all lost. But in spite of losing the election Minister Puno will not resign for some time yet.

Reagan is due in Ireland in a couple of weeks. My mother is demonstrating in a cage as a symbol of our cell, I'm told. If the Reagan protest comes to nothing, I will be thinking over the possibilities of bringing my parents out for their fiftieth wedding anniversary. It would be hard on them, but it might help the case. We will have to discuss this more. It is a dicey business – people as old as that coming out.

I have thought about what would happen if this went to the bitter end. I hope I would be able to say: Well, I have had a great life, and I would rather finish well than mess things up. And if, in spite of every possible struggle, it came to the worst, then one could accept it as God's will and use it to try and bring about a lessening of violence in the world, a growth of love and care, and a lessening of the amount of tears shed. Isn't this what life is all about? Being part of the solution rather than part of the problem? I would certainly be less sure of myself when the time came, but then God would come to my rescue, *dabitur enim vobis in illa hora quidquid loquamini* (Matthew 10:19). I am afraid that things are going to go to the bitter end.

Monday, 21 May

Last night the little eight-year-old daughter of Diutay, the tattooer, was here again. She was locked in Cell 4 with him. She cuddled up beside her father (he is some sight, with all those tattoos), and then she jumped up to play with the other prisoners, most of whom are in for murder. She is so happy to be with her father. I slip some sweets to Diutay for her; I would not like to give them myself, because it would diminish his rôle – it must be a great sorrow to a father not to be able to give little gifts to his children. (To me the most heartbreaking moment in *The Grapes of Wrath* is when Joad can't afford to buy even the sweets for his little sister.) In spite of everything, the obvious joy of the little girl and her closeness to her father are a pleasure to see, and it confounds the wise. . .

We were in the visitors' room when news came that the judge had denied our motion for dismissal. We had half expected this, but here is the shock: he has released Itik! Sounds ludicrous, because Itik was the one whom the witnesses claimed was not only carrying a machine gun but was the leader of the strike force.

A copy of the judge's decision was brought to us, and here are the vital words:

WHEREFORE IN VIEW OF of all the foregoing the instant motion to dismiss is hereby denied except with respect to Rev. Father Vicente Dangan in whose favour alone the motion is hereby granted and the case against said accused hereby ordered dismissed. The Provincial Warden of Negros Occidental is hereby directed to release the accused Rev. Father Vicente Dangan immediately upon receipt of this order unless otherwise being held for some other legal cause. Let the continuation of the trial with respect to all other accused be set at 8.30 o'clock in the morning of May 29th 1984 in Bacolod City, Philippines.

May 21st 1984   EMILIO LEGASPI, Judge

So we have a week to start preparing our witnesses. I will probably be the first on the stand. Here we go again!

Itik was deeply depressed at the news that he would be separated from us. He came straight from the hospital and as soon as he got to the gate he was cornered and got to sign a document releasing him from the prison. We had no time to plan any symbolic protest – such as him refusing to come out – because by the time he got to the cell he was officially no longer a prisoner. We persuaded him to go back to the hospital to finish his treatment. He has gone on television and spoken very strongly, announcing that he will not return to his parish until we are all out. He will work for our release. Meanwhile the bishop has made him official chaplain to the prison. We feel that the dropping of the case against him may be because they want to separate the foreigners; it's easier now to make the thing appear as foreign interference.

Wednesday, 23 May
I was asleep, taking a *siesta*, when I suddenly woke up with a brain-wave. Why not put Itik on the witness stand first? Ask him if Pancho and Boholano, the star witnesses, had accused him of being at the ambush with a machine gun. Answer: Yes, it is in the court records.

Were you there? Answer: No.

Have you any legal proof of this? Answer: Yes: the recent decision of Judge Legaspi which finds me innocent.

Why did he find you innocent? Answer: Because he has accepted that Pancho and Boholano were lying.

Having discussed this with the others, I called the lawyers immediately. We had several meetings and they decided to put Itik on the stand first. . .

Television people are arriving. Rob O'Regan and Dermot Kinlen, representatives of the Australian Bar and International Jurists, are on the way. Irish and Australian diplomats are arriving, and visitors from the Philippines and abroad, not to mention some of the one hundred and twenty-nine witnesses coming in with lawyers to go over the events.

THIRTY-TWO

Pardon Implies Guilt

Friday, 25 May
It seems there has been a serious misunderstanding regarding the Exodus march. Sister Marie came to visit me and socked it to me strongly. She had heard that we had contacted the bishop and asked that the boycott not be 'pushed' at the final rally. Others felt that the Long March protest against our imprisonment should also include the Boycott Protest against the then forthcoming elections. However, we felt that, since the final negotiations with Borromeo had been scheduled for that time, we should give him no opportunity to use anything like that against us. Unfortunately, some people read this as meaning that we were against the boycott, which is, of course, not so. Itik and the lay leaders, who have a vote, were

169

boycotting and pushing the boycott. Brian and I have remained silent on the matter.

Saturday, 26 May

Sister Marie phoned. She was worried that the frank discussion yesterday had disturbed me. She felt that in an attempt to bring the two sides together she may have put the other point of view rather strongly. She did. But I had been thinking how heroic it was of her to try and bring the two sides together and how thankless the job of the peace-maker is. If he or she wants to do the job properly they must give each of the opposing parties the other's point of view, in full and as strongly as possible. Usually it is the peace-maker who ends up by drawing the ire of both parties. I was happy to be able to tell Sister how grateful I was for what she had done. In fact Father Dodo came in yesterday and right away I took the opportunity to apologise to him, and he accepted this.

Peace-making is a thankless job – real peace-making, that is. There are those who love to be the *mediator*, which is different, because they want both parties to be in debt to them and they are not beyond speaking nice words to both parties so that their own image will not be damaged.

Of course, there is always the fellow who loves playing the devil's advocate and that can be very tiresome and exhausting, especially when it is done repeatedly, automatically and with what often turns out to be a patronising and spurious fair-mindedness – a form of pompousness which helps no one because it gets everybody's hackles up. This fellow is no peace-maker.

But far more common is my own ailment: the tendency to see in two people's conflict a subtle rising of my own stock in both their eyes. . .

A new inmate to the women's cell arrived yesterday. She has just finished twelve years in a mental asylum in Manila. She was originally detained for killing her husband's lover. I was introduced to her by some of the women prisoners. Her face shows signs of great suffering and it seems that only now is the cloud of depression lifting from her; I dare not ask any questions – too much anguish lies behind those suffering eyes. She addressed me in Tagalog, which she presumably learned in the asylum, a nightmare of a place where naked inmates hang in cages. When she was told that I was a priest, she insisted on singing the religious songs she had learned in the asylum. She sang them with feeling, maybe too much feeling, till there were tears in her eyes; I stood listening reverently and visibly approving. As I looked at her, a once-beautiful person, now overdressed in ill-fitting clothes and out-of-place make-up, I thought of that awful place and the long years and the cages. My mind wondered where her husband and children were now, and I dared not dwell further on it. I took my leave firmly. I saw her again this morning and steered myself away. I pray the cloud will lift from her.

As I write, the clanging of gates and clicking of locks is coming from outside, together with the shrill barking of dogs, as the trustees do their rounds, counting us. They have stopped locking our cell.

Tonight we examined the documents of the court case. We find that the Chief of Police, Major Yulo, says in his report that Father Dangan was the co-leader of the strike force. Star witness Pancho mentioned him three times in his affidavit and says he carried an M16, and major witness Boholano Junior identified him in court as being in the jeep on the night of the ambush. Why then was he freed?

Sunday, 27 May
After Mass, Mrs Campolargo came to our cell to announce a rise from three pesos a day to four-fifty in our food allowance. The five fish have been doubled in size, and this makes quite a difference to the prisoners. Our protests seem to have worked.

It was so hot today that everyone was complaining. I lay on my wooden bed, with my limbs aching from the heat. I kept a little towel by me and just dried the perspiration continually. Twice I doused myself with water, but in the midst of all the heat I kept telling myself it is better than the cold. I was also aware that although I was uncomfortable I was not unhappy. A simple distinction of which I constantly remind myself. . .

Henry caught Alo stealing: he must have taken one of the artifacts from our cell and given it to someone to sell for him, I feel saddened: Alo has a great sense of clowning and humour, and I hate to see him fall into this. It seems to be the second time he has done it; he took my money before. I suggested that Brian speak to Alo like a father and help him to see how self-destructive stealing is and how ungrateful – but not to correct him with others listening. Alo's parents are dead and he grew up with his grandmother, and he may have missed a strong guiding hand correcting him on elementary things like this. Parents should never be depressed when a child steals. They should thank God that it happens early and with the chance of correction, explanation and supervision. The only real mistake is the one we don't learn from.

Monday, 28 May
'You have burdened me with bitter troubles, but you will give me

171

back my life.' So goes Psalm 71 in today's breviary. I never read the psalms without finding some very appropriate line. These prayers have been prayed for three thousand years. Is there any other prayer book in the history of mankind which has carried so much the fears and expectations of the human race?

Martin Ryan from Kilkenny was here on a flying visit. He told us about the growing tide of massacres and 'salvaging' (assassination by the military) and torturing taking place in his area on the island of Mindanao in the south. Next week his parish and several others will keep a vigil day and night outside the Philippine Constabulary command in their area to protest at the disappearance of five parishioners. We decided to send a message to those keeping vigil, expressing solidarity with their struggle, and encouragement, and emphasising the power of non-violent mass action. We did this by sending them a tape-recorded message, and at the end of the recording we sang a prison song in Tagalog entitled 'High is the wall'.

I do not believe that we have even begun to plumb the depths of the possibilities of non-violence. One of its strengths lies in mass action, with many people doing some symbolic act. This has the effect of isolating the wrong-doers and helping them to realise that their action is not acceptable. The fact that the act itself is merely symbolic and often even very small allows the faint-hearted to take part. The famous noise-barrage in Manila during the last election but one was so successful that the government had to declare noise illegal and so came out in their true colours.

The article on non-violence which I wrote off the cuff for Michael Diamond in Mindanao is being printed tomorrow in the *Daily Star*. I went over it, worried that there might be some gaffe in it. I changed the title by one word from 'Non-violence the way to peace and justice' to 'Non-violence a way to peace and justice'. I noticed that my article treats of non-violence not as a Christian imperative but as a human imperative independently of the specifically new dimension which Christ brings. Non-violence is a sensible and truly human solution; Christ adds the dimension of the brotherhood and sisterhood of the human race. The eventual purpose of struggle is not only justice; it is reconciliation, which is a much more difficult achievement.

Tuesday, 29 May
Court case resumed. Itik, number one on the stand, points out that judge's dismissal of case against him shows Boholano and Pancho are lying. Foreign Minister Barry phoned and asked about speeding up the case. My article on non-violence has not appeared and will

not appear. The editor feels it would be unacceptable to the authorities: very interesting.

Wednesday, 30 May
I was on the stand today in court. Beforehand I was like a boy waiting to go into an oral examination. I was filled with mixed emotions, the desire to scupper my opponents and turn the tables on them personally, and the reluctant realisation that they are my brothers and in some way I must leave a door open for their moral and human rehabilitation; and then again I would remember that they are out to get me – one little mistake and they will try and stamp me into the ground. It was a long four-and-a-half-hour session with a break of half an hour in the middle. When I got home to the prison I lay down exhausted and thanked God. I remembered my joy years ago on singing the 'Te Deum' – the sense of almost touching God's goodness. I felt now that his promise had been fulfilled to the letter – his goodness and kindness have followed me, all the days of my life.

My mother wrote another great letter. She mentioned that some relation of mine is worried that all the adulation will go to my head. I am so grateful to have people care about me enough to worry about me. Just now I am at a loss to know what to do. We should discuss this problem of adulation among ourselves, but the real point at issue should be how we can use all this for bringing about the Kingdom.

Don Mullan phoned and gave me the latest developments in Ireland, Reagan's talk via satellite and promise to help in our case. MacBride's sending of the Amnesty report on El Salvador to the Taoiseach Garret FitzGerald for presentation to Reagan. Shultz's visit to El Salvador and Jeane Kirkpatrick's visit to Manila, where she may take up our case; my mother's imminent phone-call to the White House and Reagan's statement that Ireland is the US's gateway to Europe (that sounds ominous).

Thursday, 31 May
Yours truly in chair again. I was very tired after the long morning session in court. Phoned my parents and told them we expect them for their fiftieth anniversary. Seems my mother is up to her eyes in demonstrations!

Friday, 1 June
Reagan to arrive in Ireland today, in Galway. Casey has other engagements. Many protests: Minister Barry to bring the case up.

173

Today was an exhausting day – my third on the witness stand – and though the lads were happy with me I still found it tense. Nick Murray, our superior, and Michael Martin testified. They were excellent and Michael used the occasion to make many statements on the meaning of being a disciple of Christ.

In the afternoon I phoned Sean Rainey to discover that Dick Keelan and others have gone on hunger strike in opposition to the Reagan visit. It is the US activities with regard to Nicaragua and El Salvador that they are trying to highlight. Dick's last letter to me showed great concern for the damage the US is doing, and the gist of his letter was: what will happen when these enormous government debts in the US come home to roost? I replied to Dick as follows:

Dear Dick,

Greetings from Bacolod. Firstly, let me say how deeply moved we all were when you went on hunger strike against the Reagan visit. You know, it is strange, but though I follow with great care the goings on in the world of finance and the monetarist debate of the last five years, a remark made by you in your last letter somehow gave me a new understanding. . . like another part of a jigsaw falling into place. Hence I understood and agreed with your hunger strike all the more. The huge budget deficit means that the US is borrowing so much that dollars are scarce and the price of money goes up. Hence interest rates go up. Hence the debts of the Third World go up. They cannot pay even the interest on their debts and they ask for re-scheduling and they are given the re-scheduling provided they do several things. . . all of which means a fall in the standard of living for the people.

One of the things that the Third World countries are frequently asked to do is to de-value their currency. Like recently when it happened in the Philippines and the savings which had been amassed in ten years by the members of the community farm which I set up in the mountains were cut in half (in real buying terms) overnight! Another condition which is frequently asked of them is to make changes in their laws which will favour the entry of foreign business. So the whole economy becomes more vulnerable. When you realise that the over-spending in the US in the first place is not on goods which 'roll' so to speak and make more money and more work as the money goes round, but on 'dead end' goods, namely arms, which are stock-piled and await obsolescence (and it is even worse if they are used). And then, as you say, 'What happens when the debt comes home to roost?' I feel we must reach the stage where we can de-code the news headings which announce a half percent rise in interest rates but which really translate into more hunger in South America, Africa and the Philippines and more repression to keep the hungry people in line.

Dick, while you were on hunger strike we said Mass for you here. All the lads send their warmest regards.

God bless,

Niall

As if to confirm what I had said to Dick, a few days later Mrs Campolargo came to our cell and said; 'I want to warn you that the food won't be good tomorrow. It's not my fault: prices have all risen and the new food allowance isn't enough.' Sure enough, next morning the fish had shrunk back to their original size. What we do in the First World affects directly the stomachs of the Third World. So I feel that Dick's hunger strike is an apt commentary on what the US is doing. Coming from Dick it is all the more telling, as he is not a strident man – a human human-being is how I'd describe him. Those of us who have decided against violence as a solution are all the more bound to use the alternatives.

In court the judge pricked up his ears when I mentioned non-violent alternatives and he gave me a chance to talk about them. I missed my chance to say that the greatest alternative to violence is a clean, uncorrupt legal system. But, when I was explaining my membership of the Fellowship of Reconciliation, I took the opportunity to show that without reconciliation there is no victory. I think it is right that each of us should use this court occasion to proclaim the Good News, and the Good News is this: we are all brothers and sisters, no matter what private or limited solidarity binds us; we must go beyond these limited solidarities of nationality, race or religion and struggle to establish the larger family that we really are; we must return to each other. And this is why justice is not the end but a milestone on the way of reconciliation. Impossible? If Christ is risen the impossible is possible. . .

My mother was on the phone to the White House yesterday or the day before, and yesterday she had an appointment with the ambassador at the US Embassy. Last week she spoke on an anti-Reagan platform and came out on the television here in the Philippines in some sort of an anti-Reagan march. For her it is really a 'return to life', as it were, and I am deeply grateful that all my prayers have been answered far beyond my dreams. Indeed, if I examine my life, it is filled with prayers answered – like a tide coming in so slowly while you are reading on the beach that suddenly you look up and find it is brimming – brimming with the goodness of God. . .

Late call from Father Michael Martin: he says he has information that the case might be withdrawn tonight. He doesn't want us to be taken by surprise. The Reagan protests must be taking effect. I can't stop myself from singing. The atmosphere in the cell is electric.

Saturday, 2 June
Two calls in morning from US news agencies in New York. Apparently the various government representations, the demonstrations of the Negros Nine Committee and AFrI, the strong stand of Bishop Casey and the mysterious 'other engagements' of the entire Irish hierarchy have got the message across to the two thousand US reporters accompanying the president.

Bishop Fortich came to us at three-thirty p.m. and told us that Cardinal Sin has been speaking to Marcos about the case. Australia seems to think it is all over – phone buzzing all the time.

For the next three days keeping track of the release rumours was a nightmare. Everyone wanted to be first with the news. I kept saying to Ireland, 'We'll believe it when we see it,' and to AFrI and the Negros Nine Committee, 'Keep up the pressure.' I received a phone-call from Don who told me that they had been keeping the pressure up all the time. My mother stepped into the mock prison at the Garden of Remembrance as Reagan stepped off the helicopter in Dublin.

Sunday, 3 June
Sean MacBride visited my mother in her mock prison, and she appeared on television last night and made a statement. She is still in her 'cell' now.

An air of expectation is spreading. Noreen Trota, the wife of the Irish consul and our close friend, arrived with Helen Galanzoga, the secretary.

Walking through the yard tonight when things had quietened down, I feel a sort of sadness at all the bodies stretched out on the floor or on boards inside the cell gates. Our leaving highlights their staying. Many of them are quite sickly and have almost no hope.

Today I had a reconciliation with Alo, who took some money of mine. He admitted that he had taken it. I forgave him and gave him money for a marketing project. He got to work immediately and seemed to be a new fellow. Sister Gwendoline, faithful as ever, went and bought all the necessities for him.

Wednesday, 6 June

Brian came back to the cell from the phone a bit breathless. He waited a moment for our attention, and then said: 'On Friday they are offering us pardon and parole.' Pardon for us two, and parole for the others. I looked at him incredulously: so that's what all this has been leading up to – the same old offer in slightly new clothes, just to get the US off their backs.

'There's no way we can accept that.'

'Precisely: that's what I said, but in stronger words.'

But so far it is only a rumour and it might be wrong. We hope it is. We are still willing victims of the false hope syndrome.

Thursday, 7 June

Noreen and Helen arrived back for Mass. They had originally come down to celebrate our release, and they couldn't conceal their sadness as they knew that the water was running out of the new bowl of hope.

At about ten p.m. Bishop Fortich strode across the yard with a huge retinue of superiors, lawyers, media people. He told us what had happened. (He was at a bishops' conference in Cotobato when he got news of developments.) He flew six hundred miles from Cotobato to Manila, managed a meeting with Puno (who still has not resigned). The meeting ended with Fortich asking for the meaning of pardon. Puno admitted that it implies guilt, and Fortich replied, 'Pardon which implies guilt is unacceptable.'

We discussed the whole thing, and by the time it was over we realised that the next day's offer would probably have to be refused. I tried to phone home to prepare my parents for the worst, but the prison phone is cut off. All here are asleep early, I would say exhausted by the tension of the day. All day the lay leaders were stretched out silent. I felt they were sick with the tension of uncertainty ever since the news began to turn sour – when Brian came in with the pardon/parole offer.

Friday, 8 June

What a day! At two a.m. I was wakened by the guard to say that there were visitors. What of Brigadier General De Guzman's new regulations? The visitors apparently insisted, and, though they were not going to be let in, I could meet them at the outside gate. I wrapped myself up and went out. There were Bob Wurth of ABC, Rob O'Regan, Brian McKay and Michael McCluskey. They had spent the whole night with the prosecutor and they felt the terms of the offer *were* negotiable. I was now disturbed, so I woke Brian and asked him to think it over.

At eight a.m. the same group came back, together with Nicholas Murray, our superior, and Dermot Kinlen. We re-discussed the whole thing: maybe there was lee-way for bargaining. While we were sitting on a bench in the quadrangle, discussing the situation, trying to keep reporters at bay and also trying to keep out of the sun, word arrived twice to say the case was off till the afternoon. There would then be time for us to share these ideas with our lawyers. . . But there wasn't, because suddenly, just as we were beginning to relax, news came that we must go straight to the court: the judge was waiting. We hurriedly changed into *barongs* and the military vehicle took us to the court.

We had hardly walked into court when the next witness was called. We were confused: what of the negotiations? In feverish whispers it passed through the dock that negotiations were over. They had already taken place a few minutes before in the judge's office. The prosecutor, the judge, the bishop and our lawyers were present at that meeting, and so was at least one reporter (Carla of the *Daily Star*). Pardon had been the stumbling block: it was unacceptable because it compromised our innocence, and the bishop and the lawyers had rejected it, in accordance with our discussion with them last night. Right there, with the court in session, reporters were asking for our reactions.

Of course there was chaos after the hearing, with reporters jostling for our statements and us not too sure at the time what had taken place at the closed-door conference. The prosecutor announced to the press that we had 'slammed the door'. What is more, for the first time a rift seemed to be opening up between us and our lawyers on the one hand, and the reporters and diplomats on the other.

In our cell tonight we were analysing what had happened, when Bruce Dover, Paul Lynam and Bob Wurth arrived. They were livid. They felt that we hadn't given the negotiations a chance. *We* felt that 'negotiations' was the wrong word because, in camera, the prosecutor had given the offer in the form of an ultimatum. *They* felt that at their long discussion with the prosecutor last night they had been assured that there *was* room for negotiation. *We* felt they had been led up the garden path by the prosecutor. At this stage we were nearly shouting at one another. The Filipino lay leaders watched goggle-eyed as the group of close friends poured each other drinks, lit each other's cigarettes and simultaneously bellowed at each other.

'Maybe you fellows want to become martyrs, but what about the lay people and their families? They have to live here.'

'You just want to have the case finished so that you can get out of here.'

'Of course I want to get the hell out of here. But, by God, I want even more to see you out of here.' Bob had tears in his eyes.

The voices calmed, and in the ensuing silence they stood up to go. We had disagreed, but the visit had not been a waste of time. We assured them we would fight to keep the door open.

Saturday, 9 June

Bishop Fortich arrived with lawyers. It seems that the president will be giving a foreign press conference on Tuesday. Our case is likely to come up and we are anxious that the alleged intransigence of our side should not be used by the president for castigating us and slamming the door in a way that even he, the president, would find hard to go back on. We have agreed on the following statement:

WHILE THE OFFER of pardon for the two priests was not accepted because of the legal connotations as explained by the Minister for Justice himself, nevertheless, it is not true that we are unco-operative with the government in helping dismiss the case. We merely stated the well-known basic minimum which we require, namely:– the innocence of the accused being not compromised – in fact we welcome any move by the government to have the case dismissed and give justice to the accused.

Issued by the accused after a prolonged conference with their counsel and Bishop Antonio Y. Fortich.

On the phone to Cardinal Ó Fiaich I was wondering how they felt in Ireland about us refusing the pardon. Would they feel we had looked a gift horse in the mouth and that we had been intransigent? I explained to the cardinal the danger of civil liabilities being brought against the seven in a case which could go on for years. Ó Fiaich was in complete agreement and said that the Irish people felt that way too.

Letter came yesterday for Lydio to say he will be accepted as a Columban missionary. He has passed the psychological test. He plans to start his studies here in the jail. I will take him for various subjects, liturgical Latin being one.

Dermot Kinlen has arranged a dinner with the minister and some others, at which the forthcoming negotiations will be plumbed. Dermot has done exhaustive research into Philippine jurisprudence: he has it from the best authorities that pardon always connotes guilt. This is vital in any future negotiations – because some people think it doesn't.

Morning. Paul Lynam and crew were here. They had come from the Kinlen dinner with Puno. Two things emerged: the door is still open; the present prosecutor is not the man to do negotiations.

So the door is open, but we have been burned so often before that we plan to continue full speed ahead with the case in court. The more witnesses we produce the better.

THIRTY-THREE

Cell Nine

I take my *siesta* in Cell 9. A *siesta* is a must in the Philippines. Who wants to brave the midday sun? No one. It would seem to present no problem because one gift that Filipinos have is this: they can sleep anywhere, any time; they lie down and go out like a light. Itik is an example. Once, three of us, Father Eamonn Gill, Itik and I, were lying on the floor in my *convento* about to go to sleep. Itik was between Ned and me, and the three of us were chatting away, wide awake. Itik said, 'Good night,' and before one minute was up he was snoring away. We were so amazed we began to laugh. Now the problem with this wonderful gift is that Filipinos are apt to think that everyone else has it too, so that when *siesta* time comes visitors are still eddying around our cell. No problem to the lay leaders. They just lie down and go fast asleep despite the noise. My solution is to emigrate to Cell 9, where no one thinks of looking for me; moreover, since it is locked, no one can get in. Hence I have foiled those well-meaning visitors for a time.

Cell 9 is twenty paces by eight and has twenty-five inmates, most of them in for murder. I suspect it is not part of the original Spanish building because the end wall to the right as you come in at the gate is made, badly, from new cement; water pours down this wall in streams whenever it rains. Though very little light penetrates into the cell through the slits, nevertheless plants have started to grow where the water comes in. There are some other odd plants in tins – they say the guards own these! It is in this very damp spot that Colas has set up his bedding. They say that Colas has gone out of his mind. He sits alone, with all his belongings beside him in a plastic bag, his head shaven, and dressed in outlandish rags – usually in a dress. He has a little tin bugle which he is liable to blow at odd times. I have often looked in at the gate of the cell when they are all asleep and seen Colas awake in his isolation, carefully picking through his ragged belongings.

In the cell there are only three beds, or wooden settles, and everyone else sleeps on the floor. There are a couple of canvas folding beds and I occupy one of these at *siesta* time. Some sacking on wire covers the hole that is used for a toilet at the end of the cell. As Brian Gore says, the prison authorities provide four walls, a roof, a floor, and nothing else.

Gradually I have got to know the other prisoners in Cell 9 quite well. A great harmony exists, with very little fighting. As soon as two prisoners have a row, one of them will be asked by the others to leave and go to another cell. The authorities will facilitate this, and though there have been many such incidents since we came none has been fatal because of this sensible system. However, feuds and rivalries exist between the cells, and Brian, who has done a lot more talking with prisoners and guards than I have, tells me the guards exploit this tendency to rivalry as a means of dividing and ruling.

Most of the cases are murder or homicide, but out of twenty-five in this cell only two have been sentenced. Most of the cases I find so sad that I lack, at times, the energy to want to know any more. I do not mean that they are all in on false charges (although this is frequently the case). Sometimes they have been put in by powerful people for one reason or another. Many are in because they took the law into their own hands: some member of their family was killed, and in the heat of the moment and because the law will not catch up with the perpetrators, they decided to kill the man or men that did it.

Such is the case of Norman. A group of men came into his house and killed his mother. On the spot, his father and uncle killed two of the men. Norman, quite unaware of this, came home from ploughing the field and was greeted by blood flowing from under the door of the house. He opened the door and found his pregnant mother dead, and the two dead men beside her. His father and uncle were imprisoned, and Norman with them. Nothing was done about the other attackers. Now Norman's seven younger brothers and sisters have no mother or father or elder brother. The crops are untended and there is no one to mind the carabao. His whole home has dissolved in blood around him. Sometimes he sits and looks out of the gate of the cell, his large brown eyes focused on the middle distance and filled with inexpressible sadness. I asked him what he was thinking about. 'I am thinking of my younger brothers and sisters: they are all scattered.' I dared not continue the conversation. Today I saw the same look on his face; I felt a great emptiness. For those who have less in life, and especially an eldest child like Norman, the loss of a mother brings unspeakable grief. I wish there were more people to carry these loads.

Around the wall, prisoners' clothes are drying, and just inside the gate there is a list on the wall of those in charge of cleaning and fetching water for the week. This list is made by the *bosio* and is followed faithfully.

THIRTY-FOUR

Why Us?

Saturday, 9 June

Father Tullio,* an Italian priest, came to visit us, and we reminisced together about gregorian chant and how we miss it. We sang the 'Veni Sancte Spiritus', tomorrow being the Feast of the Holy Spirit, and compared all the pieces of gregorian music which we know and miss so much. He used to sing in the çathedral in Mantua.

During all our time in jail we had been asking ourselves precisely why Brian, Itik and I were chosen for this frame-up.

It is very obvious that on the national level, President Marcos was hard-pressed by the criticism of the Church. He had managed to hijack the state and turn a seventy-year-old democracy into his personal fiefdom. The congress and senate have been abolished, the unions and students silenced, the small middle class bought off, and the army given a slice of the action. Only the Church was left. Careful politics kept it at bay, but there was no doubt that it was becoming more and more aware and restless as the economic situation of the poor worsened.

In the early days of martial law, the bishops referred to the new régime as the '*de facto* government'. Hiding behind the Latin tag was the uncomplimentary definition: 'the government we have whether we like it or not'. It was with that in mind that Cardinal Sin announced his policy of 'critical collaboration'. The word 'collaboration' was carefully chosen and evoked memories of war-time collaboration with the enemy, the Japanese. Then as time went on Cardinal Sin moved away from collaboration and more and more towards criticism.

What was the government to do? Well, many countries in Latin America have this trouble, and from these parts has emerged a policy

* Father Tullio has since been killed by the ICHTS, a local government militia.

182

for dealing with the Church called the Banzer Plan. The plan, named after Banzer, a former President of Bolivia, outlines the classic national security policy in the face of an unco-operative Church. One of the central planks of the plan is the discrediting of the Church in the eyes of the people. The first step is the discrediting of individual priests engaged in social action. The guardians of security in the present Philippine régime have obviously adopted the substance of the Banzer plan, and one of their many victories was Father Kangleon.

Father Kangleon, a young Filipino priest who may or may not have been entangled with the Communist Party, was taken into custody and a short while later appeared on nation-wide television with the most extraordinary revelations. I watched the interview, which was released in all the media. It was chilling: with glazed, unfocused eyes he calmly told us that he used the pulpit to spread communism. I had no doubt that the man had undergone the third degree. Though most people suspected this, we had no proof as yet. So the revelations left all the bishops acutely embarrassed, as Kangleon began to name names and a witch-hunt was on. It was a coup for Marcos and for the military men who had engineered it. The whole case lent credibility to all the other even less well-documented trumped-up charges against sisters, priests and lay people throughout the country.

Now they were going for the jackpot. And if they won it, it would cast international discredit on the Church. The hunt was on for victims, and word was passed down the line.

In the sugar province of Negros the Church had for many years been an outspoken critic of the régime and its various organs, particularly the military with its liquidation squads. It therefore suited certain people to have the Church put paid to in Negros once and for all.

The military now started to search for suitable candidates. Mixing with local landlords, they soon learned that nearly all the priests were eligible in the minds of some. How they decided on the three of us is really a matter for speculation. The truth is that they would have been glad to get anyone.

In Brian's case there had been a petition against him. A few years earlier, our sacristan, Jimmy Tiaga, witnessed the rape and murder of his mother by four cowboys – employees of a well-known rancher. The murder had been made possible by the pre-planned imprisonment of Jimmy's father on the charge of stealing a cow. We fought the case in the courts and even made a petition to Rome to have the rancher deprived of a papal decoration he had received. When the judge died, the priests of Kabankalan parish agreed, after consultation with the bishop, that they would give the ordinary canonical blessing to the judge, but no trimmings. It became a *cause célèbre*, and ended with a petition by some land-owners to remove Brian, who was acting parish priest at the time.

Brian's stand in his mountain parish had always been assertive on everything, and his close network of Christian communities meant that he had the necessary organisation. One of the many clashes he had had with local powers came over the land of Nonas, where thousands of acres belonging to the agricultural school had been squatted on by landless peasants. However, some large land-holders had also moved in and occupied chunks for sugar-growing. Now the authorities began to push the peasants off, but not the *hacienderos*. Brian and his communities objected strongly: all or none, was their attitude. So the Christian communities, built up among these peasants, strengthened them in their decisions not to move, and Brian got the free legal help of the Diocesan Social Action Office and the back-up of the bishop, who came on occasion to mediate between the authorities and the peasants. Until the time we left, the peasants were still on the land.

So Brian was an obvious choice. After a crude 'plant' job, they brought several charges against him of having explosives and subversive documents and of incitement to sedition. Brian was imprisoned, but after a massive campaign by the Church in Negros he was allowed out on bail. The next time they cooked a case against him they would make it stick – and there would be no bail.

Father Vicente Dangan had been appointed to Kabankalan in his early years of ministry and had helped Brian and me in our small Christian communities work. Then he was changed to La Castellana, where he too began to try the small Christian communities approach. He encouraged the peasants not to be pushed off their land, and this may be what earned him his place on the team – one of my leaders told me that he himself was home in La Castellana on holiday and present when some drinking military were rejoicing at the arrest of Father Dangan and complaining about how he had been the one encouraging the peasants to stay on their land. From the tenor of the conversation they themselves seemed to have an unhealthy interest in the same land. When the military men realised my leader was from Kabankalan they asked him if he would like to become a witness in our case. He declined.

In my own case there were similar connections. Firstly, the parish was strongly organised into small Christian communities, and, of course, we encouraged the people to hang on to the land – in fact, we brought the diocesan lawyer up to give a special seminar to the justice committee of each Christian community on their rights according to the law. Eleven share-croppers won their case in the Land Reform Office against a local landlord.

Top - Helping with the sugar harvest at the Kibbutz 'Iwag Santa Maria' - a worker-owned sugar co-op founded by Fr O'Brien at Dakongcogon, Tall Grass Mountain. *(Columban Mission)*

Above - Fr Niall O'Brien at one of the regular meetings with members of the Kibbutz which he helped found. Fourth from the left is Renato, since stabbed to death by members of the Barangag Brigade, a local government para-militia. *(Columban Mission)*

In September of 1982, we priests were invited to meet the military in a closed-door session and register the complaints we had. I had my complaints well documented and they were particularly galling because they involved a lot of stealing on the part of the local military units. Murders could always be passed off as ambushes, but stealing was somehow more embarrassing. Some of the priests felt that it was that meeting which gave me the extra marks to make the team. I don't know. However, hardly a month had passed before I was accused with Brian and the lay leaders of murder – ordinary common or garden murder.

Now the interesting point here is that it was the head of the local task force, Colonel Hildalgo, who himself held the interview and was the source for the Reuter release that went all over the world. The army had decided that this drama would be played out and won under the eye of the international media. They would allow the media into the court-room while the witnesses against us were telling their stories, and it was 'our' colonel himself who brought them to the military headquarters while we were billetted there.

But what about all the telephone calls and the reporters and visitors? Well, as you have seen, while we were under military control it was within the colonel's power to limit our calls and visitors or eliminate them altogether. In the early stage, for example on the occasion of Brian's birthday, it suited him to use the media to show that we were being well treated, but later he planned to withdraw these privileges. It was our escape to the provincial jail which effectively stymied these plans and removed us from his jurisdiction.

Once in the provincial jail we were under local government jurisdiction. Now, local government officials are elected, and, even though it is a case of 'Hobson's choice' for the voters, for those running for election it would be disastrous to have the record of being against the priests and the Church as the Philippine people are very devout. I have also explained that in the prison there were some prisoners who received special treatment because they were related to officials. To be strict on us would invite withdrawal of the privileges their own relatives were receiving.

There is no doubt that the warden was overwhelmed by events. In a semi-feudal society the hierarchy had been turned upside-down. He could not cope, and so he absented himself most of the time. He longed for us to be gone.

However, apart from all this, there is another reason which accounts for the easy-going ways of the prison, and that is that Filipinos have been given a marvellous dollop of humanity by God, thus the ordinary man who, like our guards, is untrained in repression, finds it very hard to keep any strict régime going for long. Add to this the fact that the guards were, when all is said and done, our own parishioners. The Church is close to the people in Negros, and the guards themselves have experience of this. So, although there were strenuous attempts every now and then to tighten things up, it just could not work, unless we were condemned – and then we would have been moved to the national penitentiary, and that would have been a different matter.

THIRTY-FIVE

New Recruits

Sunday, 10 June
Feast of the Holy Spirit. Tomorrow the new recruits will leave for our formation house in Cebu. There are nine of them. We invited the newspapers and television for the good-bye Mass. Of course Lydio will not be able to go with them as he is our co-accused.

I am including now the report that appeared the next day in the *Daily Star*. It shows how much public opinion had swung around to support us, and also that the papers were becoming less afraid.

Columban Society Admits First Filipino Trainees
Another version of the NEGROS NINE has gone into 'voluntary detention' and, just like the original group, one of them has been left behind.

The eight others left for Cebu city yesterday where they will start training for the priesthood under the Columban Society. The ninth one, Lydio (Boy) Mangao, is waiting in jail because he is still facing trial for multiple murder. . .

Lydio Mangao of Oringao, Kabankalan, is one of those in the group of nine persons including three Catholic priests, two of them Columbans, and six lay-workers charged with the 1982 ambush-murder of Kabankalan Mayor Pablo Sola. . .

Meanwhile, accused priest Niall O'Brien said he and his co-accused priest Brian Gore will provide Mangao with the basic instructions for the priesthood at the Negros Occidental Provincial Jail where they are presently detained until he is free to join the rest of the new seminarians in Cebu for formal training.

O'Brien said he and several other Columban priests have talked to thousands of students on the life and duties of a missionary. On those occasions, O'Brien, who was at the time under house arrest, said he was accompanied by his guard. Even when he had entered jail early this year several applicants had still gone to him for interviews and briefing and in fact, he said, some of them actually filled up their forms in jail. . .

The jailed priest said those who applied to be Columbans had been informed that if they became missionaries they will never be able to help their family financially. They are also required to have ordinary good health, intelligence and faith and, most importantly, must be ready to work with the poor and with compassion.

'We in the Columban Society believe that God reveals himself to us in a special way through the poor,' O'Brien said, pointing out that when Christ chose to be a man, he chose to be poor.

He however stressed that the Columbans work for the reconciliation of all sectors of society.

Recruitment for the next batch of Filipino Columbans for 1985, he disclosed, begins June 19 this year.

– Carla Gomez, for the *Daily Star*

Tuesday, 12 June
Frankie Connon, our daily visitor since the beginning of the case, has gone home as his father is seriously ill. Frankie did all the photos and never missed a day coming to us. We are going to miss him.

Most people wear hardly anything here – just a pair of briefs and shorts, or even just briefs. This is because in the first place everyone is very poor and the prison does not supply any clothes. It is also very hot, so it does not cause great inconvenience, though there is a certain lack of dignity in the rags that some wear, especially as people here are very clothes-conscious.

Many visitors send in clothes, but these soon disappear. At night the prisoners get hungry and pawn their clothes to each other, and eventually to the guards. The problem comes when they have to appear in court and have nothing but briefs. They must hire clothes then. We have a set of clothes which were sent here by an itinerant preacher and which we keep for anyone who so wants. They don't fit very well, but they will do. The preacher came and stayed with us all day, and the next day he sent us his own clothes with a message saying, 'You need these more than I do.'

What with all the pawning of clothes you frequently get mixed up, as you begin to associate a certain T-shirt or pair of shorts with a certain prisoner, and the next thing is that some else owns them, or has them for the time being.

Outsiders give in clothes they don't want. Sometimes clothes that have been used in tableaux or plays or pageants, quite unsuitable for wearing in the streets, will be accepted here. So one should not be surprised when someone passes by in mediaeval costume. One poor fellow dresses in terrible rags. We have given him clothes again and again, but he collects them and finds some sort of security in them. It reminds me of Johnny Fortycoats in Blackrock long ago, the difference being that Johnny had the excuse that it was cold, and five minutes of talking to Johnny meant a real transfer of wild life from him to you. . .

Last night I started Lydio off on his studies and prayers. I gave him a rosary and a New Testament and a Psalter for daily scripture reading, the life of Charles de Foucauld, a book on the Mass, and an introduction to liturgical Latin. We decided that Father John Lucy would be his spiritual director. Lydio is a very willing student, but we don't have much time. . .

I find the court sessions excruciating. Far worse than before because I hate to see people standing up to defend me and being humiliated and tricked into contradicting themselves; it's so easy for a lawyer to do this with an untrained person. It is not enough to have the truth on your side, you must be able to express it. The witnesses against us had learned their stuff off by heart and stuck to their story. The witnesses for us are trying to remember events of more than two years ago, and by its nature this is a difficult thing to do, all the more so if you are a conscientious person, as our witnesses are.

I get so involved emotionally that I find it easier to ask to be excused to go out to the bathroom frequently, so that I can pace up and down the corridor outside. Any excuse is good enough for me to delay my return. On one such occasion I took the opportunity to make all the arrangements by phone with the local hospital for the X-raying of our Columban candidates. I was happy to get this done, but I still had to face going back into the court. . .

Some of the hearings were more tense than others, for example, when Balthazar was on the stand. Balthazar was a student in the Bacolod Diocesan Seminary. I have known him since he was only four years old and used to play in the *convento*. He had also helped me around the parish when he had finished high school; in fact, he was partly looking after the *convento* when I was in Manila at the time the mayor was killed, since he had not yet entered the seminary at that time.

Prosecutor: 'You say Father O'Brien left for Manila on 8 February and returned on 22 March. How do you remember these dates so accurately?'

Balthazar: 'I wrote them in my diary.'

Prosecutor: 'Where is the diary?'

Balthazar: 'Here,' producing, to our surprise, a diary from his pocket.

The prosecutor examined the dates in the diary and was a bit nonplussed, since it backed up Balthazar's statement.

The judge intervened in measured tones: 'Would you now read for us what you wrote in the diary on 10 March 1982, the day the mayor was killed?'

Balthazar opened the diary, and flushed slightly.

Silence in court. Could Balthazar have written something negative about the mayor that might be used as an implication?

Judge: 'Read it to the court.'

Balthazar: '10th March 1982.' Pause. 'I danced with Lydia Siplaw tonight.'

A roar of laughter and relief from the court. The entry was so transparently genuine.

Prosecutor, recovering his balance: 'Was that your first dance?'

Balthazar: 'No – but it was my last.' (He went to the seminary the following June.)

More laughter from the court.

The prosecutor now took up the diary and began to examine it. (Balthazar is left-handed, and, like all of us, writes differently at different times, and uses a different pen depending on what is at hand.)

The prosecutor began to push: 'How is it that on this date you wrote in pencil. . . but here in pen?'

Balthazar: 'It's all my writing.'

Prosecutor: 'How is it that there it is slanting and here it is not?'

Balthazar: 'I wrote every word in that myself.'

Prosecutor, raising his voice: 'Answer my question. How is it that. . .'

Balthazar: 'I've told you already that I'm the only person who wrote in that diary.'

Prosecutor, raising his voice still further: 'Answer the question.'

The crowd – including myself – was now on its feet. 'Don't shout at our witness.'

The judge gavelled the voices down.

When Balthazar came down from the witness stand he received the longest ovation I ever heard in court.

I began to dread the hearings and found myself less able to control myself.

On another occasion Lydio was on the stand being asked about his school attendance – he was at school with many companions the day the mayor was killed. The prosecutor snapped Lydio's private letter out of one of our lawyers' hands and began to quiz Lydio on the contents. (This was a letter which Lydio had made out for his own lawyer, giving the layout of his complicated class schedule.) The prosecutor now began to imply that it was a 'composition'. The lawyer, meanwhile, was dumbfounded.

I stood up in anger and said to the prosecutor, 'Can *we* take *your* private notes and read them?'

The judge gavelled me down, and as he did so, our lawyer snapped Lydio's letter back.

With all my talk of non-violence, I was an inch away from leaping over the dock and getting physical with the prosecutor. I would have made a very bad lawyer! However, one thing was becoming clearer to us: since we were already in jail, even if the judge found us guilty of contempt of court, there was nothing further he could do.

Meanwhile a development had taken place in Manila. Our 'door still open' statement had not managed to get past the Ministry of Justice to the president's desk, because the ministry had consistently refused to pass it on. The president was now about to hold his press conference. Our case would surely come up, and the president was quite likely to say: 'Well, what can I do? They slammed the door.' However, Bob Wurth of ABC had managed, at the last moment, to get our statement to the Minister for Information, Cendaña.

As the president was going down the corridor to the press conference, Cendaña collared him, so to speak, and showed him the relevant lines in the statement.

When the president got into the conference, Bob Wurth and Bruce Dover were there to throw the right ball at the right time. Here is an extract from a transcription of that conference which was given by the president to foreign correspondents:

> Wurth: 'Mr President, following the defence lawyers' rejection of your pardon for the two priests and parole for the six Church leaders on Negros island, you directed a speedy trial. I am now aware of new initiatives by the accused to continue negotiations on your offer towards an early resolution of the case. Could the wording of your offer perhaps be amended especially to ensure the safety of the six Filipinos in the case and to bring this matter to an honourable conclusion once and for all?'
>
> President: 'I would suggest that if there are any more initiatives it be taken up with the Minister of Justice so that he can recommend to me what can be done. I am open to suggestions.'
>
> Wurth: 'Just finally, sir, the minister can talk to the defence lawyers about this matter – your original offer?'

191

President: 'Anyone, I guess, not just the defence lawyers. Anyone will do.'

Dover: 'Mr President, it seems there are two main obstacles. The first is the use of the term "pardon" and an assurance of safety for the six Filipino Church workers. Secondly, can you assure in future that no charges will be brought against the six lay leaders in connection with this case?'

President: 'I would suggest that we quietly look into these possibilities and' (turning to Minister Puno) 'may I ask the Minister for Justice now to talk to the gentlemen and find out what can be done here on the premises. Don't you think that is better?'

Dover: 'Thank you.'

When we listened to the tape in our cell we realised that Wurth and Dover had not only managed to by-pass the justice ministry but had so posed their questions that the president had promised to re-open negotiations in spite of our veto on 'pardon'.

The justice ministry was not amused. However, the president's statement was public and there was no going back on it. The minister had no option but to continue discussions, knowing we would not accept pardon. So that confrontation in the cell with Wurth, Dover and Lynam had been very much worth it!

Brian and I walked up and down the yard. It was time to face a topic both of us had been avoiding. The door was now open to negotiations. Pardon would not be part of the final formula, but our leaving certainly would be. We both agreed that we would prefer to face the thing to the end; however, we could not escape the fact that we were not the only ones involved. There were others – others with wives and children.

I was haunted by the possibility that the judge would suddenly declare us innocent and the six guilty. Anything was possible after the Itik decision. Then there was the remark made by Paul Lynam: 'Are you fellows trying to make martyrs of yourselves?'

If our leaving was the price to pay for the safety of the others, then that was how it would have to be. We tried to console ourselves that legally we would not be forbidden to come back, but we had no illusions. The Philippines owe their economic soul to US-backed international institutions, who are going to demand their pound of flesh – and procuring it is a nasty operation which requires a strong long-term dictatorial government prepared to wield the knife. The future does not look good.

Both of us lapsed into silence, our thoughts drifting back over the years – the happy years. It would be hard to say goodbye.

THIRTY-SIX

'Have You No Pity?'

Michael Martin, our superior, visited us on 22 June and said he wanted us to do a reflection on being in prison. We felt too exhausted. However, together we isolated some points for reflection, and later I wrote them down:

Is the court a waste of time?

Me: 'Well, it is corrupt, but it can be used to proclaim the Good News as did Michael himself, or Karl Gaspar, or Christ, for that matter.'

Brian: 'You don't only proclaim the Good News by words. You proclaim by actions. Every witness, no matter how inarticulate, who stood in the court and risked his life is a witness to the truth. Any witness to the truth is a witness to Christ, who said, "I am the Truth."'

By using the court have we accepted their terms?

Me: 'I feel that a court is the last bastion, however corrupt, between us and unrestrained violence, and it can also be the smoke-screen behind which institutional violence works. It is the myth which we are struggling to make a reality.'

What have we learned from being here?

Michael: 'The poor reveal God's face to us. They are a sacrament of God. Only the poor can get the full message from the Bible. They recognise their God and themselves in the Scriptures. Riches are a barrier to seeing God – to even understanding the word of God. The poor teach us. You are in here to study. This is a retreat.'

Why do all not learn from the poor (A good question!)

Me: 'The three things we have learned here are:

1. The generosity of the prisoners. They share everything with each other. For them food and sharing are two words which always go together.

2. As I read the Scriptures they take on new meaning. Psalms which seemed to me out of date or preposterous have taken on a deadly accuracy for our situation. For instance, Psalm 142:

> In the path where I walk
> > they have hidden a trap for me. . .
> Deliver me from my persecutors,
> > for they are too strong for me.

Bring me out of prison,
that I may give thanks to thy name. . .
These psalms seem to have been written from prison or from a situation of great oppression. Then there are the Captivity Epistles of Saint Paul, and then so much of the Old Testament is written from captivity.

3. One thing that used to annoy me when I came to the prison first was that when prisoners asked for help they would say in Ilongo, *"Diin ang imo kalo-oy?"* (Have you no pity on me?) It used to embarrass me and make me feel that I was being turned into a patroniser. Later I understood that what they were saying was, "Have you no *compassion?* Can you not get inside my skin and see with my eyes?" Ultimately, compassion is faith. They are saying to me, "Have you no faith? Can you not see? I am your brother."'

THIRTY-SEVEN

Opium or Dynamite?

On 23 June I received the following letter:

Dear Father O'Brien,

I am writing you because I feel I should share with you a piece of vital information from an insider who is not an inmate but both close to the inmates and the guards.

Here is what I learned. There exists a brewing enmity among cells 8, 9, 10 and another I can't recall, as against the occupants of cell 11. Accordingly a 'rumble' is planned to fall on a day when there are visitors and will likely be on Sunday, 24th June – Saint John's Day. The people in cell 11 are said to be preparing their sharpened stainless weapons.

You two, Father Brian and Father Niall, do take care. You're not in good health.

Yours in Christ, love,

Antonia (member of VIPS)

From my diary:

Saturday, 23 June
We have noticed that two fellows have voluntarily moved out of Cell

10 and into the *bartolina*. We asked them why, and they said they wanted to avoid trouble. (They must be expecting something. The *bartolina* is a rough spot, but apparently they consider it the lesser of two evils.) We have also heard that Cell 11 is loaded with weapons (as the VIPS letter says).

Two sick fellows from Cell 11 asked me for medicine. I asked them to come to our cell to collect it, but they said they were afraid to come down to our end of the quadrangle.

Brian called for a meeting of all the *bosios*. They came to our cell. We gave all the reasons we could against rioting, making them as practical and down-to-earth as possible:
1. you'll end up with another case and many years more;
2. you'll be injured yourself;
3. it will make the guards happy to see you fighting each other;
4. what's to be gained?
5. the other prisoners are our brothers.

Sunday, 24 June: Feast of Saint John
Last night at four in the morning I was awakened by many voices in the next cell. It turned out that Boy Chris and two others had escaped from the cell by fiddling with the lock (the warden was right when he complained about the price of locks!). Then, with the aid of an iron rod (normally used for cleaning out the sewers) which they hooked up on the wall, they climbed onto the guards' washing-place. From there they got to the outer wall and fled.

Boy Chris was the one who borrowed the extra shoes and *barong* which we keep in our cell for his last hearing in court. The shoes were too big and the long-sleeved *barong* too large. He looked a sight. He pranced around the yard doing imitation Philippine folk-dancing. Some evangelical group had a prayer-meeting on, and they could not have been amused with the distraction.

Boy Chris tried to escape before, and was put in the *bartolina*. His young wife used to visit him. She would stay all day and even remain all night, looking in at the gate of the *bartolina*, and someone would put a blanket on her to keep her warm. She must have slept standing.

Another wife literally lived outside the gate of Cell 6 for a couple of weeks – she and her six children – with no cover whatsoever from the elements. She was so thin and tubercular-looking that it was a wonder she could survive in the cement crevices of the quadrangle. . .

Meanwhile, those indefatigable reporters, Carla and Nympha from the local papers, came to see us, and I gave them a look at some of the hundreds of letters we had been receiving. They took out one from a little boy who had sent us his very first letter ever; another from the niece of the famous Monsignor Flaherty of the film *The Scarlet and the Black,* which everybody here has seen; another from the playwright J. B. Keane; and yet another with the pope's own signature – it was sent to these nuns and they sent it to us. And then there was a copy of one of those cards being sent by AFrI, with a picture of us behind bars.

During the meal I let drop some reference to the escape last night. Carla leapt up and said, 'And you told us that there was no news!' She abandoned her lunch on the table and disappeared off to Cell 6 to get her scoop. It never struck us that it would be news! But it was headlines in the paper next day.

Monday, 25 June
A prisoner came to me to say he is going to escape. I asked him why he didn't try to get his case dismissed, so I arranged for him to meet Ben Alayon, our barefoot lawyer. The prisoner was doubtful. He said that the police and the prosecution were in cahoots in his and his friend's case – frustrated homicide – and they hadn't a chance. He had already been here two years. However, I pushed and he agreed to have a last try. Later he came back and said that they couldn't wait: they are going to escape to the mountains and join the NPA. They want to buy a gun, and they have an electric fan which they want us to buy so that they'll have money. I said, 'No way,' and told them that if they plan to go ahead, that part of the plan is no good. 'You don't need a gun, and it will bring more trouble. In the last analysis it is a doubtful defence.' Later I thought it might be a plan to involve us, but at the time I didn't think of that.

Brian and I are disturbed by some of the evangelical groups who gain admission here. They take advantage of the prisoners' low self-esteem and reduce it still further. With over-fundamentalistic interpretations they reduce religion to opium. Sad, because true religion is dynamite.

THIRTY-EIGHT

Thou Dost Protest Too Much

Tuesday, 26 June

We are still preparing busily for our court case each day, and negotiations are still going on all the time.

I was called to the phone. It was the bishop. He was excited: 'The sun is shining. About a week now and all will be well.'

I said, 'Monsignor, answer me one thing: is the word "pardon" included?'

'No,' he said. 'Don't tell anyone. Everything depends on secrecy.'

We've had so many false hopes, that I am beyond excitement.

Frank O'Donovan is here from the Irish government and he took me aside and gave me a personal letter from Taoiseach Garret FitzGerald.

Wednesday, 27 June

News coming all day about the case. Brian woke me at two o'clock in the afternoon to say that Bruce Dover had phoned the justice ministry and they had said: 1. all parties are meeting now in Columban headquarters in Manila; 2. the government will ask for dismissal of the case and will use our own motion for dismissal (the one that was rejected last time); 3. all seem to be agreed.

Phone-call later from Charlie Bird to say that they have actually signed the document in the presence of Minister Puno and Nick Murray, our superior, and that Puno phoned the president in their presence. The story is not yet verified. . .

At tea-time Baby Gordoncillo, the Social Action Director, arrived with the lawyers and the bishop himself. They brought a document with them – the final document to be presented in court tomorrow. We all signed it. According to this document, all the cases will be dropped against the eight of us, with no possibility of being brought up again even in the civil courts; the priests will leave the country; and the lay leaders will be guaranteed protection.

I phoned my mother and told her the news. She had had so many false alarms and false hopes, that I had decided that I would never be the one to give her such hopes, so that up to this I had always cautioned her against an early end to it. This was the first time I had said anything positive. So when I said it she knew it must be true.

Thursday, 28 June

Brian was interviewed by some eight radio stations and various newspapers.

Well, the court met at two o'clock in the afternoon today in a very formal way. Johnny Hagad, our chief lawyer, asked for the dismissal of the case because of the new evidence. He was joined by the public prosecutor, then by the private prosecutor, and they co-signed our motion – the very one that had been rejected a few weeks earlier.

There was an air of good humour in the court. The prosecutor got some applause, and then he said that he wanted to point out that it was the first time he had been clapped since the very beginning of the case. Finally, when all the lawyers had spoken, the prosecutor asked permission to speak: he said that he apologised for the inconvenience; he congratulated the accused for their patience, and just as he was doing so a catch came in his voice and he was overcome with emotion and had to walk away. Strange, really. I thought he was more hard-hearted!

Then, in a long-winded speech, the judge said he could not decide immediately, lest the independence of the judiciary be compromised. He was obviously standing on his head in order to prove that he was an independent judge! 'Thou dost protest too much' was what everyone felt. So he said he would make his decision in a very short time, banged his gavel and dismissed the court. And off he went for five days to decide whether we were guilty, even though the prosecution had signed a document in court to say we were innocent. Anyway, the end is in sight.

But first back to the jail.

THIRTY-NINE

Farewell

Tuesday, 3 July

Last day in prison. We gave away all our things: every last little bit of wire, or nail, in the cell was booked. One fellow followed me around waiting for me to take off my short pants, which he had 'booked', and change into my long trousers to go to the court. We all felt deeply for the prisoners we were leaving. We packed our bags, left them in our cell, climbed into the military vehicles, and set out for the court for the last time.

The judge came in and banged his gavel, asking the court to stand. We stood, but we did not smile. Before he got down to business, he threw in the usual bits of piety – he had had to go to Mass last Saturday for something or other – and then in a less than magnanimous address he said that 'the evidence for the defence tended to weaken the evidence for the prosecution' so he was accepting the motion for dismissal. (The motion, by the way, says we are *innocent*.) We did not applaud. He banged his gavel, and the last of some fifty hearings was over.

We were driven back to the prison to get our bags, be fingerprinted and given our release papers. Going out of the gate, I was asked by NBC for a statement, and I said, 'I am filled with deep joy to be out of this terrible prison, but it is no worse than the conditions under which many people must live. We have been in prison because we worked to change these conditions – we will continue to work to change them because we believe that as long as half the world is hungry no one is free.'

We walked up the road to the *plaza*, with camera people running in front of us. On the way people came out to cheer. Some were very emotional. We got to the bishop's house, and then the interviews began.

After a meal I slipped away for a *siesta* to my old friends the Gonzales' house, knowing no one would find me there. It will be heavy going in the days ahead, and I need a bit of sleep.

Wednesday, 4 July
I woke up at Batang, our headquarters in Himamaylan, with the sun streaming in at the windows and beckoning me to investigate sea and field, like the first day of summer holidays as a child.

Hundreds of visitors from all over began to pour in. I don't know how our bursar, Geoff Revatto, managed, but he did wonderfully. Of all the special things said by everyone after the meal, I remember particularly one of the Australian journalists who had played a vital part in the whole story right up to the denouement and who said, 'You praised us, but we couldn't hold a candle to the local Filipinos who have risked their lives so often right through this whole affair.' We all knew he was referring to Nympha and Carla.

Thursday, 5 July
Back to Kabankalan. The last thing we wanted was display – among other things, it was dangerous – but the new Filipino priests who had just taken over from Father Mark Kavanagh would not have it said that they didn't pull out all the stops, so as soon as we got to

Above - Frs Gore, O'Brien, (with Roney, a thirteen-year-old who was accused of murder) and Dangan entering the parish of Oringao after their release. *(Far East)*
Left - Fr O'Brien's parishioners welcome him back. *(Far East)*

the town we were met by a band with majorettes and the whole works.

After Mass at Kabankalan it was up to Oringao, where, of course, Brian's people had us walk the last two miles. They were the people who had worked and suffered more and risked more than anyone else and they were going to squeeze the last ounce from this occasion.

I slipped away to Tabugon for an evening with my old leaders, those who had built the Basic Christian Communities with me. All the core groups from each mini-parish were present and I slept for the last time in my own room.

Friday, 6 July
All the Christian communities came in for Mass. The bishop arrived, bringing the news that my Uncle Donal had died: he had held out until the end. The Mass was in the open outside the church, because the church wouldn't hold the people. It was an emotional moment for me, saying goodbye. Tom Fawthrop was vainly trying to interview me when a man from an outlying community approached. He was in his bare feet, the ends of his trousers were rolled up, and he was thin and worn. In his hand he held a plastic bag of new rice. His eyes were literally shining with affection as he held the bag out and told me that the rice was for me. For me it was a symbol of all the love I have always received from the first day I set foot in the Philippines.

As I went down the mountains I called into the kibbutz farm I had started more than ten years before. They were all waiting for me. I made my farewells. It was an emotional occasion: I had walked in there many a time myself in my bare feet because of the mud, and I had had many a row with them and many a song. I went away quickly, leaving so many memories behind.

Saturday, 7 July
In Bacolod, about to emplane for Manila, I paid my last visit to the prison. There was Juanito; there was Alo; there was Nene. Jun Herbolario came to me with a large ledger I had given him. He had filled it with writing: 'That's my life-story, Father. You remember you asked me to write it?' (He was dead within a month, killed by the son of one of the prison authorities; but his story will be known.)

All the cells were locked, our cell was empty, strange and stripped. Every footstep towards the gate was difficult, as the prisoners stretched their arms through the bars calling out desperately, like a scene from *Les Misérables*.

Then the airport. . . old friends, dear friends. . . The plane was delayed, so it was harrowing for me.

The Negros Nine pose behind the iron gate of Cell 7 at Bacolod Provincial Jail.
(Fr Frank Connon)

Sunday, 8 July

In Manila, more goodbyes to personal friends, and many who had witnessed for me at what could have been great personal cost. Our house in Manila overflowed with well-wishers, and Cardinal Sin came to say goodbye. Brian, Itik and the bishop joined the lay people, the diplomats, the witnesses. At the farewell, Cardinal Sin stood to speak. He told the following story, which in a way tells as much about him as about us. He said that the other day he had gone to visit President Marcos, taking him a present of a video-tape: 'Mr President, I want you to see this.'

'What's it about?'

'Well, it's called *The Scarlet and the Black*, and it's about a Vatican priest, Monsignor Flaherty, who used to hide Jews during the war. Monsignor Flaherty had Vatican immunity. The head of the Nazis came to the pope and said, "We know what Flaherty is doing, Your Holiness, and if we catch him we will kill him." The pope replied, "If you kill him, he will be replaced by another." I think you will enjoy it, Mr President.'

My parents met me at Amsterdam, together with Father Michael O'Neill who had been our first spokesman nearly two years before, when the whole thing started. After an interview with Dutch television we left for Dublin.

I could hardly believe my eyes when I saw the welcome at the airport, and I felt unworthy of it. After that we went to Whitehall and Sean McDermott Street, where they did a street drama releasing us (my mother and me) from a mock cell as they declared me innocent. The joy and spontaneity and poverty of Sean McDermott Street took me back for a moment to the Philippines.

Then to the Lord Mayor's House, where there was an old-time razzamatazz band playing, and as soon as I heard it I said to myself, 'I'm going to enjoy this.' The mayor had an oak tree tied with yellow ribbons for me to plant, and among the crowd I saw many old friends, all with yellow ribbons.

One of the funny incidents was that on the journey from Sean McDermott Street to the Lord Mayor's House, two fellows had just crashed into each other and were in the middle of an altercation, but when the mini-motorcade passed by they stopped fighting and both began to wave to me.

Next night it was Mass at the Pro-Cathedral. The atmosphere was really wonderful – more like Mexico than Marlborough Street – and I had a chance to say why I felt unworthy. I said simply that sisters and priests and lay people had been out on the mission for years and had experienced leprosaria and prisons a-plenty but had not got the attention

I was getting. Many had died, and others were killed, and I felt like an up-start. However, I accepted this wonderful welcome on their behalf and as their representative.

Then a wonderful Mass in my own parish, and on to Dalgan Park, where I had done my seminary training. Once again I felt humbled. Men who had spent years in prison, been tortured and been expelled were there welcoming me. And the sun shone all the way.

I had one special journey to make, and that was a visit to my mother's home town of Dunmanway, Co. Cork. All my family came, and it would take a whole chapter to tell that story. It was a sentimental journey for my mother, and for me it was a great gift to become a member of the Dohenys, as my grandfather had been before me. Then to Ballyvourney to say thank you to Saint Gobnait, and a special Mass in Irish. The sun still shining.

I am sure you do not want to visit the whole of Ireland with me, so just let me tell you this last one.

I decided I had to go the Aran Islands (the Club na nÓg there had been very supportive), so off I went on my own. On my way to Doolin, after I had crossed on the Tarbert ferry, I picked up a German hitch-hiker who was also going my way. He guided me, as I had never been on that road before and he had it all worked out. It was a relief not to be recognised for a bit. We decided to stop and have a cup of tea at a pub; we chose one together, and in we went. I went straight to the counter and ordered the tea and sandwiches, and with my head well down returned to a seat with him. In a few minutes there was a bit of a buzz. A woman asked me for my autograph, and then so did several others. People came and shook my hand, and someone produced a camera. . . then more cameras. . . more people in from outside, and there was quite a cuffuffle. Some people had serious problems in the family and they told me about them there and then, and asked me to pray for them.

When he got a chance, my German friend said, 'But you said you were never here before.' 'No, I wasn't,' I said. He was silent for a moment, and then he tried again: 'Do you know these people?' 'No,' I said, 'I never saw them before.' A smile dawned on his face, and he said triumphantly, 'You're an actor.' 'No, no way,' I said. He lapsed into silence. Things were getting a bit out of hand now with the number of people. We finally got into the car and said goodbye to quite a crowd, but the car was stopped several times for a last hand-shake or a blessing. My German friend lost all his talk, and when he got out and said goodbye he looked at me long and carefully – and with, I thought, a touch of suspicion.

EPILOGUE

Seeds of Injustice

Grasp the Barbed Wire

All through our case we constantly discussed our duty to forgive and its apparent clash with our duty to stand up for our rights, and we discussed what form this stand should take. Frequently after the Gospel reading we would agonise over these things. However, it was not only while in prison but for years before that I had been captivated by the whole concept of non-violence. Let me share it for a moment with you.

Violence has a source, and that source is injustice. Violence is the fruit of the tree of injustice, and hate is its evil flower. If we sow seeds of injustice, we reap violence. If we want to remove violence, we must first remove injustice. Injustice begets violence, and violence begets counter-violence. The cycle takes on its own momentum.

In proposing non-violence as a solution, one must be very careful to explain the terms. An earlier name for non-violence was pacifism, but pacifism seems to denote an absence of action and even a quiescence, and could even leave the door open to fatalism and the wrong use of the concept of 'This is the will of God' to which we are prone. On the other hand, though it too is a negative word, the reality of the non-violence movement is not at all negative. It is in fact an assertive, carefully planned struggle for justice, using the techniques of non-violence.

Though thousands of volumes have been written on the art of war down the centuries from Caesar's *Gallic Wars* to Churchill's *Second World War*, almost nothing, comparatively speaking, has been written on the art, techniques and strategy of non-violence. Not that non-violence was not being practised – it was, and is – but it has not been examined, evaluated and improved the way weapons of war are all the time. In the arena of war we have come from using the jaw-bones of animals for killing an enemy to today's megaton nuclear war-heads which can destroy a city of millions in minutes. On the other hand, in the history of non-violence we are still in the palaeolithic age.

It was Gandhi, in our century, who tried to show the world that non-violence leads not just to victory for the oppressed but to liberation also for the tyrant. Behind the philosophy of non-violence is the belief that your enemy is never completely bad and also that his own best interests lie in stopping his oppression and being liberated from the

Top - Squatters' houses demolished by police at Bacolod – they were later rebuilt as a result of Church action, 1984. *(Fr Frank Connon)*
Above - Neighbours making a coffin for one of the victims of the Masaling (South Negros) massacre, when three farmers were taken from their homes at night and shot, 20 June 1983. *(Winston)*

effects on himself of his own injustice. However, for the person who would be a disciple of Christ there is the added fact that the heart of the Good News is precisely that we are all brothers and sisters – even those who would make lampshades from our skin are our brothers and sisters. To forget this is to lapse into atheism, because if we are not brothers and sisters then there is no God.

One of the great alternatives to non-violence which the human race has given birth to through much labour is the system of justice through the courts. If we regard the Magna Carta as the starting point for our present system of law courts, then it has taken some seven hundred years of struggle – much of it two steps forward and one step back – to reach our present level of justice in the courts. Courts are supposed to offer non-violent means of undoing injustice; in them, justice must not only be done, but it must be seen to be done. If it is not *seen* to be done, then the sense of injustice remains and the spectre of violence reappears.

Non-violence is a continent which we have just discovered; but we have not yet gone inland. During our attempt to build small Christian communities we evolved four basics which we found essential in this approach.
1. Truth: the truth is lethal against lies, the truth shines out, and it is feared by those who deal in lies; it has its own inner power; it rises out of the grave of the dead man to confront his killers.
2. Faith: faith is opposed to fatalism. To believe that good is more powerful than evil is ultimately to believe in God, whether you verbalise that belief or not. To believe passionately in the dignity of man is ultimately to believe in God. Conversely, to ignore and trample on the dignity of man makes you into a practising atheist, no matter what church you attend.
3. Imagination: Gandhi, Martin Luther King, Dorothy Day, Saul Alinsky, the Berrigans, Câmara, Romero – all have shown in our age a resourceful use of imagination and humour in their specifically non-violent strategy to win the battle for human dignity.
4. Courage: most oppressive rulers rule just by fear – the *threat* of the grenade thrown into the crowd, rather than the actual grenade. Fear is catching, and so is courage. Start showing courage even in the little things and suddenly one day you will discover that the king has no clothes at all.

One of the most beautiful symbols of non-violence is one we had embroidered on our Mass-stoles. It is that of a human hand grasping the barbed wire, absorbing the pain of the barbs, so that the dove of peace can find a place to land. So it is in the spiral of anger and violence and killings: someone must be the first to stop; someone must grasp the sharp barbs with their naked hand so that the dove of peace can descend. And if you think for a moment, you will see that this is just what Christ did.

Who Killed Mayor Sola?

And now we come to the end. And we must ask the question: If the ordinary people of the world long for peace, as they most surely do, how come there is so much killing all around us? And if what we said above is true – if the level of violence is normally related to the level of injustice – we must then ask the questions:
Who allowed this injustice to continue?
Who wrote it in the first place into the structures of society?
Who turned a blind eye to it?
Who was too busy about many things to hear the cry of the poor as they called out?

If the problem of violence
ultimately resolves itself into the problem of injustice,
then,
to the degree that we have allowed
injustice to prevail,
you or I might well answer the questions:
Who killed Mayor Sola?
Who buried those peasants alive?
Who is responsible for this ever-widening stain of violent death?
with the words,
'Is it I, Lord?'